# Ballistic Missile Defense
## ⬤ and the ⬤
# Future of American Security

## Agendas, Perceptions, Technology, and Policy

Roger Handberg

 PRAEGER

Westport, Connecticut
London

Property of Library
Cape Fear Comm College
Wilmington, N. C.

**Library of Congress Cataloging-in-Publication Data**

Handberg, Roger, 1945–
  Ballistic missile defense and the future of American security : agendas, perceptions, technology, and policy / Roger Handberg.
    p.  cm.
  Includes bibliographical references and index.
  ISBN 0–275–97009–4 (alk. paper)
    1. Ballistic missile defenses—United States.  2. United States—Military policy.  3. National security—United States.  I. Title.
  UG743.H36  2002
  358.1'7185'0973—dc21        2001034579

British Library Cataloguing in Publication Data is available.

Copyright © 2002 by Roger Handberg

All rights reserved. No portion of this book may be reproduced, by any process or technique, without the express written consent of the publisher.

Library of Congress Catalog Card Number: 2001034579
ISBN: 0–275–97009–4

First published in 2002

Praeger Publishers, 88 Post Road West, Westport, CT 06881
An imprint of Greenwood Publishing Group, Inc.
www.praeger.com

Printed in the United States of America

The paper used in this book complies with the Permanent Paper Standard issued by the National Information Standards Organization (Z39.48–1984).

10 9 8 7 6 5 4 3 2 1

# Contents

# Acknowledgments

All projects have roots in the past. This one is no different since my professional training took place against the background of the original debate over national missile defense and whether to deploy a system and if so, in what configuration. My interests were different at that time, but the issue has intrigued me intellectually since the crossover back and forth from science to government policy was so clear as scientists put themselves on the line over the question of deployment.

In this new generation, the issue draws less visibility despite the fact that the Cold War has ended and the United States is, comparatively speaking, at peace. The puzzle becomes, Why does the issue draw such fervent support from certain groups when there exist larger defense policy questions that are more immediate and pressing? The answer is that you find the interaction between traditional American views regarding technology and the expression of worldviews regarding the state of the world as a hostile, or a more benign, place within which the United States must live now and in the future. American views are very optimistic with regard to the ability of technology to solve hard problems, but many perceive the world outside American shores as alien and threatening. These attitudes persist despite the alleged effects of globalization upon what states do. That essentially economic concept has been expanded to encompass a world of peace and order although several benighted areas still exist; however, their future will be one of increasing pacifism with regard to the use of force against other states.

On a personal level, I wish to thank Bob Bledsoe for his support and the use of his library, which he has accumulated over the years. Jess Nakaska and Anastasia Theodoridou provided bibliographic and organizational support while Stewart French was a major help in tracking down references and generating additional ones, all of which I appreciated. Mary Ann Parker provided her usual efficient, though on occasion caustic, assistance for which I am grateful. Also, I appreciate the "girls" (Raven, Rahab, Rachel, Becky, and Priscilla) and their willingness to go out in the backyard to do whatever dogs do while allowing me to write. My wife, Angel, has provided a great environment within which to work even though at times her cleaning patterns drove me to distraction. Angel also found herself helping put the manuscript in final form, an assistance I found above and beyond the normal. Finally, this work is dedicated to Robert, Sierra, and Ellie whose generation will live under whatever is decided regarding national missile defense—for theirs is the first generation since the 1940s to know only peace, however tenuous that is at times.

# Abbreviations

| | |
|---|---|
| ABL | Airborne Laser |
| ABM | Anti-Ballistic Missile |
| ASAT | Anti-Satellite Weapon |
| BM | Ballistic Missile |
| BM/C3 | Battle Management/Command, Control, and Communications Systems |
| BMD | Ballistic Missile Defense |
| BMDO | Ballistic Missile Defense Organization |
| BUR | Bottom-Up Review |
| CBO | Congressional Budget Office |
| CEP | Circular Error Probable |
| CIA | Central Intelligence Agency |
| CONUS | Continental United States |
| CTBT | Comprehensive Test Ban Treaty |
| DEW(1) | Defense Early Warning |
| DEW(2) | Directed Energy Weapons |
| DoD | Department of Defense |
| DRR | Deployment Readiness Review |
| DSP | Defense Support Program |
| EKV | Exo-Atmospheric Kill Vehicle |
| EMP | Electromagnetic Pulse |
| ERINT | Extended Range Interceptor |
| EW | Electronic Warfare |
| ICBM | Intercontinental Ballistic Missile |
| INF | Intermediate Nuclear Forces Treaty |
| IRBM | Intermediate-Range Ballistic Missile |
| GBI | Ground-Based Interceptor |
| GPALS | Global Protection against Limited Strikes |
| HTK | Hit-to-Kill |
| LSI | Lead System Integrator |
| MAD | Mutually Assured Destruction |
| MARV | Maneuvering Reentry Vehicle |
| MEADS | Medium Extended Air Defense System |

| | |
|---|---|
| MIDAS | Missile Launch Detection Alarm System |
| MIRV | Multiple Independently Targeted Reentry Vehicle |
| MOS | Military Operation Specialties |
| MRBM | Medium-Range Ballistic Missile |
| MTCR | Missile Technology Control Regime |
| MWC | Minimum Winning Coalition |
| NASA | National Aeronautics and Space Administration |
| NASP | National Aerospace Plane |
| NATO | North Atlantic Treaty Organization |
| NIMBY | Not in My Backyard |
| NMD | National Missile Defense |
| NORAD | North America Aerospace Defense Command |
| NTW | Navy Theater Wide |
| QDR | Quadrennial Defense Review |
| R&D | Research and Development |
| RMA | Revolution in Military Affairs |
| SAC | Strategic Air Command |
| SALT | Strategic Arms Limitation Talks |
| SBI | Space-Based Interceptor |
| SBIRS | Space-Based Infrared System |
| SBL | Space-Based Laser |
| SDI | Strategic Defense Initiative |
| SDIO | Strategic Defense Initiative Organization |
| SEATO | Southeast Asia Treaty Organization |
| SLBM | Submarine-Launched Ballistic Missile |
| SRBM | Short-Range Ballistic Missile |
| START | Strategic Arms Reduction Talks |
| TAV | Transatmospheric Vehicles |
| TBMD | Theater Ballistic Missile Defense |
| THAAD | Theater High Altitude Area Defense |
| TMD | Theater Missile Defense |
| UAV | Unmanned Aerial Vehicle |
| UEWR | Upgraded Early Warning Radars |
| WMD | Weapons of Mass Destruction |
| XBR | X-Band Radars |

# 1
# Introduction

## INTRODUCTION

Ballistic missile defense (BMD) as a distinct technological and political issue is now embarking upon its fifth decade of controversy and technological development, dating back to the mid-1950s. In fact, the first consideration of BMD as a concept took place in 1946—two short years after the first V-2 attack fell on London. This long-running political saga reflects many factors, but one major underlying theme has been BMD's presumed capacity to alter international politics in both unknown and unpredictable ways. This work presents an analysis of ballistic missile defense as a policy issue, traces its development (historically and in terms of the worldviews underlying the policy antagonists, politically and technologically), and assesses national missile defense's (NMD) future impact upon U.S. security interests. The stakes are high in that the wrong decisions could lead to possible national military and economic disaster down the road. By its very nature, NMD especially in the nuclear age deals with issues of national life and death. A failed defensive system could conceivably lead to a devastated society because of leadership overconfidence in its effectiveness or if those in power are cowered by enemies' threats due to excessive uncertainty concerning the technology's effectiveness. Effectiveness is measured empirically by NMD's capacity to reliably and repeatedly intercept incoming warheads, including weapons of mass destruction (WMD), in the chaos of battle.

Achieving technical success, however, raises other troubling questions concerning the future shape of world politics. The relationship between the United States and other states is altered significantly and in possibly unforeseen and unfortunate ways if NMD actually works. Therefore, judgments have to be made evaluating the likely reaction of other states to this altered strategic environment. It is unclear how much of the rhetoric expressed by Russia, China, and even the European states reflects their actual willingness to do something drastic or is simply an effort to deter the United States from altering the strategic environment. Predictions appear to be based on one's worldview going into the debate rather than actual information evaluation. Much of what passes for analysis of the likely impacts of NMD upon future American foreign policy is wishful thinking or preordained ideological judgments.

What lends particular urgency to this analysis is the intense and mounting domestic political momentum for starting national missile defense deployment among some groups. Political pressures generated by such groups are building up to render such a decision quickly. To use John Kingdon's terminology, a policy window appears to be opening—that is: "an opportunity for advocates to push their pet solutions, or to push attention to their special problems."[1] The presidential decision was to have been made in late 2000 but was put off until early 2001, which means that deployment is expected by 2005 or 2007 at the latest; but even that deployment date remains entirely contingent on the pace of NMD technology improvement and what different approaches are pursued. Those groups and individuals pushing for NMD deployment represent an interesting mix of internationalists and isolationists. Thus, the issue contains hidden agendas as well as possibly not well thought out military and political postures. The appeal is often made to nationalism in the narrowest sense of that emotion-laden term. BMD allows the United States in the view of some NMD advocates to retreat from any engagement in the world's problems, truly establishing again a "Fortress America" concept. From the other side, NMD is perceived as effectively granting the United States the freedom to operate in the world according to its desires alone—the other side of Fortress America, a redoubt of total security from which to do good. In effect, the United States will be placed in the unique category of becoming a "isolationist global power"— capable of intervention at its discretion with no effective response by those affected by its actions.[2] This is a posture thought by many to eventually lead to irresponsible behavior because the only effective restraint becomes the U.S. sense of self-restraint.[3]

Embedded in some critiques of the NMD question are assumptions about American leadership and how that has been and will be exercised in the world. Many are critical, seeing U.S. policy as erratic, lurching from issue to issue with no general framework or strategic goal to guide decisions. Those evaluations are often premised upon highly partisan and/or personalized views of American policy. Much of the fervor of the debate is provided by NMD partisans' visceral dislike for President Bill Clinton who presided over the latest round in this lengthy controversy. The purpose here is to move somewhat outside that context to consider long-term implications and the deeper historical roots underpinning the NMD controversy. Presidents are not "so to speak" froth on the wave but this question preceded President Clinton and will endure past his administration. The conversation is about the future directions of U.S. policy in the world, not just in relation to its potential foes but also its allies and neutrals.

The NMD deployment decision has not been finalized (as of this writing, in early March 2001) so that understanding the fundamental political dynamics inherent in this debate becomes critical for all concerned regardless of their perspective on the question.  One must also recognize that even preliminary deployment decisions are reversible as conclusively demonstrated by the subsequent cancellation of the original NMD 1967 and 1969 deployment decisions.  The technical issues clearly being emphasized in the present debate shape the specifics, but the ultimate decisions whether or not to actually deploy are more likely driven by preexisting worldviews or ideologies rather than technological issues.  This situation reflects the essential malleability of the NMD technology, at least politically speaking.  BMD is an issue heavily encrusted with multiple policy and ideological considerations lying outside the general parameters of whether or not the critical intercept technologies actually work.  For example, from the fall of 1999 until the end of 2000, only one successful intercept out of three tests was achieved in the sense that the target vehicle was struck.  Even that success was challenged by critics as being too easy to achieve and not a true test of the technology.  Technology, it will be argued here, becomes merely fodder within that larger debate, but it is not as central as one might suppose in determining the final conclusions to be drawn by the respective antagonists.  Both sides observe the same glass of water filled to 50 percent of volume and draw totally divergent policy recommendations.  One perceives a high likelihood of operational failure and disaster while the other sees future possibilities and ultimate success.

Ironically, as a result, ballistic missile defense represents a prime example of the influence of ideas rather than the technology itself upon American policy development; in this case, its security and foreign policy dimensions.  The central idea is simply the physical protection, as much as possible, of the United States from ballistic missile attack.  This simple concept then splits into whether the primary focus is upon protection of the society and its population (the most encompassing) or military forces in order to deter any attack upon the United States (a two-step relationship but clearly more limited in scope).  The variations within this theme become enormous in their extent and ramifications.  All of this takes place in the absence of any present credible experience, not merely tests that BMD will work reliably in the field.  In fact, persistent testing clearly establishes that the technological task at hand remains extraordinarily difficult to implement effectively.  All of this becomes fodder for the fine grinding of the intellectual debate—one flavored by few data points, and those are usually bitterly disputed facts.

Too often, in the analysis of public policy, the explanation put forth is premised largely upon some expectation that the parties involved either benefit economically from the outcomes or are engaged in a series of maneuvers aimed at pressuring decision makers.  Economic expectations obviously impact the calculations of some corporate or bureaucratic participants, but the crux of the matter is that BMD policy, especially in its national-level manifestation, has become an *idée fixe* for certain groups who are almost totally immune to the ravages of political and military reality.  The debate is not always abstract and intellectual in tone, but, at its root, the concept encapsulated by the term NMD drives the participants. Equivalent discussions occur regarding such issues as human rights and the environment and how one approaches those realities in a manner that is complete and self-contained. Our task becomes one of examining the playing out of these ideas within the NMD realm.

This focus upon ideas reflects the reality that NMD still remains a concept not an actuality–the calculations that go into structuring deployment and use decisions are still abstractions, albeit ones often overlaid with a thin veneer of fact on both sides. In that sense, they mirror the larger Cold War debate over nuclear deterrents in which firmly held viewpoints were propounded with great authority and no relevant experience. The latter situation allowed full range for one's views regarding the world as projected through the prism of this single issue. The debate was unresolved, at least temporarily, without being put to the test and without the great human cost involved if carried out. Ignorance is not bliss, but the absence of experience does allow full run to the imagination.[4]

## SOME TECHNICAL ASPECTS TO CONSIDER

Ballistic missile defense as a concept embodies two distinct but interrelated facets: theater missile defense (TMD) and national missile defense (NMD). The former envisions implementing defensive systems capable of protecting U.S. and allied military forces that are deployed operationally from missile attacks by immediate adversaries (e.g., battlefield or regional defense). Such systems, therefore, must be mobile, robust, and quickly deployable across a wide diversity of geographic environments including the desert, jungle, mountains, and arctic. National missile defense by contrast envisions protecting the United States, especially its continental territory, from missile attacks by either submarine-launched ballistic missiles (SLBMs) or intercontinental ballistic missiles (ICBMs). While both situations are similar in nature, each demands counter- or anti-missile technologies capable of responding to very different threat profiles.

Intercepting a ballistic missile and/or its warhead is an extremely difficult feat under perfect testing conditions, but the task would have to be accomplished in an environment for which there has been no real experience. Models and exercises have been constructed to simulate such a disruptive environment; but no one truly knows the environmental effects of large-scale nuclear events. The task of interception has been conceptualized generally in terms of four phases within the arc of the ICBM's flight to the target.[5]

The boost phase (lasting possibly three to five minutes) involves the missile lifting itself into space while shedding stages to reduce mass and increase its speed. During this phase, the ICBM is most vulnerable if successfully attacked by the defensive force. The other value is that the missile, if destroyed, will fall back upon the party that launched it, creating additional damage. Usually outside the atmosphere, the missile enters the post-boost phase (lasting around five to six minutes). At this point, the "bus" or warhead carrier begins dispensing its payload in the form of warheads and penetration aids. The interception task clearly becomes exponentially more difficult as the defender must identify quickly whether or not an object is a warhead. The bus and its passengers are in outer space, a near vacuum, so there is effectively no drag. All objects move together in a cloud of apparent missiles. Target discrimination becomes an issue.

The third phase, or mid-course phase, lasts the longest depending upon the distance traveled and the angle of the flight (fifteen to twenty minutes), and continues to present the same problems of the previous phase. Multiple targets move through space at a height of 1,200 kilometers more or less at speeds up to Mach 20; all present a credible profile for a warhead inbound to the target. Near the end of this great arc in space, atmospheric drag will begin to separate out most of the decoys, allowing for greater target discrimination by the defender. However, this dispersion based on atmospheric effects occurs just before entering the terminal or fourth phase (lasting between thirty and 100 seconds). It was this phase on which earlier, more primitive, NMD focused.

In this latter phase, the warheads enter the atmosphere, closing on the target at hypersonic speeds. Defense at this point becomes extremely difficult due to the time and velocity of closure. Effectively, NMD becomes literally a computer war with little or no human agency possible. In addition, the tactical environment is likely to be polluted by nuclear blasts in the atmosphere aimed at disrupting defenses through electromagnetic pulse (EMP) effects. Even more stressful are tactical or theater-level ballistic missiles that, as with submarine-launched ballistic missiles (SLBM), have even more truncated flight paths, further complicating the interception tasks. TMD, however, copes with lower speeds than NMD.

Additionally, approaches to BMD generally track one of two pathways: either an area defense methodology or a point terminal defense modality is pursued. The former envisions interception occurring outside the atmosphere, and is an exo-atmospheric interceptor. In the latter case, interception occurs inside the atmosphere, and is an endo-atmospheric approach. An exo-atmospheric system must discriminate between warheads and decoys in an environment where those differences may be obscured because of minimal drag (no atmosphere). Endo-atmospheric systems usually confront situations that are that are much more simplified because decoys are affected by atmospheric drag. Decoys disintegrate or are buffeted by the atmosphere while warheads come in more quickly, separating out, as it were, the wheat from the chaff. In both cases, interception remains extraordinarily difficult due to the speed of the vehicles.

In Table 1.1, ballistic missiles types are generally classified, based upon the longest range achieved by the specific systems. The classification is presented in order to provide a framework for considering the various statements made regarding the comparative missile threat posed by other states. During the Cold War, the Soviet threat spanned the entire spectrum of possible missile types. Presently, most missile threats lie at the lower three levels with future development of the ICBM threat capability the question that roils the political waters. Capability reflects intentions—for example, the willingness of a possibly poor state to commit scarce resources to such an enterprise.

Capabilities thus may not directly translate into actions. A similar situation occurred with regard to nuclear weapons. South Africa and Argentina did not pursue such weapons to deployment despite their apparent technical capability to do so. Both, for reasons unique to their national politics, terminated their already existing nuclear weapon programs.

Later, the discussion will focus on the more explicit threats posed by different national missile systems. Differences in missile range change flight profiles, both in terms of the time elapsed from launch to impact plus the height the missile achieves prior to its descent toward the target. These parameters produce major changes in the technological requirements that must be met by any intercepting system depending upon what point in the missile's flight interception is desired.

NMD represents the most technologically challenging facet, given the extreme speeds and great distances involved, but both NMD and TMD remain extraordinarily difficult feats to achieve, shooting one missile down with another missile. For example, TMD confronts the problem of an extreme shortage of time, given the comparatively short duration of missile flight to target. Even this scenario is in fact an unrealistic simplification since many attacks are likely to involve multiple missiles traveling in deliberately evasive patterns and target profiles. Decoys may be deployed to further confuse the situation. In fact, the duel in the desert in 1991 during the Gulf War saw the largely futile Patriot antimissile defensive efforts complicated by the physical breakup of the incoming Scuds; their very obsolescence enhanced their survivability against U.S. efforts at mounting an effective counterattack. Fortunately, that situation likewise prevented the Iraqis from achieving any real accuracy in warhead delivery. Even more futuristic scenarios envision the employment of lasers and particle beams (directed energy weapons) to shoot down attacking missiles. None of these latter interception technologies—neither from missile interception nor attack from some other form of weapon—presently work outside the test range. Protecting American society from external threat, especially nuclear weapons, always remains a critical national priority. Unfortunately, the policy choices become more complicated than merely agreeing to pursue a particular type of defensive methodology.

**Table 1.1**
**Classification of Ballistic Missiles by Range**

| Ballistic Missile Type | Range Parameters |
|---|---|
| Short-range ballistic missile (SRBM) | Under 1,000 km |
| Medium-range ballistic missile (MRBM) | 1,000 to 3,000 km |
| Intermediate range ballistic missile (IRBM) | 3,000 to 5,000 km |
| Intercontinental range ballistic missile (ICBM) | Over 5,000 km |

*Source*: National Intelligence Council, "Foreign Missile Developments and the Ballistic Missile Threat to the United States through 2015," Central Intelligence Agency, September 1999.

Different choices impact the future in often unpredictable ways. Plus, the very real specter of technological breakdown during combat haunts the field. What if the defenses being so confidently relied upon fail? It is these unanswered, possibly unanswerable, questions that help keep the debate alive. Such questions may be unanswered at present, but they are unavoidable if final resolution is to occur. Judgments must be rendered in the absence of hard battle experience, hopefully a continuing problem, but one that complicates the debate. Presidents, except notably Ronald Reagan, have been unwilling to commit unequivocally to national missile defense; hedging their bets has been the usual choice. The politics of national security make it impossible for a president to ignore the issue completely but most prefer that it remain on the periphery of public concern. That concern, unfortunately from their perspective, ebbs and flows with events—with the tide now rising.

## THE PROGRESSION OF THE ANALYSIS

The analysis presented here is organized in fairly straightforward fashion. The present chapter lays out briefly the changing U.S. worldview, one which underlies the general BMD debate, being a continuing generalized argument about the present and future role of the United States in world affairs. In that discussion, the security dilemma encountered by the United States is analyzed, along with the technology fixation so often thought of as characteristic of American security policy. Both of these factors have driven the policy protagonists in how they articulate their approaches to BMD generally and NMD specifically. This discussion will be generally cast in terms of shifting national agendas or priorities. In chapter 2, an abbreviated historical sketch of the NMD debate is laid out through 1997. Theater missile defense has been less controversial, being tied directly to protecting American forces in the field. The events highlighted are those that have impacted the tenor and direction of the continuing national discussions regarding missile defense. Chapter 3 discusses the apparent breakdown in the long-standing reliance upon deterrence in its various forms to forestall foreign aggression against the United States and its policies. This failure of deterrence, it is argued, makes BMD at all levels a political necessity if a coherent U.S. foreign policy is to be sustained. As a result, BMD is not simply a military technology program; rather it becomes a political litmus test regarding perceived American capacity to continue operating successfully as a global superpower. The difficult part is that the same answer can be used to support either an interventionist or an isolationist posture.

Chapter 4 picks up the historical sketch from 1997–1998 onward, plus it presents in more detail the arguments being advanced for implementing missile defense at both the theater and national levels with particular emphasis being placed upon theater-level activity. The current U.S. TMD program is presented with some detail to illustrate recent technology developments and enduring issues. Subsequently, in chapter 5, the discussion explicitly hones in upon the NMD debate and whether or not to deploy such a complex and expensive system. At this point, we further elaborate the ideas concerning U.S. foreign and security policy that influence the arguments being made by the protagonists. Whether or not the presidential and congressional decision is to deploy NMD, chapter 6 briefly lays out the basing alternatives being suggested. Such a discussion is obviously tentative, given likely technological and fiscal uncertainties but the broad parameters can be identified and analyzed (albeit with possibly large margins of error, especially fiscally). Finally, in chapter 7, the analytic focus shifts back to the possible domestic and international political and psychological ramifications if national level deployment occurs—whether it is successful or not. Those ramifications are likely wide sweeping and move in unanticipated directions. Important questions regarding its future U.S. relations with other states and their perceptions of our country's likely behavior will confront the Americans.

## THE CHANGING U.S. WORLDVIEW

Ballistic missile defense did not spring like the Greek goddess Minerva from the forehead of Zeus fully formed but rather reflects the historical but incremental evolution of American foreign and security policy development across the past fifty-years a process in which BMD is merely one component. Understanding this general historical context becomes essential for comprehending the strong attraction BMD as a concept possesses for American policy makers. Eight presidents (now nine with the most recent—George W. Bush) plus various Congresses have explicitly grappled with the technology's uncertainties, only to be repeatedly confronted by new technical permutations supposedly solving the earlier problems but in reality often encountering new ones. Those changes have repeatedly set off renewed searches for policy finality, continually receding goal. That search, in fact, was initiated even earlier by a dramatic shift in American elite perceptions regarding the United States and its future world role. BMD policy at one level becomes another metaphor for that larger process of seeking a secure American future in an increasingly complicated and dangerous world.

BMD as a concept strongly benefits from an almost visceral yearning for a restoration of that profound sense of national security provided by U.S. geographic isolation from the rest of the world. An inwardly looking people despite their immigrant heritage, Americans have with some trepidation and resistance embarked upon a different voyage through history than previously thought necessary. Building upon earlier national experience during and after World War I, World War II proved to be a watershed event for the United States in terms of its national self-perception. The bold statements made earlier regarding an expanded American role and power in the world seemed to have finally come to fruition. The United States had long been considered the laggard in world politics, possessing great potential military and economic strength but little follow through in terms of international engagement. Many European statesmen were not unhappy with that situation although they considered it potentially destabilizing over the long term. Despite intense and often emotional domestic opposition from both the left and the right after the war's end, national political elites firmly concluded that the United States could no longer retreat back into the isolationism characteristic of its national history up to that point. The collapse of the old Eurocentric political order (dating from the Peace of Westphalia in 1648) had left the world, especially Western Europe (the area of most critical and immediate American interest), subject to the Soviet Union's— the only other global power left standing by war's end—tender mercies.

The former European imperial powers, France and Great Britain, were noticeably in decline while Germany was prostrate after its crushing defeat. In the Pacific, China was in the midst of a civil war and Japan was devastated after its defeat. France and Great Britain were confronting their reduced capacity to wage successful war without major assistance from outsiders. The Soviet Union, while terribly damaged by the Nazis and its own actions, possessed the world's largest army and the most effective one left on the Eurasian continent. The U.S. military had disintegrated through immediate demobilization once hostilities ceased. Soviet intentions were clearly hostile to the capitalist democracies despite their former wartime alliance against Germany (and belatedly, Japan). Arguments concerning Soviet intentions during that period became irrelevant in one sense since U.S. policymakers were moving toward a more assertive global role. The United States had become fully aware through bitter experience that waiting until late in a conflict, even if conventionally fought, would likely be a recipe for defeat in the future. Greater German efficiency, for example, in waging war could have led to the defeat of the United Kingdom, leaving the United States isolated and alone. Nazi Germany would then have matched the United States and the Soviet Union in terms of accessible natural resources and population.

Even more dangerous for any sense of American national security was the obvious fact that new military technologies had greatly diminished the protection formerly embodied by the two broad oceans while nuclear weapons opened wide the very real possibility for total societal devastation. The protection previously provided by the vast distances of the Atlantic and the Pacific did not completely or immediately vanish but first air power and later ballistic missiles drastically reduced, if not eliminated, that vital cushion of time and distance. Voyages formerly covering a number of weeks were reduced to hours and finally mere minutes. More importantly, the oceans' vast size meant that adversaries could hide from American surveillance until a blow was struck. The Japanese fleet in December 1941 evaded aircraft and ship detection—both coming and going toward Hawaii and Pearl Harbor specifically. Enemies could now strike from a great distance, creating the potential for nuclear Pearl Harbors, the ultimate military disaster in American history. No longer could the United States simply rely upon those physical features to provide sufficient time to mobilize any defenses. Even Canada's great territory to the north did not provide much protection in the age of the missile and jet plane. Aircraft armed with nuclear weapons had minimized distance as a defense. Missiles effectively eliminated any cushion at all.

As one of the two remaining superpowers, the United States therefore somewhat reluctantly assumed a proactive posture of internationalism. This meant that the United States would now immerse itself in other states' affairs along multiple lines besides trade, the traditional venue, including possible military action. This proactive military commitment reversed a historical tradition dating back to the George Washington presidency with his fervent advocacy of the avoidance of entangling alliances. This new policy assumed even greater prominence when the Soviet Union extended its political control over ever larger areas, especially in Europe and Asia, with the potential for threatening putative U.S. allies globally. In a belated response, spurred on by the Korean War, U.S. military forces grew in both size and technological sophistication in order to provide both strategic and tactical combat support for its allies.

A strategy of political *cum* military containment formally rationalized this expanded international role.[6] Such an approach, however, assumed a long-term global American commitment to resist communist expansion. The long-term nature of this engagement was embedded in the containment concept, a constant source of social strain as many quickly wearied of the unending marathon. At different points in time, arguments were made for pursuing more proactive strategies, including "rolling back communism." The confrontational aspects of this approach limited its political realism in a nuclear age. Military action, likely nuclear, would be devastating for both sides. So, the United States embarked on a series of actions, usually conventional, in terms of weaponry employed, but these were ultimately buttressed by the U.S. nuclear arsenal. The John F. Kennedy inaugural address in 1961 with its espousal of an American destiny to preserve world peace and order in the face of communism and other international threats represented the high point. Later, the expressed attitudes remained much the same, but the aggressiveness became more publicly muted. In doing so, the United States assumed and acted upon the presumption that regional allies would remain absolutely essential for achieving containment success. However, in most instances, direct U.S. military involvement became central for establishing the allies' credibility in standing firm against possible Soviet expansion. The North Atlantic Treaty Organization (NATO) in 1949 became the poster child for that expanded American military role, but other treaties such as the Southeast Asia Treaty Organization (SEATO) also cemented an expanded U.S. engagement in world affairs. Whether or not all the alliances so eagerly created in the 1950s were realistic extensions of U.S. power and interest was an issue left unresolved but clearly highlighted by the Vietnam War.

As a result, two threads run prominently through the American international experience since World War II—or, at least, two threads that feed directly into this analysis. First, as we have discussed, the United States or, more accurately, its national leadership has been driven by an intense desire to impact the flow of international events. Their stated purpose focused upon the furtherance of American interests across the entire spectrum of international issues. No longer was the United States to be the powerful though passive actor on the world stage on an entire spectrum of issues, we refer to a broad span of engagement, ranging from the earlier traditional ones such as economics in various forms, especially trade and military security, to questions of environmental protection and human rights. Such a long menu suggests a very activist international presence although the reality is that trade and military always remain most central to U.S. concerns while the others fluctuate, depending upon the degree of attention extended to them. The larger problem is that the perceived security ramifications proliferate when one's agenda expands so greatly. Potential points of friction with other societies increase exponentially, especially with less developed societies not imbued with Western views of human rights, economics, and world order. Being the "have-nots," their perspective is somewhat jaundiced when regarding the "haves" and their sanctimonious claims to virtue and precedence.

Consequently, American security interests became broadly defined beyond merely protecting the country's physical security to fostering those values in other societies that will, broadly speaking, eventually become supportive of U.S. objectives. Thus, for example, one concerted push becomes fostering democracy and market economies under the assumption that such societies are likely to be less hostile to the United States as they are also another democracies. The "democratic peace" idea is obviously attractive although its empirical roots may be weaker or, at least, narrower than often thought by its exponents.[7] The new century will likely find the question revisited as more democracies' interests collide in situations where military conflict is feasible.

This activist foreign policy strain can be tracked through the various American presidents and their policy choices. Earlier presidents, from Harry Truman onward, felt compelled to focus upon international issues, given their dire implications for the United States in the context of the Cold War. But even Bill Clinton, the president least personally focused upon international affairs, found external events intruding upon his domestic political plans even prior to the "Monica Chronicles" in his second term. Across the ebb and flow of events, the consistent theme remains that of the United States as an active participant and shaper of international events.

More pragmatically, as a society, the United States has been largely protected from the worst consequences of its actions if a failure or misjudgment occurs. Overwhelming U.S. military strength and sheer physical distance from many crisis locations combine to provide a margin of protection from immediate retaliation. The apparent shrinking of these safety margins is what heightens uncertainty about the future. Part of the justification for NMD builds upon this international activism and the adverse reactions it might possibly provoke from those states being threatened by the United States.

However, conversely, there also exists an elite awareness that the general public, while generally supportive of the broad thrust of American international policy, often remains extremely skeptical about specifics. Public attitudes, for example, while fundamentally hostile to Soviet expansionism were unsupportive when it came to actually engaging in Cold War military encounters. Such events were perceived as either potentially threatening to the society's survival, given the possible use of nuclear weapons, or, indecisive as to outcome, effectively reiterations of the *status quo, quo ante.* This latter characteristic was inherent in the containment concept as compared to more assertive views such as "rolling back the Iron Curtain." The latter inconclusive result plays particularly poorly when contrasted to the earlier world wars when the United States (in the public's judgment) was an unequivocal victor, acting on the side of justice. The ambiguities of that earlier history were washed out by the passage of time while the inadequacies of the present situation are always graphically evident. For example, the Korean War (1950–1953) dragged out to a stalemate with a truce finally freezing the antagonists in place. The larger political point regarding a demonstrated U.S. willingness to intervene militarily washed out in the domestic political process, although not internationally. Other states remain fully aware of such American interventions, especially through employment of surrogates such as occurred in Iran and Guatemala in the early 1950s.

Subsequent events in Vietnam conveyed a similar somewhat mixed message regarding U.S. willingness to intervene militarily at least initially, but raised serious questions regarding its ultimate will to succeed. The importance here of both wars, Korea and Vietnam, is in the realization that the contours of American internationalism become clearer. The political limits on U.S. military forces and their employment were established, albeit after the fact, in both cases. Arguments that the difficulties encountered in both wars were explainable as temporary aberrations and should not influence future policy decisions ignore the clear reality that in a robust democracy there do exist clear limits to military interventionism in the absence of a direct security threat against the United States. The United States however is not unique in that behavior. Other governments, whether they are democratic or authoritarian, operate under similar domestic constraints. The difference comes in the visibility of American public reaction rather than the fact of its existence. In more authoritarian situations, erosion of military service or effective pacifism are the means employed by the public to register its dissatisfaction.

Clearly, American political leaders, if interested in pursuing an activist foreign policy, have to significantly reduce, if not eliminate, what may be perceived as intolerable demands upon society. The difficulty is that there exists no fixed standard by which to judge when enough becomes enough or even too much for the public. Clearly, public acceptance of a certain level of burden was heavily affected by their perceptions of the seriousness of the security threat posed by outsiders. When the perception of threat was thought high, greater sacrifices could be demanded and received with minimal adverse political reaction although even in World War II, the good war, the burdens imposed on the American people were minimized as much as possible.[8] As further support for this view of the public, later, a peacetime military draft was initiated in the face of a perceived active Soviet threat in Europe (Korea came later). But the draft, was in fact, seen as the lesser evil to implementing universal military service.[9] The Vietnam and Korean wars tracked this phenomenon of a changing public willingness to support and continue the original commitment. However, in both instances, the political commitment shifted toward a more expanded concept, only to retreat under the pressure of publicly adverse events (the Chinese December 1950 military intervention and the 1968 Tet offensive).[10] Given the growing ambiguity in the public mind regarding the specific goals being pursued, their support slid downward, further encouraging political opposition. Policy makers often become so absorbed in the details of the game that they lose track of the larger picture, including the steady accumulation of social costs. This occurs because the perceived costs of "losing" grow higher, especially when withdrawal negotiations or stalemate is perceived as reflecting upon the leaders' inability to create an acceptable outcome. Such tunnel vision is reenforced by a barrage of criticism by political opponents, reinforcing the leadership's sense of paranoia. Lines are drawn that further exacerbate the conflicts.[11]

The cost-benefit analysis made regarding a specific military action is calculated at two levels. First, the public assesses in some fashion their evaluation of the general worth of the particular policy—a process often very personalized in terms of burdens (e.g., increased taxes and military draft chances). Second, political opponents of the administration continually calculate their position regarding the intervention. Usually the latter argue for general support for American forces overseas, combined with often-detailed criticisms of specific government actions. The two calculations interact as the opponents attempt to convince the public to support their perspective. What is often left ambiguous for the public becomes the fact that the elites are often disputing over how to best manage the problem, not whether the original decision was correct. The opposition argues that the different approach being suggested by them would have produced much more positive results. Isolationist views are often articulated, especially in Congress, but administrations have usually assumed a more internationalist posture, reflecting differences in institutional perspective. Congress is being constituency focused in terms of burdens while an administration pursues larger themes. Administrations were not indifferent to constituency needs or views, just somewhat less intimately connected because their perspective differed from that of Congress.

Retrospectively, the original decision may be attacked, but that usually reflects longer-term policy failure. As John Kennedy stated after the Bay of Pigs debacle in 1961 (slightly paraphrased): Victory has many parents, defeat is an orphan. American elites have often vocally disagreed concerning the specifics, but internationalism in some form has been an elite priority since World War II and especially has been strong the Korean conflict. The world has become too dangerous for the United States to completely abstain or withdraw. An isolationist America is no longer perceived as a realistic option. There are disputes over how best to handle specific crises or dangers, but all occur within a generally internationalist framework. The difficulty comes in sustaining public support in specific contexts, ones that are often difficult and dangerous endeavors. Fortunately, most international crises rise and fall quickly, not fully testing U.S. national resolve. This allows elites to temporarily operate on their own, as it were. That reality has helped defuse some of the institutional conflict inherent in the War Powers Resolution, an attempt by Congress to force executive accountability (at least in terms of reporting) when American forces are committed in harm's way.[12] That resolution was part of a larger congressional distrust of executive branch ones, choices that became accomplished facts for Congress. The difficulty of voting against funding U.S. troops engaged in combat was too high for retrospective reaction. Instead, the intent was to get congressional involvement upfront before irrevocable or difficult to rescind choices were made. All administrations since Nixon's have resisted such efforts, cooperating with the War Powers Resolution provisions in the most minimal manner possible.

This thread is interwoven with the other great thread running through the tapestry of late twentieth-century and beyond American security policy. That thread traces out the continual search for technological solutions suitable for solving national security problems. Prior to World War II, technological solutions generally referred to advances in weaponry and the mobilization of American industrial might. The latter was, in fact, more important than the former since warfare still remained an affair of massed military formations. Great armies, encompassing hundreds of thousands of tanks and troops, and vast bomber raids, totaling a thousand or more bombers, were necessary in order to bring decisive force to bear. Naval task forces roaming the Pacific during the island-hopping campaigns contained multiple aircraft carriers.[13] The American capacity to equip such formations and, more critically, to continually resupply and replace them as necessary was decisive in achieving victory. Germany and Japan both lost that industrial production race to the Allies. During World War II, that productive capacity proved overwhelming, but, at the same time, military technology began expanding in sophistication and flexibility.[14] Military technology's full flowering awaited the nuclear age and the concurrent explosive development of electronics. The former clearly negated the large military formations employed earlier (those mass formations merely became targets) while the latter opened new frontiers, which are only now being fully explored. The search for technological solutions has become an unceasing one since 1945. The intensity of that effort has accelerated in more recent years as the Cold War's bipolar military and political structure recedes into historic memory. BMD as a concept has benefited substantially from this technological obsession since it is totally compatible with this trend: the use of high-tech weaponry to achieve political-military goals wrapped up nicely in a neat package.

The analysis presented here will not directly explore the question of whether a Revolution in Military Affairs (RMA) is in fact occurring.[15] Clearly, military technologies have been dramatically enhanced by improvements in sensors, artificial intelligence, and communications, but while BMD has benefited generally from those enhancements, the field has moved forward regardless of its BMD applications. BMD as a policy question would be on the table whether or not an RMA was occurring. Certain facets, especially those listed above, clearly push NMD closer to success but do not guarantee it. BMD generally benefits from the overall thrust of modern weapons' policy, which emphasizes high-tech solutions, but that emphasis has deeper roots than BMD.

## TECHNOLOGY AND PERSONNEL REPLACEMENT

Searching for military technological solutions occurs in several ways, reflecting both the state of existing technology (both civilian and military) and the equally strongly felt needs of political necessity. Each factor may have great effect at particular points in history. The longest running example has been the increasing substitution of more sophisticated technology for personnel. In a nation-state, whose history is often rhetorically bellicose but not as militaristic in behavior, military service has not been an admired or highly esteemed social occupation. The agrarian South, with its earlier aristocratic pretensions and general economic backwardness, was long disproportionately represented in the American military. The officer corps and many career noncommissioned officers represented both ends of southern society. As the South becomes more fully integrated into the larger American economy and society, regional attitudes became more similar to the national norm. American conservatism, unlike its European aristocratic counterpart has been driven by a capitalistic ethos, one often in fact very hostile to the military as an institution.[16] In addition, the more politically liberal elements of society are also imbued with a great hostility to the military except during periods of national crisis, but after it is over they quickly revert to their usual state of animosity. As a result, personnel recruitment has long been a problem during times of peace or, at least, no war. Earlier, the result was often a "hollow military" that is, a military that on paper appeared potent but in fact lacked sufficient personnel or equipment to carry out its missions when called upon. Prior to World War I, the U.S. Army was rarely able to conduct exercises beyond the battalion level because bases were widely scattered and budgets were small. For example, more recently, a brigade would be reduced by a battalion while each battalion lost a company, and so forth. On paper, the organization appeared strong; reality was much more daunting.[17] That situation arose prior to the Korean War as forces shrank to fit available budgetary resources. Presently in 2001, divisions are undermanned and warships sail short of crew. When those shortages adversely affect efficiency and effectiveness is not easy to judge.[18]

The result is that advanced technological capabilities, especially since the post–World War II period, becomes the mechanism by which an effective American military presence is maintained. Substitution of technology for scarce personnel is the hallmark of the American military. Originally, the mix was somewhat different in that U.S. military formations during World War II were already more technology intensive than their counterparts in other nations and were also larger in numbers.[19] As military technologies have become more flexible and efficient, their use has openly been transmuted into a replacement modality while hopefully retaining the enhanced combat capabilities implied by such technologies.

Explicit examples of this substitution process include the Eisenhower military innovations that culminated during the 1950s in the "New Look," followed by the "New New Look."[20] These innovations involved combining nuclear weapons and air power with the doctrines of massive retaliation and containment. Strategic doctrine over the Eisenhower years ultimately evolved into "finite deterrent" and finally later in the 1960s and beyond into strong and weak versions of "mutually assured destruction" (MAD). Each policy iteration was a refinement of the pressing question: How much is enough? All approaches, however, were fundamentally premised upon this substitution of technology for personnel or numbers in order to maximize combat effectiveness.

The United States along with its NATO allies almost immediately confronted in 1949 the reality that apparent Soviet willingness to maintain large troop concentrations was not going to be matched by equivalent Western military formations. This inequality (depending upon the definition used) resulted in five to ten times more Soviet divisions in the field than NATO could deploy.[21] Political realities within the Western democracies made matching such exertions politically unsustainable. The disparity in forces declined somewhat if sufficient time existed to mobilize reserves and deploy forces from the United States. That necessary time interval was thought highly unlikely to exist under the weight of a Soviet onslaught.[22] Therefore, nuclear weapons became the equalizer, especially when tactical nuclear weapons became available in large numbers and were deployed overseas. The Strategic Air Command (SAC) became the primary means through which nuclear weapons could be delivered directly against the Soviet Union and its allies.

The personnel implications of smaller military forces allowed the United States to stabilize and then to reduce its conventional forces, especially the army. Consistently, army formations have proven the most difficult and controversial to sustain in terms of recruitment because of their higher demand for numbers and the brutal, personalized nature of ground combat. Fiscally, reducing the army's size also produced the largest immediate budget savings— an especially critical question constantly occupying the Eisenhower administration's attention when achieving balanced budgets was the president's first priority. The navy, by contrast, developed the supercarrier as a mechanism through which it could remain militarily relevant in the new order while not significantly increasing its size. The key became guaranteeing each service's relative budget, position with each providing a critical component within the larger defense effort. Navy carriers were capable of handling the heavy aircraft necessary for sustaining a strategic nuclear role. Nuclear weapons had significantly larger payloads than conventional ones for many years; aircraft as a result grew to accommodate this heavy payload requirement. Ultimately, the Polaris submarine with its nuclear-tipped missiles firmly secured the navy's long-term strategic role, being effectively unfindable compared to the aircraft carrier. Instead, the carrier battle group gradually assumed the symbolic role held earlier by the battleship of "showing the flag" as a token of U.S. engagement in resolving a particular controversy.

The Vietnam War further intensified this linkage between military technology and personnel policy. The conduct of the war was predicated upon the intensive employment of such technology to overcome the twin perils of adverse terrain and uncertain political will. Regarding the former, there were successes, but the latter could not be changed through such devices. The United States, for example, deployed electronic devices in an attempt to detect and guide intense air and ground attacks upon the enemy's movements. While air power carried the war to the north, airmobile units in the south sought out the enemy on the ground, employing firepower to reduce casualties among American forces. None of this extensive technology usage overcame the political questions that were ultimately decisive in deciding the outcome—within both the United States and Vietnam itself. Technology replacement, however, was further bolstered as the only political answer—given the emotional domestic debate over the draft and the heightened concerns about being bogged down in an unending Asian war of attrition. The failure of technology to overcome a militarily inferior opponent did not undermine its appeal but temporarily moderated excessive enthusiasm.

Technology in and of itself could not compensate for faltering political will and deteriorating troop quality. The volunteer military, instituted by the end of the Vietnam War, encountered turbulence in resolving drug and racial problems but, once controlled, upgraded the overall quality of performance. Technology, despite its shortcomings due to poor doctrine and operational choices, became even more critical to the future due to its force multiplication features along with its potential for reduced casualties. A volunteer military is almost by definition more removed from the civil society, reducing some of the pressures that rose during Vietnam as casualties rose. More critically, when future conflicts occurred, the initial response would be by a more professional force, likely equipped and trained to handle the enhanced technologies. The full implications of this enhancement were not well understood because they were always measured against the Soviets, a peer force capable of overwhelming U.S. forces through numbers and quality of equipment.

Thus, more recent political enthusiasms concerning technology and its usefulness reflect the increasing time interval between that earlier mixed experience in Vietnam and the present with the Gulf War again highlighting the potentialities of such technology. The Soviet army faded into history without the final test occurring. The Gulf War as an example of the new military technology enhancement represented a difficult model to evaluate, given the flat desert terrain that maximized air power efficiency and the clear Iraqi military inferiority. Later air power difficulties in fixing and destroying Serbian ground targets in early 1999 further fed ambivalence about technology, but other more pressing political realities have forced if not accelerated continuation of the substitution pattern. The critical political lessons drawn now are those of minimizing American casualties. Zero air crew casualties, as in the Serbian air campaign, are obviously an overwhelmingly attractive proposition. Repeated military engagements in other unpleasant situations in geographically isolated parts of the world have reinforced technology's appeal as a substitute for personnel.

Across the Reagan era (the 1980s) and into the present, this substitution pattern persists, even across those earlier expansive years when force sizes were re-inflated after the post-Vietnam reductions. The intention shifted to creating a military force more powerful than that simply indicated by its size, especially in terms of personnel. As indicated earlier, the Soviets still outgunned the opposed

NATO forces. The debate now intensified across that period as to whether technologically sophisticated forces could, in fact, fully compensate for their smaller size. The all-volunteer military after Vietnam was a further goad to increase technology use as each individual became more expensive, but each member was now in theory more capable of operating sophisticated weaponry and support equipment. In addition, high-tech systems were increasingly "black boxed" in order to simplify maintenance—replacement of system components rather than actual repair became the modus operandi.[23]

The down side was that this further increased costs—despite reducing the aggregate number of units purchased, fewer tanks and planes, for example. In a circular fashion, the pressures grew to acquire ever more sophisticated technology in order to compensate for their smaller numbers and fewer personnel. Finally, with the draft's end, American society also returned to its long-standing avoidance of military service as a normal career choice, putting further pressure on the military to compensate with technology. Thus, the trend, especially with the Cold War's end by 1991, becomes even more a process of technology substitution as overseas bases decline in numbers and size. The U.S. military is moving toward an expeditionary force model in which its forces are dispatched to distant points from bases in the continental United States. Using sensor and communications systems truly global in nature, the U.S. forces will in principle be locally overwhelming both in effectiveness and lethality when in conflict with indigenous forces.

## TECHNOLOGY AND ACHIEVING TOTAL SECURITY

The second long-term pattern has not been singularly American although this country has pursued this particular approach with unusual vigor and enthusiasm. Until the arrival of the industrial age, military technology continually advanced, but it did so comparatively slowly over long time periods. For example, the British navy operated wooden ships of the line for literally decades, reflecting gradual changes in naval armaments and propulsion. That era ended dramatically with, first, the arrival of steam propulsion, followed by the ironclad. Entire navies were rendered effectively obsolete in a matter of a few short years. Now, technology and its anticipated advances are perceived as providing a dramatically enhanced capability for defending the United States from any external attack. The search for technological advantage has long characterized all military efforts, but for the United States, the combination of continued technological improvement and, comparatively speaking, possessing unlimited national resources has fueled the search for the ultimate weapon or defensive system. Most states confront hard economic choices, limiting their ability to pursue such options. However, in certain circumstances, those limits are overridden. Nuclear weapons once held that allure; the capacity existed to so intimidate potential adversaries as to be the ultimate military deterrent. Dogged pursuit of that goal drove several generations of military technologists and strategists. Unfortunately, the quest for the ultimate offensive weapon has floundered on technological inadequacies and human frailties. Certainty became a continual quest, rather than a reality or end state. As weapon platforms grew in size and complexity, their very growth left them vulnerable to countermeasures. Like the battleship, the energy expended in order to protect the system from counterattack was often sufficient to render it ineffectual or of limited use.[24] Weapons systems have grown in complexity and cost to the point that their loss becomes unacceptable. For example, there was concern expressed that a $2 billion B-2 might be lost during operations against Serbia. This contrasted to experience during World War II when the production of replacement units meant that losses were clearly disruptive but not self-defeating in themselves. German panzer tanks were individually superior but significantly fewer in number compared to the herds of Allied tanks. Quantity, within limits, overcame quality.

The reverse side of that coin becomes the search for the perfect defense. Previously, sheer physical distance from likely military threats provided that sense of security for the United States. Technology has now been made so overwhelming that unpunished external aggression becomes effectively impossible. Offensive weapons punish after the attack; and here the attacker is rendered ineffectual when the attack occurs. The Strategic Defense Initiative (SDI), begun in 1983 by President Ronald Reagan, was the clearest manifestation of this particular pathway. That enterprise represents a linear continuation of air and missile defense efforts, begun on paper in the 1940s and, more concretely, in the 1950s, and which have evolved into the present. Psychologically and politically, SDI represented a paradigm shift upward in public expectations concerning the role of technology in protecting America. The technology would be so overwhelming as to literally overcome the stupidity of leaders who too often place their nation in jeopardy. Running automatically of necessity, a BMD system becomes at one level a modern metaphor for *deus ex machina*, protecting a society from all harms. That loss of control by humans is an issue that is skirted but real in that the automatic nature of the process could worsen the outcomes.

Since BMD is the subject of this analysis, we will obviously return to consider in detail it and a variety of other questions associated with the search for an effective national missile defense. The larger point is that the United States has consistently striven to employ technology along several historically well defined pathways. Such behavior patterns are also found in other states as each society within its resource limits develops a distinct national style of defense policy making that persists across governments and even historical periods. Change occurs but at least superficially the forms and methods pursued often remain largely the same. Such change when it is truly fundamental in nature can force drastic shifts, but that event is much less likely to occur than rhetoric suggests, barring catastrophic events such as military defeat or persistent national challenge. For the U.S. military, the theme is one of consistency in terms of the military's role in society with its concurrent heavy emphasis upon technology to compensate for certain weaknesses, including personnel issues.

## TECHNOLOGY AS POWER PROJECTION

A third pattern, power projection, while more recent in development, reflects the accelerating military capabilities made possible by the new technologies. The Department of Defense articulated this view of the employment of high-tech capabilities most clearly in its Joint Vision 2010 (JV 2010).[25] The stated emphasis is upon rapidly deployable forces capable of global reach with overwhelming fire-power, and able to dominate the entire spectrum of military conflict.

The central concepts were dominant maneuver, precision engagement, full dimensional protection, and focused logistics. The third one, full dimensional protection, is particularly important because it focused upon enhancing U.S. capacity to protect its committed forces from all possible threats including ballistic missiles.    In effect, the military through this officially approved statement agrees that U.S. forces will be committed globally but under the provision that maximum efforts will be exerted to protect those forces from harm.    The other facets, especially dominant maneuver and precision engagement, draw directly from the expectation that U.S. forces will be capable of engaging the enemy in a manner maximizing the opportunity for success. That success is predicated upon the possession by the United States of technological superiority since often the will be fewer U.S. and allied forces than those of the enemy. Technology becomes the multiplier. Precision-guided munitions aided by near real-time intelligence gathered by extraordinarily accurate sensors will ensure maximum lethality and the ability to rapidly and accurately position U.S. forces in the best location possible to defeat the adversary.

These capabilities hold out the prospect that American military power can be multiplied (already alluded to earlier) exponentially.    Thus, possessing capabilities potentially allows implementing global-reach military operations in pursuit of American national interests.    The United States will have the capability to reach other locations, no matter how geographically remote, and impose its military will upon others, even when they actively resist.    In effect, the United States becomes what the British empire could only aspire to achieve, a truly global-reach power, capable of operating along all possible dimensions of warfare including air, sea, space, and ground.    The DoD has embarked on that developmental process, one fraught with some uncertainty since technologies do fail or are only partially successful in achieving objectives.    The process also involves changing how very traditional organizations, the military services, operate in reality not just on paper. Real change is demanded, not pro forma gestures.

Critics such as Michael O'Hanlon have suggested that the potentialities of military technology are vastly overstated.[26]    The argument is that the physical limitations of space and time are more difficult to overcome than advocates either understand or are willing to acknowledge.    Sensors, for example, limited how much improvement can be achieved.    More importantly, air power cannot physically lift sufficient fighting power to make a difference quickly against a well-armed opponent.    Ground units remain heavy and are consequently slow to deploy.    Those ground forces (i.e., light infantry or paratroopers) easily deployed lack the sufficient fighting power to dominate the battlefield.    Air power can severely damage the enemy but may prove insufficient to achieve political control.    The Serbian air campaign has already become a source of dispute over air power's real effectiveness.[27]    Despite these caveats, the political consensus defines such technology as absolutely essential for power projection as efficiently and effectively as possible.

JV 2010 or, its more recent permutation, Joint Vision 2020, represents but another stage in this technology developmental process, one that was initiated in the 1920s with the enthusiasts' bold predictions regarding air power's capacity to wage total war anywhere.    The bombers would get through regardless of the circumstances. Reality proved significantly more mundane until the 1950s when air power (with several technical improvements, including in-flight refueling) and ballistic missiles, combined with nuclear weapons, provided an early form of global reach.    Their deficiencies lay in the relative political bluntness of the weapons used—nuclear warheads of varying sizes, both tactical and strategic. Once a nuclear weapon is detonated, either the situation abruptly ends or the nuclear escalation process is a direct result, a terrible scenario for most. Military conflicts below the nuclear level remained difficult to access physically and affect quickly, witness Vietnam.    The newest military methodologies emphasize precision targeting with maximum lethality but employing conventional warheads.    This development process simply becomes the newest iteration in the "bigger bang for the buck" mantra permeating U.S. military policy.    As such, this aspect of military technology development lies at the heart of American post–Cold War foreign policy.    U.S. words may appear to lack forcefulness, but they are now backed by the demonstrated capacity to damage potential adversaries severely.    The Tomahawk cruise missile and stealth aircraft become the punishment of choice.    However, Iraq and Serbia have both endured that punishment and survived (or, at least, the regimes did so in the short term— nearly ten years at this writing in the case of Iraq).    Other means are required, if not in place of military force, at least as a complementary source of pressure.

## THE TECHNOLOGY IMPERATIVE AND OPTIMISM

All three of the above impulses interact to shape the direction and content of American security policy.    The increasing capabilities of such technologies expand the range and precision of military actions thought possible, but their limitations also leave one vulnerable in unexpected ways.    For example, dependence upon specific types of sensors may create uncertainties if the enemy is able to mask its actions from their scrutiny.    High-tech systems tend to be so expensive to develop and acquire that the spectrum redundancy existing earlier often atrophies.    For example, in time, the migration of surveillance sensors to space-based systems reduces the availability of aerial systems, decreasing flexibility and coverage at least in the short term.[28]    In the existing international context, when future wars are likely to remain small scale although possibly high intensity in nature, such cost factors impinge severely upon the military choices available. If a technology apparently works and covers the need, why do we require a second system, one that is likely expensive to maintain, operate, and continually upgrade, especially when the latter remains possibly more vulnerable to destruction by the enemy? That issue has arisen with regard to electronic warfare (EW)—"jamming" of enemy sensors by overload or spoofing—in support of air operations. Earlier decisions to scale back redundant capabilities are being reversed in some cases so current military deployments can continue successfully.[29]

One effect of this technology fixation can be summarized as the "technological imperative" along with its sibling, "technological optimism." The technological imperative refers simply to the understanding or belief, almost ideological in nature, that following the technology trail relentlessly to its logical conclusion becomes the only rational course for policy makers.[30] If a technology is thought to be physically possible and holds military consequences, then its development becomes the next logical step in a chain of naturally sequencing events. This primitive version of progressivism assumes as a matter of course that future technological advance is both inevitable and always for the better. Whether the technology imperative exists in reality is often heavily debated, depending upon what type of evidence is considered.[31]

The most extreme posture, in effect, states that there exist no real limits except the laws of physics and human imagination. And, the former can be manipulated or more fully understood, reaching unanticipated positive results. So, engineering imagination becomes the real limit. Serendipity also becomes an integral factor in this developmental process. We set out along a particular direction where unknowable but positive results are likely to occur as a matter of course. Computers, for example, have changed the manner of war because of their capacity to manipulate immense masses of data well beyond human capabilities to handle them in miniscule amounts of time. As a result or extension of this thought process, BMD now becomes a realistic possibility because the variables involved in achieving interception change so quickly that no human observer could anticipate and intercept such hypersonic objects. But, in principle, computers can successfully complete those functions. Improvements in military technologies are therefore presumed to reflect scenarios of steady advancement, illuminated by flashes of dramatic acceleration. In this sense, the American military and its supporters after its positive experiences in World War II have bought totally into the technology imperative.

Their initial enthusiasm after World War II may have been as much bureaucratically defensive in nature as that of convinced adherents since the military services wish to be in charge of any change process as much as possible, rather than being passive recipients or victims from their perspective. Being in charge allows some discrete even blatant channeling toward directions more compatible with their long-term institutional interests and objectives. Overt resistance did occur, for example, the air force's fixation on the manned bomber across the late 1940s and early 1950s led to the effective exclusion of ballistic missiles.[32] In the post–World War II budget-short situation, the service aggressively protected its current core technology, delaying newer and unproven technologies as long as possible.    After the Korean War began, the air force moved to systematically improve its missile programs.    This effort was partially a response to larger defense budgets; the air force could now possess both bomber and missile systems.    The threat existed that the other military services might attempt to assume control.    The secretary of defense had to adjudicate which service pursued which ballistic missile technology.[33]    The air force was not hostile to new technology; the service just desired to control its implementation in defense of the service's other, more critical organizational interests.    Organizational priorities differed from national priorities, at least in the short term.

The technology imperative is usually accompanied by a profound sense of optimism.    This optimism is only partially a direct consequence of experience. Rather, it also reflects an almost naïve faith in science and technology.    For laypersons, including many military leaders, the observed results are often close to magic, but magic that is doing their bidding.    This faith assumes that simply exerting the necessary political will with adequate resources leads to the desired outcome.    Inklings that some militarily-relevant activity is possible on paper or in theory becomes quickly translated into a position of eager expectation of success.    This sense of expectation is often not tempered by adversity, even when it occurs.    Indeed, adverse or negative results are routinely explained away as being inherent during the developmental process, a process almost by definition fraught with obstacles due to the enterprise's path-breaking nature. Given sufficient (often vast) resources and time, the requisite results or a facsimile thereof will be produced as a matter of course.    From this perspective, failure is routinely excused or explained away on the grounds that insufficient resources and/or time were provided for completing the effort.    In this accountability exercise, Congress or the civilians in DoD become the scapegoats, not the military.    The technology and the technologists are also normally not faulted although on occasion their competence may be drawn into question if a particularly strongly desired technological goal is not achieved.

The technological imperative and its attendant optimism flourish most strongly within the recesses of the classified world where public scrutiny can usually be avoided.    Within the "black" world of secret projects and agendas, mistakes are only belatedly, if ever, acknowledged openly.    Unrealistic programs or objectives can be sustained long beyond their natural life spans. What is most likely is that the technology being pursued will prove marginally successful or else demonstrate sufficient progress to justify continued effort. The project instead slips into the nether world of demonstration project: meaning ultimate success is not in theory the goal of the project.    Something is learned from this effort that is applicable to the next round.    Technological optimism does not demand an extraordinarily high standard of proof in the short term in order to maintain a program's existence.    Skilled bureaucratic players can normally meet the minimal standards necessary to sustain a secret program. The result is that the research and development budget is often confronted by extraordinary demands upon its resources, some of which are not visible to those who are unauthorized to access such sensitive information. Killing programs off becomes a difficult process. In fact, dying programs are routinely cannibalized to support a successor variation, which continues the pursuit since the goal is not discredited just the particular effort.

BMD has continually confronted the critics' question of whether its continuation as a program reflects reality or the triumph of fervent hope over experience. Generally, sufficient progress always occurs technologically to encourage those already predisposed to support the BMD effort while any failures (whether acknowledged or not) persist in keeping skepticism alive. The power of the technological imperative along with its attendant optimism, it can be argued, has kept BMD programmatically afloat where other less ideologically driven programs fell by the wayside. These somewhat emotional responses continue to drive the debate. Interestingly, opponents, like BMD proponents, also operate from within this general technological perspective. The former fears its success while the latter push for that outcome. This disparity in views reflects their very different perceptions of the world and the international system rather than any disagreement over the possibility of technological success. Time and money will cure all deficiencies.

## CONCEPTUALIZING THE POLICY PROCESS

Debating BMD policy has been an active though episodic blood sport for national elites for many years, a debate largely divorced, however, from the larger concerns of the American people. At a conceptual level, BMD mirrors national health policy, specifically health insurance, in that at intervals the issue resurfaces as a major national question—one that appears only to be partially resolvable at any point despite the often global rhetoric employed by partisans. Ballistic missile defense, however, represents an issue that continually circulates among the national elites, but remains somewhat below the national political horizon. No one has been elected or defeated for political office on this narrow issue. External events such as heightened threats from "rogue states" (now "states of concern") or the former Soviet Union earlier raised the question's visibility periodically but final resolution never occurred. This failure to achieve closure reflects the uncertainties inherent in the field plus its political disabilities. Few members of Congress demand to have missile interceptors based within their constituency while the military cost-benefit ratio remains suspect. Cost projections fluctuate drastically but usually go steadily upward while resource constraints remain very real.

BMD remains a policy concept continually struggling for more space on the national political agenda. As a concept, the issue remains very much alive within the specialized publics that focus upon national security issues, but only on occasion has it been able to achieve the status of being viable and visible on congressional and presidential decision agendas. That episodic quality reflects the impact of the changing national mood regarding external threats, changes in presidential administrations, and turnover in Congress. Those factors have undergone dramatic shifts across fairly brief time periods as will be discussed in chapters 2 and 4.

Public opinion regarding ballistic missile defense has been characteristically volatile because the issue remains peripheral to most individuals' interests. Despite the fact that NMD in principle acts to protect the population from annihilation, the debate has been arcane rather than focused upon issues immediately germane to private individuals. Much like the nuclear arms race generally, BMD becomes part of the background "noise" permeating the political process.[34] An individual president can lead on the NMD issue, Ronald Reagan did so, but his legacy proved more tenuous than most expected, even in the successor Bush administration. More usually, presidents are publicly ambivalent about BMD, especially in the form of NMD, because of costs and technical issues.

Thomas W. Graham and Bernard M. Kramer collected all the relevant surveys through late 1985 regarding BMD.[35] This period covered through the early stages of Star Wars, announced in March 1983. Their compilation showed that public awareness was usually high in terms of issue recognition although details were fuzzy. Support remained high until one factored in questions of cost and effectiveness. For example, in June 1968, 59 percent saw anti-ballistic missile (ABM) deployment as very desirable, a result that shrank to 34 percent when a $40 billion price tag was attached. A similar effect was seen when the question of system effectiveness was introduced (33 percent).[36] However, when the question was asked purely abstractly, Should an ABM be deployed? support ranged from 72 to 86 percent. But, when cost considerations are introduced, support generally declined.[37] The point is not to belabor the numbers since these survey questions are particularly difficult to evaluate. The reported results clearly reflected the interactive effects of question format, especially the preliminary statements to the actual question. The difficulty is that the public has remained largely disengaged; the issue is not too difficult intellectually, but it is just totally alien from their daily lives with no real reference points for judgment. Efforts in a survey to provide that context run the risk of contaminating the responses.

As a result, political elites and their views almost exclusively drive this question. The groups, individuals, and worldviews that influence them become the critical variables explaining decisions, not the general public's response or lack thereof. Appealing to the public is rarely successful unless the issue is directly related to their personal lives. For example, the original deployment in 1967-1968 became publicly controversial in many urban areas because ABM batteries would likely be sited near their homes since it was a terminal defense configuration. That localized connection made the issue real—groups in Washington and their local allies opposed to the ABM exploited that fact to leverage a public response that would undermine congressional reaction to the program. The current debate, and even the Star Wars controversy in the 1980s, while publicly divisive is confined within the Beltway. Public awareness and citizen activism have not been central to the controversy except at very rare and brief intervals. Modern technology, e-mail, and faxes can simulate public interest and outrage, but much like the U.S. space program, the degree of public interest and engagement remained both small and largely episodic in nature, heavily influenced by specific events. In a manner similar to gun control, public opinion is in a vague fashion supportive of NMD, but that support shifts as the question becomes more narrow in nature.

Specific topics pursued within the general BMD debate often become very esoteric in substance, and are cloaked in a technical jargon far removed from the common experience of both policy makers and the public. Hypothetical constructs constitute a large portion of the information being exchanged or, more accurately, hurled between opponents. Any technological advances have been incremental and/or theoretical, meaning they are difficult to evaluate without some degree of specialized technical understanding although each advance is much hyped by NMD advocates. As a result, much of the public debate has been largely framed in symbolic terms or through metaphors aimed at fostering understanding by the uninitiated. The "shield" concept of President Reagan is the most obvious example; but it never was a reality in practice. The paucity of successful interceptions has been a continuing and major disadvantage for NMD proponents. For example, the number of successful interception events depends on how one defines "success," passing near the target or directly striking the target vehicle. That slipperiness in definition causes political difficulties when those already skeptical or, at least, uncertain concerning NMD hear the facts as interpreted by various sides. Frances Fitzgerald and others have pointed out this recurring pattern of contested evaluation of test results.[38] Thus, NMD opponents merely point to the continued difficulties in achieving successful target interception and, by implication, suggest this pattern will continue indefinitely.

As a result, public engagement has not come directly through NMD itself as an issue but rather occurs when the question is cast more broadly. For example, public attention can be focused more quickly upon questions of general national well-being and evaluations of future directions set by the government.[39] These evaluations, however, are heavily driven by domestic concerns, for example, the state of the economy, but foreign policy and security issues can become an important component when those policies visibly fail or perceptions grow that the United States has become weaker in some fashion. The furor in 1999 over Chinese nuclear espionage, chronicled in the Cox Report, is a good example of asserting national vulnerability by an administration's opponents.[40] In a similar manner, that controversy tracks the earlier 1940s and 1950s debates over Soviet spies and the atomic bomb. The effort is one of engaging public attention if possible in pursuit of some larger political agenda. Final resolution is often not necessary or even possible on such matters—witness the continuing controversy over the extent of Soviet spying in the United States during the early Cold War. New facts are merely subsumed into the larger debate without appearing to change participant attitudes or their conclusions.[41]

Such evaluations are obviously not spontaneous political occurrences but grow out of the give and take of partisan politics. The NMD issue was not originally the property of a single political party, but, over time, significant segments of the Republican and Democratic parties shifted to opposite ends of the debate. The Republicans have become the most adamant NMD supporters while Democrats have remained and grown more skeptical over time. Recent vote totals (through November 2000) have not clearly reflected that division since each political party seeks to manipulate the issue for its benefit. Democrats maneuvered to decrease any adverse political effects while Republicans continually strove to leverage the issue as a critique of the Clinton administration. For example, in 1995, the Republican attempt to enforce the "Contract with America" section calling for immediate NMD deployment was defeated 218–212 in the House. Later in 1999, the Senate voted 97–3 to deploy an NMD system as soon as technologically possible—a position that only symbolically changed the situation. Such protective actions meant NMD remained below the horizon despite the best efforts of NMD proponents.

The disappearance of conservative Southern Democrats has severely reduced the core group of NMD supporters within the Democratic party. There have been instances of nearly unanimous congressional support for NMD initiatives, but those episodes represent largely symbolic actions. Democratic support often occurs in the form of a political vaccination—inoculating themselves against the charge of being "soft" on national defense issues. The dominant factions within the Democratic Party are well aware that NMD costs can severely impinge upon their domestic priorities by reducing the available funds for other purposes. At the party's most liberal end, this domestic priority perspective also rejects any significant funding for National Aeronautics and Space Administration (NASA), for example, as a wasteful diversion of scarce societal resources for purposes unrelated to critical priorities. Former Vice President Walter Mondale strongly pursued that particular view while serving as a senator in the 1960's and 1970's. Describing the Apollo Program as "moon-doggle" is the most famous academic articulation of that attitude.[42] This understanding of the fiscal linkage between NMD and domestic social priorities becomes even clearer if balanced federal budgets continue to occur. The available pot of money shrinks especially when domestic economic growth slows. Rising tides lift all boats, but ebbing economic tides have the opposite effect. Hard choices will then have to be made between equally important national priorities. Starving social programs to ward off a distant military threat may prove politically challenging in terms of economic adversity and the claims made by constituents for relief.

Republicans, rhetorically at least, argue NMD as a higher national priority than most social programs although that stance often gets compromised in the legislative process. In an era characterized as not the Cold War but a twilight zone of uncertainty, mobilizing support for domestic priorities is easier than for foreign policy or defense matters. The public presently does not perceive the enemy as massing at the gates, so deferring or stretching out NMD does not raise intense alarms. The international context will impact which way the decisions fall—in favor of domestic or NMD programs.

Proponents of NMD confront a dilemma if public support is sought for the effort. When a party does not hold the presidency, raising the alarm can become another weapon in its arsenal. But, if a party holds the presidency, the problem becomes more complicated.  Raising the political temperature requires that one portray the country as at risk due to the failure to deploy NMD.  That, however, reflects upon the administration, undermining its ability to govern.  So, NMD advocates in the absence of unambiguous external threat tread a fine line between strident alarmism and informed criticism.  Presidents, regardless of their political party affiliation, have been erratic in their support for NMD, reflecting their considered but evolving judgments as to potential threats, technological progress, and available resources; and a balance must be struck. Policy as a result has zigzagged over the years.

Over time, the BMD policy debate has gradually coalesced into several distinct constellations of supporters.  These groupings are organized into a policy community tied together by its linkages to individual members of Congress and the various committees and subcommittees dealing with the BMD issue, along with relevant executive agencies.  Presently, NMD proponents are tied most closely to Congress while opponents gravitate toward the executive branch.  This reflects the reality that Congress remains most supportive (being Republican controlled) while the executive (being Democratic through 2000) has been clearly more skeptical.  This reverses the earlier relationship of Republican presidents supporting BMD with vocal Democratic congressional opposition, for example, to SDI.  The changeover occurred between 1993 and 1995 when George Bush left the presidency, succeeded by Bill Clinton, and the Republican congressional majority assumed office after the 1994 elections.  As a result, 1993 and 1994 became years of policy flux while BMD programs shifted in emphasis and new players entered the long-running debate.  The capture of the presidency in January 2001 by the Republicans and the near stalemate in Congress complicates things, but clearly the tide is flowing toward some form of NMD deployment.

There are clearly economic interests involved, but those stakeholders (e.g., defense contractors) have not driven the larger debate, at least as overtly as many assume, because other facets of the controversy, especially feasibility, have dominated the issues.[43]  The restructuring and downsizing of the American defense industry in the aftermath of the Cold War has further consolidated the players into basically a few clusters or industrial teams whose memberships fluctuate across one weapon system to another.  For example, Boeing is the Lead System Integrator (LSI) for the present NMD program while Lockheed Martin heads the consortium building the most prominent TMD program component, the Theater High Altitude Area Defense (THAAD) program.[44] Raytheon is the other large corporate player, developing the navy's Theater Wide program, and is also a major subcontractor within the larger BMD program.

What is more interesting is that unlike the first ABM deployment debates, there is no military service per se arguing for the program.  The Ballistic Missile Defense Organization (BMDO) like the earlier Strategic Defense Initiative Organization (SDIO) represents a distinct organizational entity, led by air force generals but clearly not a single service program.  The earlier Nike X was clearly an army initiative, fully supported by that service.  Conceptually, this translates into a bureaucratic situation in which the individual military services, the traditional budget players, find the BMDO a potent competitor, drawing funds from their service priorities.  Recent DoD supplemental appropriations have disproportionately favored the BMDO despite the services' arguments regarding their shortfalls and especially the modernization needs. Organizational politics, therefore, have not disappeared but may track more complicated configurations.  The consistent pattern since the late 1950s has been to centralize authority in the DoD.  BMD further accelerates that process both organizationally and budgetarily.  Unlike the U.S. Space Command, the BMDO does not present the potential threat of another military service arising out of the shell of BMDO.  Conversely, many of the organization's functions due to their highly technical nature, are completed by civilians.  That allows for continuity of service (no rotation necessary) and the payment of competitive salaries. Military personnel are in the command positions but their workforce is mixed not only in terms of military service but also whether an employee is civilian or military.

Essentially, the interest (advocacy) groups located outside the government (see Table 1.2) have provided Congress with proposals and technical evaluations with which to challenge administration proposals.  These concepts are also debated by groups outside the administration that are supportive of its agenda. A reciprocal feedback loop ensues as the various players enter into the congressional-executive debate and then go back out to the interest groups. Participants often transfer institutional positions, depending upon the changing contours of the debate.  BMD experts in exile look to their return or, at least, the return of their views to power, but meanwhile they strive to maintain their credibility and visibility while waiting.  One thing that impresses is the important role of ideas in fueling the debate.  In another context, John Kingdon alluded to the fact that "the content of ideas themselves, far from being mere smokescreens or rationalizations, are integral parts of decision making in and around government."[45]    Those ideas are developed, expressed, and sold through the medium of different advocacy groups.

**Table 1.2**
**Rough Classification of Advocacy Organizations**

| Pro-NMD Deployment | Anti-NMD Deployment |
|---|---|
| Heritage Foundation | Federation of American Scientists |
| Cato Institute | Union of Concerned Scientists |
| Stimson Center | Carnegie Endowment for |
| Marshall Center | International Peace |
| National Intelligence Council | Coalition for a Livable World |
| Nixon Center | Arms Control Association |
| Center for Security Policy | MIT Security Studies Program |
| Coalition to Protect Americans Now | Greenpeace |
| Citizens for a Strong America | Physicians for Social Responsibility |
| America's Future | |

One thing that impresses is the important role of ideas in fueling the debate. In another context, John Kingdon alluded to the fact that "the content of ideas themselves, far from being mere smokescreens or rationalizations, are integral parts of decision making in and around government."[46]    Those ideas are developed, expressed, and sold through the medium of different advocacy groups. For example, the Heritage Foundation runs a continuing commentary upon the BMD debate with an emphasis toward accelerating deployment. The Union of Concerned Scientists in conjunction with the MIT Security Studies Program has engaged in a series of technical critiques of BMD technology generally and in particular on NMD specifically dealing with its responsiveness to decoys and other deceptions. One public advocacy group was the Coalition to Protect Americans Now, which ran ads in the media supporting NMD deployment and also attempted to heighten public awareness by providing on it's web site the ability for an individual to specify his or her location and find out its vulnerability to missile attack through what was labeled the "Missile Threat Calculator."[47] The goal was to heighten public awareness in the context of the 2000 presidential election. Greenpeace and the Physicians for Social Responsibility on the other side had petitions posted on the web that concerned citizens could sign and transmit to selected public officials. Nongovernmental organizations here as elsewhere have been major contributors to the controversy through analysis and publicity pushing their particular positions. High Frontier, for example was instrumental in pushing the original SDI decision in 1983 and continues to be active into the present although the Center for Security Policy is now the acknowledged leader of the pro-NMD deployment forces.

Other occasional participants in this struggle over concepts and ideologies have included the Government Accounting Office and the Congressional Budget Office.    These official agencies provided analyses of NMD options, DoD progress toward successful deployment, and, most critically, estimated costs of implementation. The Brookings Institution and the International Institute for Strategic Studies, for example, published several works dealing with the NMD issue along with more general analyses of American defense policy and its future directions, including assessments of the effects of NMD on relations with other states.    The latter analyses were less obviously political in their analysis but individual authors put forth their positions as to what should be done—all of which became fodder for the larger debate.

In this study, however, the primary focus will not be directly upon these specific participants, although their efforts will be cited at times when relevant, but rather the general policy views espoused, which are more fundamental than those of passing celebrities and often-transitory organizations. Fundamentally, one must be aware that there exists an intense intellectual ferment surrounding the questions embodied in the BMD concept whether at the theater or national level. These interactions provide the intellectual framework within which the overall debate has proceeded and all new information has been assimilated.

In fact, the movement of individuals back and forth facilitates the intellectual interchange between official and unofficial participants. The revolving door is mostly from government to private but the original ties still exist and expedite communications. The policy network is both robust and contentious in part because of the issue's specialized audience. Only on occasion does the issue rise to the top of the policy pyramid and absorb elite attention. As will be discussed, NMD is much like a minor league baseball player who rises to triple-A ball but only gets a "cup of coffee" in the big leagues before being sent back to the minors. NMD is presently in the high minors, struggling to make the leap to the top of the national issue hierarchy. For that to occur, luck and circumstance must converge to provide the right context.

Conceptually, the overall policy debate fits the incrementalist developmental model in that, despite extreme flights of rhetoric, including presidential ones on occasion, reality has proven much more mundane and difficult to change. A series of marginal changes have driven the field technologically closer to ensuring successful deployment. On the surface, such singular policy initiatives as President Reagan's SDI proposal in 1983 appeared to break the mold, holding forth the prospect for truly revolutionary change. At a political level, the proposed change was potentially profound, but only for a time, until economic reality quickly pulled the program back to earth. Fiscal, technical, and international political realities served to make the SDI program innovative in intent but ultimately much more routine in execution. This more mundane reality contrasts to the often-bombastic rhetoric employed to mobilize public support for and against deployment. Possibly if deployment does occur successfully (that is, if the system in principle works under all conditions) then the implications truly may become revolutionary, creating discontinuous international political change.

## CONCLUSION

The BMD policy debate, as it will be described, can be best characterized as a program concept engaged in a continual quest for the "magic bullet"—that is, the technological breakthrough that will shatter the chains of existing incomplete technologies by effectively and reliably intercepting attacking missiles. A variety of technological options is being vigorously pursued, but progress has characteristically been significantly less rapid than anticipated or proclaimed. Therefore, the policy arena remains one in which marginal choices are made in dogged pursuit of more dramatic technological breakthroughs. The assumption underlying many decisions is that the technological barriers can in fact be broken, given sufficient time and resources. That technological optimism permeates the entire argument advanced by proponents (an assumption also shared by their opponents).

Given that profound sense of inevitability, the defeat or delay of a particular proposal does not constitute a final end to the issue, nor is it fatal to either side. Rather, the question retreats into the political nether land of more peripheral issues, only to be resurrected at some later point when conditions are thought more propitious. In fact, the very size of the DoD budget permits continuation of the effort. One must realize that the U.S. government across all presidential administrations has decided implicitly that some modicum of a BMD technology effort remains necessary. The squabble then becomes one over how fast and far to pursue this exotic and often troubled military technology, given other equally pressing societal needs and priorities.

In this analysis, we address the underlying pressures that sustain BMD as a viable program, especially the NMD's political component, even when the technological progress remains slow and erratic. A significant part of that motivation comes from observing a world that is changing in ways deemed possibly inimical to American national interests. From one perspective, NMD in its largest sense represents the United States fervent hope of the reasserting control over its destiny rather than being constantly battered by the shifting tides of events. Others perceive NMD as totally disruptive of existing international understandings, destabilizing a basically peaceful world for no significant enhancement in American security. These conflicting worldviews drive the entire debate, providing the edginess characteristic of this often-subterranean controversy. NMD represents an important public issue but one generally lost to public view or interest—a situation that allows wide latitude to presidents and Congress. That reality has been replayed multiple times as will be seen.

## NOTES

1. John W. Kingdon, *Agendas, Alternatives, and Public Policies*, 2d. ed. (New York: HarperCollins, 1995), 165.

2. Michael O'Hanlon, *Technological Change and the Future of Warfare* (Washington, DC: Brookings Institution Press, 2000) 151.

3. This view echoes the arguments made against the U.S. Supreme Court in its exercise of the power of judicial review: that is; the power to declare acts of Congress unconstitutional. As Justice Harlan Stone asserted: "the only check upon our own exercise of power is our own sense of restraint." *United States v. Butler*, 297 U.S. 1 (1936). The United States with effective missile defense becomes analogous— answerable to no one but itself.

4. Robert Jervis, *The Meaning of the Nuclear Revolution* (Ithaca, NY: Cornell University Press, 1989). The lack of experience did not deter theorists from constructing scenarios based on projections into the future.

5. The description presented here is generic and is derived from the earlier discussion in Roger Handberg, *New World Vistas: Militarization of Space* (Westport, CT: Praeger, 2000), 77–78.

6. Mr. X [George F. Kennan], "The Sources of Soviet Conduct," *Foreign Affairs* 25 (July 1947): 566–582.

7. The idea of whether a democratic peace exists in fact remains a debatable question. Cf. Michael E. Brown, Sean M. Lynn-Jones, and Steven E. Miller, eds., *Debating the Democratic Peace* (Cambridge, MA: MIT Press, 1996).

8. John Keegan, *The Second World War* (New York: Penguin Books, 1989) 218–219.

9. Samuel P. Huntington, *The Common Defense: Strategic Programs in National Politics* (New York: Columbia University Press, 1961), 58–59.

10. John F. Mueller, *War, Presidents and Public Opinion* (reprint of 1973 edition Lanham, MD: University Press of America 1985.) Mueller traces the pattern of support then decline as interpreted through the prism of public opinion relative to the president.

11.   Lyndon Johnson was highly sensitive to the political costs inflicted by the Vietnam War upon his domestic programs, but felt locked into a no–win situation, given repeated U.S. commitments of its prestige to the war.

12.   *War Powers Resolution*, 87 Stat. 555 (1973).

13.   Samuel Eliot Morrison, *The Two Ocean Navy* (1963, reprinted; New York: Galahad Books 1997), Clark G. Reynolds, *The Fast Carriers: The Forging of an Air Navy* (Annapolis, MD: Naval Institute Press, 1968). Both provide an overview of the use of aircraft carriers in the new form of naval warfare.

14.   Keegan, *Second World War* 578–584.

15.   For an eclectic sampling of the RMA issue, see Colin S. Gray, *The American Revolution in Military Affairs: An Interim Assessment*, (Occasional Paper No. 28. London: The Strategic and Combat Services Institute1997); Andrew F. Krepinevich, "Cavalry to Computer: The Pattern of Military Revolutions," *Public Interest* (Fall 1994); 30–40; George Friedman and Meredith Friedman, *The Future of War* (New York: Crown Publishers, 1996).

16.   Samuel P. Huntington, *The Soldier and the State* (New York: Vintage Books, 1957), 143–162.

17.   Huntington, *Common Defense,* 39–47.

18.   For example, during the 2000 election, the Republican candidates made continual references to declines in defense preparedness. Those became a source of controversy since some complaints were very specific and thus were challenged by the Democrats. The reality of stretched military forces was not challenged, but the question of responsibility was debated. Cf. Terry M. Neal, "Cheney Defends Attacks on Military Preparedness," *Washington Post* August 28, 2000, A8.

19.   Richard A. Gabriel and Paul L. Savage, *Crisis in Command: Mismanagement in the Army* (New York: Hill & Wang, 1978) Russell F. Weigley, *Eisenhower's Lieutenants* (Bloomington: Indiana University Press, 1981), chapter 2.

20.   Huntington, *Common Defense,* 69–113.

21.   The key question was the respective size and firepower of the divisions. U.S. divisions historically have been among the largest in terms of personnel. Their efficiency or effectiveness in combat was a matter of some controversy during World War II when smaller German divisions operated more aggressively. See the discussion in Weigley, *Eisenhower's Lieutenants* 24–28.

22.   See Edward Luttwak, *Strategy: The Logic of War & Peace* (Cambridge: Belknap Press, 1987), for an analysis of the numerical differences between Soviet and NATO forces in the mid 1980s.

23.   Stephen Peter Rosen, *Winning the Next War: Innovation and the Modern Military* (Ithaca, NY: Cornell University Press, 1991).

24.   Friedman and Friedman, *The Future of War*, 113–118.

25.   The original document is reprinted as "Joint Vision 2010," *Joint Forces Quarterly* (Summer 1996): 34–49 can also be found at http://www.dtic.mil/doctrine/jv2010.

26.   O' Hanlon, *Technological Change and the Future of Warfare.*

27.   Daniel A. Byman and Mathew C. Waxman, "Kosovo and the Great Airpower Debate," *International Security* 24 (Spring 2000): 5–38.

28.   Roger Handberg, *New World Vistas* 239–241.

29.   David A. Fulghum, "U.S. Air Force Receives Two New Long-Range Intelligence Aircraft," *Aviation Week & Space Technology* (December 6, 1999): 66–67 Robert Wall, "Pentagon's EW Efforts Seen in Shambles," *Aviation Week & Space Technology* (April 24, 2000): 29–32.

30. Herbert F. York, *The Race to Oblivion: A Participant's View of the Arms Race* (New York: Simon & Schuster, 1970).

31. Ernest J. Yanarella, *The Missile Defense Controversy: Strategy, Technology and, Politics, 1955–1972* (Lexington: University Press of Kentucky, 1977), 4–5

32. David N. Spires, *Beyond Horizons: A Half Century of Air Force Space Leadership* (Peterson Air Force Base, CO: Air Force Space Command, 1997), 16–21.

33. For one perspective, see Jacob Neufeld, *The Development of Ballistic Missiles in the Air Force* (Washington, DC: Office of Air Force History, United States Air Force, 1990).

34. Ernest J. Yanarella reported with respect to the original ABM deployment controversy: "Throughout the 1950s and 1960s, the extent of public knowledge and interest in BMD was virtually nil." *Missile Defense Controversy*, 146.

35. Thomas W. Graham and Bernard M. Kramer, "The Polls: ABM and Star Wars: Attitudes toward Nuclear Defense, 1945-1985," *Public Opinion Quarterly* 50 (Spring 1986): 125–134.

36. Ibid., 128.

37. Ibid.,129, 130.

38. Frances Fitzgerald, *Way Out There in the Blue: Reagan, Star Wars and the End of the Cold War* (New York: Simon & Schuster, 2000), 242–248.

39. For an overview of the role of issues in presidential elections, see Nelson W. Polsby and Aaron Wildavsky, *Presidential Elections,* 10th edition (New York: Chatham House, 2000).

40. Select Committee, *Report of the Select Committee on U.S. National Security and Military/Commercial Concerns with Peoples' Republic of China* (Washington, DC: Government Printing Office, January 3, 1999).

41. John Earl Haynes and Harvey Klehr, Veona: *Decoding Soviet Espionage in America* (New York: Yale University Press, 1999).

42. Amaiti Etzionim, *The Moon-doggle: Domestic and International Implications of the Space Race* (Garden City, NJ: Doubleday, 1964); Vernon Van Dyke, *Pride & Power: The Rationale for the Space Program* (Urbana: University of Illinois Press, 1964).

43. Kerry Hunter, *The Reign of Fantasy: The Political Roots of Reagan's Star Wars Policy,* (New York: Peter Lang, 1992), 144–147. Professor Hunter argues that economic considerations are critical in assessing why Star Wars was kept alive despite persistent doubts as to its technical possibilities.

44. Boeing has changed its title from LSI to general contractor in order to shed some public criticism of the contract competition and resulting difficulties. The change is cosmetic rather than substantive.

45. Kingdon, Agenda, Alternatives, 125.

46. The Web site was http://www.protectamericanow.com/.

47. Earlier work by author had predisposed one to perceive BMD as policy arena best characterized by a "punctuated equilibrium" model. That involves the perspective that American politics are often characterized by long periods of incremental decision-making, but are then struck by brief periods of fervent activity and change, and then

proceed forward from the new political equilibrium.   For a brief overview of this perspective, see James L. True, Brian D. Jones, and Frank M. Baumgartner, "Punctuated-Equilibrium Theory:  Explaining Stability and Change in American Policymaking," in Paul A. Sabatier, ed, *Theories of the Policy Process* (Boulder, CO:   Westview Press, 1999), 97–115.

# 2

# Ballistic Missile Defense, Still Trying after All These Years

## INTRODUCTION

As becomes quickly clear, ballistic missile defense (BMD) in its various guises has a lengthy history, one that grows steadily longer and more complicated with each passing year. Initially, the constraints upon the concept of ballistic missile defense were entirely technological. Later, the constraints became more mixed, a combination of policy judgments and technology development issues, especially the latter at critical points. The issue of ballistic missile defense has now been paraded across nearly five decades, beginning in the 1950s. Within this chapter, the focus is one of delineating the larger historical events and trends against which the controversy over BMD occurs. Discussions and evaluations of BMD options at both the theater and national level have not occurred in a vacuum, rather external events have impacted what was deemed relevant or at particular points in time. They included technology and military and political events with the exact mix varying across time. At certain points, technology appeared more compelling than previously, but it was still influenced by those other factors. When threat perceptions rose in intensity, the search for solutions, possibly including national missile defense grew more frantic. Risks unacceptable at another point in time might now become viable options to be pursued more aggressively. NMD always contains the potential for failure in combat, a factor influencing the degree to which decision makers rely upon that pathway to national security.

This changing context is what makes the policy process appear interminable. Rather than reaching a decision point (in some rational design sense) and then pushing on into implementation, the question appears to hang fire perpetually in part because critical decision makers did not lack agreement about NMD's most critical functions. In a very graphic way, NMD never found a policy window open wide enough to sustain long-term deployment. Instead, BMD became a question perennially on the edges of the larger strategic arms debates. The earlier focus always remained upon intercontinental ballistic missiles based on judgments regarding their essential invulnerability to interception despite defenders' best efforts.

In order to explain this phenomenon, the effort here becomes one of synthesizing earlier historical treatments of the issue rather than providing an in-depth historical analysis.[1] The broad outlines will be traced out, some details will be provided as necessary, and then they will be linked to current debate questions. BMD was clearly embedded in the intense debate over strategic weapons policy that traversed the entire Cold War era. Ironically, only in the post–Cold War period is the concept returning on its own in a context very dissimilar from the original deployment decision in 1967 but also in many ways very similar to that event: that is providing missile defense against comparatively primitive ballistic missiles rather than the Russian Federation (strategic weapons' successor to the Soviet Union) with its large and sophisticated missile arsenal. The critical difference presently is the reduced concern with the prospect of a global bipolar nuclear confrontation, a context that highlights what would previously have been considered minor players on the strategic weapons stage.

## ONLY A CONCEPT

Crude ballistic missiles or rockets (albeit of extremely limited range) have existed since at least the 13th century when Chinese and later Indian armies employed gunpowder-propelled rockets to attack enemy formations. Based on European observations of such usage, rockets were refined, albeit sporadically, across the centuries in the quest for greater range, accuracy, and lethality. William Congreve's rockets flying over Baltimore and Fort McHenry became the most visible example for Americans (the "rockets' red glare" memorialized in the "Star Spangled Banner").[2] Militarily speaking, however, all armies experienced great difficulty in controlling the missile's direction of flight while artillery continually improved in its accuracy, rate of fire, and lethality, ultimately superseding rockets. The rockets' military value was clearly suspect although their terroristic aspects were already clear. The Big Bertha cannon of World War I fame was in concept similar to a crude ballistic missile, hurling shells (warheads) seventy-some miles into the city of Paris. The military limitations of such super-cannon (lack of accuracy) were obvious although the concept remained attractive, striking at such a vast distance that civilians are terrorized by the attack's abruptness, and falling without warning or possible defense since no counter-battery fire could strike that far. In the 1990s, missiles were used with similar terroristic intent against Taiwan.

At the end of World War I, a defeated Germany was largely demilitarized in terms of military formations and possession of first-line military equipment although not in its attitude. Being severely limited regarding the availability of treaty-compliant armaments, the search began for those alternatives not covered or prohibited by the Versailles treaty, an early non-American example of the search for technological solutions to personnel deficiencies. Rockets and, by implication, missiles became one avenue among many being pursued. The primary goal remained one of extending the range and effectiveness of German artillery. At the same time, within the Soviet Union, similar military rocket developmental activities were underway.[3] In other countries such as Great Britain and the United States, isolated groups of civilian rocket enthusiasts pursuing development of rockets for space exploration existed, but national military interest remained minimal until World War II.[4] The Jet Propulsion Lab at the California Institute of Technology under U.S. Army direction became one marker of this heightened military interest. In both societies, shrunken military budgets minimized the likelihood of innovative programs outside those technologies that had already demonstrated immediate pay-off. Within the U.S. military establishment, the central struggle was over air power and its employment—rockets lay clearly over the horizon, not visible or critical at that point.

Regardless, from its modern inception, the dual-use character inherent in any rocket technology became clear. Civilian space enthusiasts may have pursued the peaceful goal of reaching outer space for scientific exploration and growth of the human spirit, but governments, if at all interested in the technology, evaluated the new devices in terms of their potential as instruments for war. Missile development subsequently became a priority within Nazi Germany, springing forth publicly with the first surprise V-2 attack falling upon London on September 8, 1944. The V-1 represented an early version of a cruise missile, albeit both a vulnerable and inaccurate one. The V-2 as a weapon failed to stem the tide of Allied victory but provided a preview of the military potential for such missiles. V-2s rained down on London and Antwerp. In fact, the argument has been advanced that the V-2 program diverted sufficient scarce resources (materials and personnel) from the German war effort in terms of more immediately useful projects (jet aircraft for one) as to actually aid the final Allied victory. At that critical juncture in the war, super-weapons such as these were a diversion rather than an addition, coming too late to save Nazi Germany.[5] The contrast to nuclear weapons in terms of military value was clear. Regardless, falling from the sky with little or no warning, such missiles proved an unstoppable weapon once launched. The only effective countermeasures immediately available for the target society involved disrupting the missiles prior to launch, destroying the industrial facilities manufacturing them, or putting the population being attacked in shelters. All of these strategies were implemented, but success proved problematic in that those early missiles were comparatively mobile and extremely difficult to locate prior to launch. Also, early warning remained difficult to carry out although it was possible.

Fortunately, for the allies, the missiles' inaccuracy and flight failure rate helped reduce their military potential dramatically.

This first encounter with the missile age laid the general foundation for all subsequent military efforts to suppress such activity.  Interception of the V-2 was, practically speaking, impossible unlike the V-1, which was effectively an early cruise missile, a drone jet aircraft.  The latter could be destroyed by either gunfire from the ground or by interceptor aircraft.  Therefore, suppression of any possible ballistic missile attacks had to be preemptive; otherwise, the defender could only react by striking back at equivalent or more valuable targets held by the enemy since the launch site was empty—unlike an airfield to which planes eventually returned if able.  Missile flight was a one-way journey.

In the missile age, therefore, great intellectual energy has been expended pondering various missile-basing modes and assessing their vulnerability to surprise attack.  Given the enormous uncertainties involved, the question could never be definitively resolved.  Earlier, however, the V-2 was comparatively limited in range (200 miles or so) with a great deal of inaccuracy.  That range, however, was substantially longer than any artillery equivalent.  Plans on the drawing boards projected a missile capable of reaching 3,500 miles—a true intercontinental ballistic missile (ICBM) spanning the Atlantic to strike New York City.[6]  When Allied armies plunged deeper into Europe, however, the Nazi missiles were forced back out of range or their launch sites were overrun by ground forces.  During the war, London and Antwerp were heavily bombarded, the first cities to suffer ballistic missile attack against which there existed no defense once successfully launched.

Clearly, the V-2 range limitation could have gradually been overcome, as more powerful rocket engines and accurate guidance systems became operational.  Earlier German plans included rocket planes spanning the oceans as part of a larger scheme that envisioned travel both beyond the edge of the atmosphere and just within it.[7]  The drag coefficient inherent in such flights along with heat generation hampered efficient military operations. Transatmospheric vehicles (TAVs) have been an eternal item on the military's long-range wish list but their usefulness remains suspect in part due to their hypersonic speed.  At those speeds, the turning radius becomes excessively larger, hindering target tracking and responsiveness.  Warheads can more efficiently and be delivered cheaply by ballistic missiles although there is no recall once launched, unlike a manned bomber.  TAVs are one derivative of the crewed bomber, dear to the Air Force's heart, but not otherwise militarily relevant in comparison to air-breathing systems or purely space-based ones. Missiles and sophisticated satellites have largely superseded the TAV—best known militarily by the cancelled 1960s Dyna-Soar program and later in the early 1990s as the National Aerospace Plane (NASP) program.[8]  Therefore, the flight paths actually flown saw rockets reach even higher beyond the atmosphere to reenter far downrange.  During reentry, atmospheric drag created excessive friction that burned up the payload or warhead.  Continued research saw the development of the "blunt nose" solution along with ablative materials that dramatically reduced heat buildup, allowing for effective reentry of the warhead on target.  At this point, the missile moved conceptually from a short-range weapon to one with intercontinental potential.  Solving this reentry problem also allowed for recovery of payloads returning from orbit.  Such recovery still remains a significant technological feat, moving a state into the category of a true space-faring state.  Other solutions for achieving safe reentry were pursued in the form of the Space Shuttle's heat tiles and particular angles of attack employed during the journey through the atmosphere.[9]

Two factors continued to limit the military potential of ballistic missiles; system reliability and payload lift capacity.  Launch failures persisted as a problem, reflecting the developmental process.  Gradually, the missiles became more reliable, reflecting both greater flight experience and quality improvements in the manufacturing processes.  Liquid fueled engines were particularly sensitive to irregularities during flight operations.  Any minor manufacturing or flight-processing errors existing in the missiles being launched cascade quickly into total catastrophic failures while in flight.  That quality control issue continues into the present with launch failures plaguing the space industry.  New launch vehicles have the highest failure rate as the bugs are worked out.[10]  For NMD, this raises questions since the launch vehicle is scheduled to be among the last components tested before the system is declared operational.

More limiting militarily was the inability at first to lift sufficient weight to carry nuclear warheads.  Early on, missiles plus nuclear warheads were widely considered to be the ultimate weapon, unstoppable once launched and totally devastating upon impact.  The ultimate doomsday weapon was finally at hand at least on paper.  The difficulty was that early atomic weapons were too heavy for flight on any available rockets.  They frankly lacked the capacity to lift the cumbersome bombs of the day.  In fact, even B-29 heavy bombers (the workhorses of the Pacific bombing campaign and the early strategic bombing force) had difficulties handling the larger weapons.  Their range was significantly reduced due to this weight problem.  The ponderous B-36 with its ten engines, for example, was the only available bomber capable of easily carrying such heavy and awkward weapons.  Unfortunately, its size and slowness left the B-36 vulnerable to Soviet air defenses.  Missile development steadily progressed toward lifting larger payload capabilities but simultaneously, due to the arrival of the hydrogen or H-bomb, warhead size shrank dramatically with no diminishment in destructive potential.  Weapons went from kilotons to megatons in explosive power.  The fusion weapon in fact—due to its extraordinary power—reduced the intense pressure upon ICBMs to become as accurate as previously thought necessary. Missile accuracy increased over the years but larger weapon yields allowed near misses to become the equivalent to direct hits.  The second nuclear strike in Japan missed the designated target point by three miles; but the devastation inflicted was still enormous.  Their accuracy grew even tighter in the early 1960s with the arrival of the CORONA reconnaissance satellites that pinpointed targets.[11]

Prior to the successful development of the national reconnaissance satellites in the early 1960s, the United States had only approximate coordinates for the most likely military targets.  In fact, vast areas of the Soviet Union remained virtually unmapped since the last outsiders had been present there during the Civil War raging in the early 1920s. Soviet secrecy meant that many cities, military bases, and research facilities were virtually unknown or only approximately located. Maps were either classified secret or printed with deliberate errors as to exact location. For example, the launch of the first *Sputnik* in 1957 was identified as occurring from a launch location, Baikonour Cosmodrome, geographically removed from the actual site, Tyuratam, nearly 370 miles away. Attacking aircraft in theory could hunt for their target if the original location was found to be in error. A missile would just impact the designated location without regard to whether the target was physically there or not. The new reconnaissance satellites, growing in accuracy and sophistication, allowed for even more precise targeting. ICBM targeting and guidance systems took several years to catch up to the accuracy made possible through the new space technologies. More critically, development was also initiated to provide more effective early warning of missile attacks—moving beyond the ground and air based warning systems available up to that point.[12] This capability extended the time available after any warning was provided; a critical factor if an effective defense was to be mounted.[13] Such warning capabilities were absolutely essential if a successful NMD was to be implemented. Otherwise, the time lines grew too compressed for effective counteraction.

The larger issue, however, was the anti-ballistic missile (ABM) and its feasibility. In fact, earlier, in 1946, the first such antimissile projects were initiated on paper—laying out the problem in greater technical detail. These early theoretical exercises were hampered by continued developmental issues in basic technologies, especially the building of boosters capable of lifting the interceptors. By the Korean War's end in 1953, ballistic missile development entered into a new age with the Atlas, Thor, and Titan programs underway or in the process of being initiated. The Atlas and Titan rockets represented the first-generation intercontinental ballistic missile (ICBM), fully capable of spanning the globe, striking deep inside the Soviet heartland. As liquid-fueled rockets, these missiles were new designs although still linear descendants conceptually of the earlier V-2 and its derivatives such as the Redstone and Jupiter. Such missiles remained slow to launch, comparatively speaking, so that successful ballistic missile defense at this point still meant striking them prior to launch. Such vulnerability led to fears that both sides might launch preemptive missile strikes in order to avoid having their missile forces being caught literally on the pad. The outcome was a heightened possibility for nuclear exchanges occurring during a crisis, especially if one side or the other perceived or assumed it was going to be preempted. That liquid-fueled launch limitation led to the initiation of two distinct missile pathways in the future.

The first, the new Minuteman ICBM series, incorporated solid-fueled boosters launched from hardened silos buried in the ground. These missiles incorporated two critical features, quick launch—effectively achieving launch on command—plus increased protection from surprise attack. The earlier generation liquid-fueled missiles were, comparatively speaking, unprotected because the fuels and oxidizers had to be loaded at the last moment, as accumulating vapors in a silo increased the explosive hazards. In fact, these issues delayed navy willingness to pursue building ship-based ICBMs whether for surface ships or submarines until solid-fueled boosters became feasible. The second, the submarine-launched ballistic missile (SLBM), beginning with the Polaris submarine fleet, employed stealth by hiding within the vast oceans covering the earth. Concealment within the ocean depths provided the naval analogue to a hardened missile silo since available Soviet anti-submarine technologies were inadequate to achieve assured destruction of such submarines, especially when hiding in the middle-ocean depths. Nuclear propulsion allowed such vessels to lurk anywhere, including out of immediate missile range, and then move closer, in order to launch their attack.

Both of these innovations, eventually duplicated by the Soviet Union, minimized the likelihood that sufficient damage could be inflicted by a surprise nuclear attack to abort a possible missile counterattack. A successful surprise attack might be mounted, but the residual forces remaining were sufficient to annihilate viable life on both sides. Successfully preventing a missile attack through preemption became more problematic despite intense efforts aimed at better targeting and improved penetrating warheads. The logical alternative became destroying the warhead in flight prior to striking the target. If one did not, or could not, destroy the missile prior to launch, then interception became the primary defensive option left.

Thus, ballistic missile defense in the general form being debated presently made its debut at least as a concept. In fact, its active development served as notice that the more proactive preemptive strike approaches had failed the test of reality or, at least, simulation, while "in 1955, Bell Telephone Laboratories completed a study using analog computer simulations that indicated it is possible to hit a missile with another missile."[14] The physical realities of achieving such an interception remain daunting to say the least given the speeds of 5 kilometer or more per second at which missiles and their warheads close on target. The continued failures of proactive search-and-destroy strategies to work effectively were evident later in the Gulf War when Scud hunters were unsuccessful despite strong, albeit belated, efforts.[15] In that context, the Patriot antimissile batteries became the only show in town with basically negative military results but positive political ones.[16]

The other alternative pursued with clearly minimal political enthusiasm was civil defense. In effect, society itself would be sufficiently hardened to minimize the population loss since no antimissile defense was practical. The physical damage to society would still be enormous, raising questions as to civil defense's usefulness. This option, although much discussed, never took hold for several reasons. First, ideologically, such an approach required drastic changes in American life—a level of regimentation thought inimical to traditional American values of individualism and freedom. Second, even if such physical measures were implemented, including a massive population shelter program, the entire effort could be negated by an increased Soviet willingness to target those same cities with a number of larger weapons—in effect, multiplying the destruction. Even if the population survived this onslaught, the society would be in shambles, nonfunctional in almost all critical spheres. By the mid-1960s, civil defense as a military response largely faded from view—the future solutions would be military in nature. This also reflected the cost factor if effective national civil defense was to be provided. Civil defense focuses more on disaster relief efforts than on a military survival exercise. The earlier Gaither Report had proposed spending $22 billion on radiation shelters but that ranked clearly as a secondary priority, far behind the need to ensure the strategic forces' survivability.[17] Deterrence through maintaining strong and invulnerable nuclear forces was the ultimate bulwark against any Soviet missile attack.

However, achieving successful interception demands that the anti-ballistic missile weapons have to track and strike their targets across a diversity of situations. That situational complexity, combined with the hypersonic closing speeds, made success, practically speaking, completely impossible until computers came of age. From the onset, BMD was irrevocably tied to advances in technologies not necessarily being developed for that purpose. Computers, communications technologies and architectures, and sensors had to advance along with development of solid fueled missile interceptors capable of effectively attaining nearly instaneous response. All of those loomed as feasible concepts, but development lagged behind the leapfrogging advances in ICBM offensive technologies. The offensive side of the equation was thought clearly dominant and likely to remain so indefinitely.

Development of an American ballistic missile defense capability also lagged for other technical and bureaucratic reasons. Missile defense in the larger scheme of things lacked political "sex" appeal. Unlike Russian doctrine and history and despite the name "Department of Defense," U.S. military policy has traditionally emphasized the offensive side when at all possible. Recurrently, across the 1940s and 1950s, civil defense along with other defensive options took a back seat to the more glamorous and politically rewarding strategic offensive weapons programs in terms of service budget share. The navy, for example, created the supercarrier in an effort to remain engaged in the strategic bombing mission mix; as, the attacking aircraft were too big and heavy for its earlier carriers.[18]

The *Sputnik* launch, October 4, 1957, provided a shot of adrenaline for all three military services' efforts to pursue control over the U.S. space program. In a series of actions that need not detain us, the U.S. Army was abruptly removed from the interservice competition to run the U.S. space program.[19] The air force and a brand new civilian agency, the National Aeronautics and Space Administration (NASA), were charged with that function, now split between the military and civilians. By 1960, the army was forcibly divested of its embryonic space arm when NASA assumed control of the Redstone Arsenal, home to the Army Ballistic Missile Agency; Wernher von Braun's organization was thus transferred to NASA, becoming the Marshall Spaceflight Center.[20] The air force solidified its control over land-based ballistic missiles, both intermediate and intercontinental in range, while the army was reduced to only short-range battlefield missiles. The navy continued its sea-based systems.

Amid the bureaucratic shuffling, however, the army was again expressly delegated the mission of providing ballistic missile defense. The decision on January 16, 1958, was driven more by the recommendations of the Gaither Report than *Sputnik* but became part of the justification for the army's removal from strategic weapons and space activities.[21] The air force resisted being ousted from the NMD field but to no avail; the program duplication argument used to defang the army of its missiles now conversely worked against the air force. This decision represented a further extension of the army's traditional role in ground-based air defense (ratified originally in 1947 when the Department of Defense was created) and symbolized by the Nike series of air defense missiles. For example, fixed Nike Ajax and Hercules batteries (the latter being nuclear tipped) protected military bases, especially along the nation's coastal areas and overseas. Their mission was to destroy incoming Soviet air-breathing bombers and primitive cruise missiles. Their effectiveness was never challenged in combat and was gradually phased out by the 1970s as the Soviet bomber threat declined in relation to their growing ICBM arsenal and the imperatives of mutually assured destruction. Successor air defense programs were developed and deployed over seas primarily especially in Europe, for use in any possible confrontation with the Soviets.

In some ways, NMD at first constituted merely a bone thrown to the army since the reality was that the technological issues made immediate battlefield success improbable. The requisite technologies did not exist, nor was there firm evidence despite great optimism that such success was imminent. The army had begun in 1955 developments that led ultimately to the Nike Zeus, a three-staged interceptor employing a nuclear warhead. The difficulties were that the Nike Zeus proved relatively easy to fool with decoys, and the system could be readily saturated with multiple launches.[22] But, within the context of American defense policy, NMD now had two critical components in place. First, the general concept of BMD had been part of the Gaither Report (among many other items)—a report accepted and partially implemented by President Eisenhower. In the report, ABM systems were to protect Strategic Air Command (SAC) bases with national area deployment to follow later if at all. That meant that high-level political support existed at least in the abstract for the general weapon concept, moving it beyond the realm of mere possibilities to an initiative with at least some growth potential, an important issue for the Army which always remained fearful of losing even more budget share. The 1960s were not kind to the army, in comparison to the other services in terms of aggregate budget share, reflecting its low-tech reality.

Second, designating the army as the lead agency meant that there was now an organizational sponsor committed at least nominally to the program. NMD was not the army's highest priority (rebuilding its divisions after the post–Korean War reductions was the highest), but it was now on the table as an issue that demanded army support. For certain organizational elements within the army, this program constituted their only entry into the new world of high-tech warfare. So, NMD now possessed some degree of high-level political support and an organizational identity. Even large-scale programs can disappear into oblivion if such organizational assets are not put in place. There exist too many other competing programs with powerful and aggressive bureaucratic sponsors capable of obliterating weak competitors. As a concept, NMD was now underway, albeit still a side issue within the larger military agenda.

## OPERATIONALIZING THE CONCEPT

The goal, in 1958, when the U.S. Army was formally charged with NMD, became achieving a high rate of successful interception with the effective destruction of incoming missile warheads prior to their reaching the target. Prior work had identified the problems; solutions were being worked out. In fact, for FY 1959, the army pushed for preliminary Nike Zeus deployment in 1962. Eisenhower, in the first of a series of recurring presidential decisions agreed to pursue technology development but not to implement deployment. The technical issues remained too daunting. This original focus was upon national-level defense in part due to the cumbersome nature of the technology; it was not mobile or robust enough for possible deployment with forces in the field, especially overseas. This mission in a programmatic sense meant that accomplishment of several distinct but interrelated tasks was demanded simultaneously. One must be able to accurately identify that a missile launch has in fact occurred first in the Soviet Union and ultimately globally when missile technologies proliferated to other states. In that identification process, the unknown missile's direction of travel and speed must be accurately, quickly, and continually assessed if successful interception is to occur. The time pressures are immense, especially during the terminal stage of the missile's flight. That identification and specification process must eliminate any false positives, while minimizing false negatives. Failure to successfully complete any of these tasks means that one's weaponry may be prematurely expended chasing false alarms, exhausting irreplaceable assets prior to actual need. Or, conversely, ignoring actual missile attacks due to faulty or inaccurate information leads to annihilation because no action is taken. These issues are not trivial and remain central to the technical accomplishment of missile interception.

So, from the start, technology development at several levels was deeply embedded in achieving a successful defensive effort. Fudging any single issue meant a possible catastrophe for the United States if the government relied upon NMD as its primary defense. In that situation, there existed no backup position—an inability to accurately and swiftly identify that a hostile missile attack has occurred becomes tantamount to national suicide. This was a high hurdle to overcome but one thought achievable since it built upon technologies already under development. The MIDAS program had been initiated by the air force in the mid-1950s as part of their applications satellite program. This included the Samos, an observation satellite, and the early warning satellite, Midas.[23] In time, this effort evolved into the Defense Support Program (DSP), a global missile early warning satellite constellation.[24] Such a system provided the  initial   launch   warning   so   critical   for   survival   and   successful countermeasures. The SAC bomber wings were totally dependent upon early warning in order not to be caught on the ground. Airborne alert was a possible option to avoid surprise, especially for short periods, but the drain upon aircrews, their planes, and budget meant the numbers of necessity would be limited. Adequate warning allows less stressful reaction options. Ground-based radar systems such as the Defense Early Warning (DEW) line were the original versions, but with missiles, warning times were cut dramatically. Space-based detectors permitted longer warning times although submarine-launched ballistic missiles still meant extremely short intervals to impact.

The Defense Support Program system is winding down in the early twenty-first century to be replaced by two interrelated systems oriented to provide more accurate and complete coverage. During the 1991 Gulf War, the DSP had to be reoriented properly in orbit in order to detect the Scud launches since the system's primary mission was to survey the Soviet Union and China, the two missile threats capable of reaching the United States. In a world (post-2000) characterized by missile proliferation globally, that degree of coverage was clearly inadequate. The Space-Based Infrared System (SBIRS) in its High and Low configuration provides that comprehensive coverage.[25] The SBIRS-High, slated for launch in 2004, is a four-geosynchronous-orbiting satellite constellation, designed to detect the hot plumes of missiles during launch phase. The SBIRS-Low is a flotilla of 24 low-earth-orbiting satellites that will track missiles after their motors burn out, the mid-flight stage. Projected SBIRS-Low system launch is scheduled tentatively for 2007 or later, having encountered major developmental delays. The original intent of all these missile early warning systems was to provide sufficient warning for U.S. strategic nuclear forces, thereby preventing a successful enemy surprise attack. NMD builds upon these early warning systems with other detectors used for actually cueing the missile batteries.

Once accurate launch identification has been accomplished, the warhead must be tracked until actual interception occurs. The chosen interception instrument was another ballistic missile. This choice occurred for several reasons: the alternatives, mostly various forms of energy beams, lasers, and particle beams, were too difficult to scale up to become effective weapons. Atmospheric effects also significantly distorted their range, accuracy, and lethality. Such weapons are most efficient in outer space, a continuing and unresolved issue politically. Other possibilities such as scattering obstacles along the projected flight path had multiple disabilities related to the peaceful uses of outer space, plus such devices impact all space objects regardless of their nationality. One could not subsequently enter the region of outer space until the objects are removed. Plus, warning would likely not come early enough to allow dispersal of the objects prior to the missile bus's, passage through the area. Also, space debris takes a long time to return to the atmosphere and burn up, (objects orbited during the earliest days of the space program still are up there). The effect would be to continue damaging satellites possibly including U.S. spacecraft, long after the crisis ended. In one sense, this scenario is analogous to the problems that exist after a conventional war where land mines are still buried across the battlefield and even in areas remote from the actual fighting as perimeter security measures. Casualties persist long after the conflict has officially ended and the combatants have left.

Striking an object along the fringes of outer space or the edges of the atmosphere requires a ballistic missile capable of virtually instant launch response with hypersonic acceleration along with significant capacity for close-in maneuver. Controlling the weapon in flight becomes a matter of milliseconds or less course corrections. That directional capability clearly lies beyond the capacity of humans and, initially, the guidance technology. Hit-to-kill (HTK) technologies proved extremely prone to failure or near misses (the functional equivalent to total failure). Therefore, the solution was to employ area burst effects, the missile version of antiaircraft gunfire with proximity fuses. However, the distances and speeds involved meant failure was still highly probable. In order to ensure the kill, nuclear-tipped missiles were to be employed. The high altitude electromagnetic pulse (EMP) effects, however, meant that everyone's battlespace communications and detection sensors were temporarily disrupted. An enemy could launch a first missile wave, promptly followed by a second wave, partially protected at least from initial detection by the electromagnetic disturbances produced by the original defensive volley. This problem persisted but in the short term (the 1960s) there was no alternative since kinetic energy or HTK methods remained too failure prone. In addition, depending upon altitude and weapon yield, nuclear blasts inside the atmosphere could inflict extensive damage on the areas being protected, a perverse outcome for a defensive system.

From the army's institutional perspective, NMD was an obvious extension of its traditional air defense role. This attitude can be seen in the naming of the initial missiles, Nike Zeus and Nike X, reflecting their organizational lineage as part of the Nike missile family. The developmental effort concentrated on solving all the various facets of the interception problem with the publicly most visible manifestation being a July 1962 successful Nike Zeus near-interception of a dummy ICBM warhead. The interceptor passed within meters of the target, but since the warhead would have been nuclear, that was deemed close enough to claim success. A Soviet V-1000 missile had completed such an exercise the previous year in March 1961.[26] In effect, a bullet had been struck deliberately by another bullet. That test range success did not signal anywhere close to 100 percent reliability, but it did suggest that a NMD option was, in fact, physically possible, not just a simulation artifact. The artificiality of the test situation, however, did not convince critics who focused upon the failure potential of the technology and politically destabilizing nature of NMD.

Similar doubts have been expressed over the years regarding the reliability of U.S. strategic missile forces. Will they work when the bell rings? Realistic test situations have proven difficult to test operationally since the ICBM fields lie inside the heartland of the United States. Firing missiles over population centers is not considered a prudent thing to do since flight failures do occur even under the best of circumstances. Therefore, missiles are transported to Vandenberg Air Force Base for testing, a process during which the missile moves completely outside its operational milieu with new parts substituted for existing computer hardware in order to run the test. How reliable or accurate an evaluation this process is best in fact, proved troubling to many, but no realistic alternative has ever been developed. Thus, the heart of the American strategic nuclear forces rested upon a series of assumptions that the systems would work when needed. Given the high failure rate of military equipment during routine operations, this remains an interesting assumption.[27]

Based upon that success plus strong evidence that technological development was occurring in other critical areas, the political debate in the mid-1960s picked up momentum over the question of whether or not NMD deployment should occur immediately. Deployment at this point obviously included only the national level rather than the theater level, reflecting the bulkiness and delicacy of the system's command, control, and computer elements. Computing facilities especially represented particularly delicate operational environments, characterized by large workforces. In an era when air conditioning was still comparatively rare, computer centers were generally arctic-like environments. Communications networks likewise consisted of extremely dense hardwired arrangements linked to fixed location detector sites for battle-space management. Space-based detectors made the initial contact, but the existing BMD technology was a terminal point, or limited area defensive arrangement, which meant the detectors handling the actual interception, must be placed comparatively close at hand for ease and speed of operation. The vulnerability of these facilities to destruction or electronic disruption was a particularly thorny problem, but was not in itself disabling since larger policy questions drove the debate.

The existence of a purported workable alternative to continued total national vulnerability to Soviet missiles meant that the issue of deployment would be pursued at some level. In a sense, the existence of a possibly workable solution moved the question higher on the domestic policy agenda, but was insufficient in itself to force an immediate choice. Several factors strengthened arguments for seeking immediate deployment. First, the technological imperative had full play since proponents consistently argued that future technology developmental efforts would, of course, conquer the obvious inadequacies existing in their early prototypes. However, the Zeus system continued to have major problems dealing with decoys and multiple targets. This situation reflected the state of the art in radar technology. Plus, it was also argued that actual experience with a deployed weapons system was necessary in order to work the bugs out and to identify any unanticipated problems. Effectively, the argument became that the first deployment was a prototype from which more sophisticated ABM systems would eventually evolve. This view reflects technological optimism but also the presumption that sufficient funds would automatically flow to support such an incremental approach. In the mid-and late 1960s, those necessary funds were becoming scarce, given other pressing national priorities. Domestic programs including the Great Society initiative plus the Vietnam War were absorbing resources. By 1963, responding to the technology and other questions being raised, the Nike Zeus mutated into the Nike X. This system was actually two missiles. The Nike Zeus was renamed the Spartan, capable of interception out toward a range of seventy to 100 miles. The second missile was the Sprint, a short-range missile with a twenty-to-thirty-mile range. The latter was intended to clean up those warheads missed by the Spartan, possibly a large number.

Technological optimism has two sides, offensive and defensive. The counterassumption was that ICBMs would continue to be developed, employing even more sophisticated penetration aids. Thus, defensive efforts could not afford to stand still but would continue to evolve in response to the offensive side of the house. The obvious analogy was to air power, which has experienced a continual competition between defense and offense for nearly a century. At different points, one side or the other lunges ahead, only to be caught eventually by the other. The growing optimism concerning NMD, therefore, always remained a qualified one, conditioned by continual pressures to pursue technological improvement. Proponents clearly felt that was a doable proposition, reflecting their deep faith in the possibility of technological progress.

Second, the difficulties associated with the Vietnam War further accentuated the perception of an increasingly threatening world, one extremely hostile to U.S. interests. The Chinese nuclear program by October 1964 was visibly being tested—with evidence that a thermonuclear device has been exploded by 1966. The lack of U.S. success in accomplishing its Vietnam War aims further inflamed those who already perceived the world as extremely threatening. Nikita Khrushchev's proclaiming of "wars of national liberation" in January 1961 as the avenue for achieving world revolution appeared to be coming to fruition.

Third, the Soviet strategic forces buildup was well underway and accelerating. The Soviet humiliation during the Cuban Missile Crisis in October 1962, due to their strategic military inferiority, provided the domestic impetus fueling their dramatic and apparently unending missile buildup. The United States under Secretary McNamara had largely stabilized its nuclear forces in terms of numbers by the mid-1960s, so the apparent military imbalance grew worse.[28]

Fourth, the vulnerability of the U.S. population to nuclear coercion had become increasingly troubling for at least some decision makers. Mutually assured destruction (MAD), as a concept, was less comforting in its moral starkness than many expected. The probity of such deliberate population vulnerability was also questioned. What if one "lost"? American society became the forfeit. Taking no defensive action at all would truly be a travesty for a people dependent upon their government to protect them to the best of its ability. In addition, the Soviets had begun deploying their Galosh ABM system by late 1966. That deployment was cited by proponents as obvious proof of the concept—if the Soviets thought it worked then ABM did in fact work. This perception was buttressed by their early space spectaculars that had conclusively demonstrated their technological competence.[29]

## THE FIRST AND SECOND BMD DEPLOYMENT DECISIONS[30]

The Johnson administration, despite its strong continued support for BMD, developmentally speaking was opposed to immediate deployment.[31] The issues framing that debate concerned the two perennials of combat effectiveness and cost. The effectiveness issue came in several forms. One was the simple question of whether the Nike X could in fact make the requisite interceptions; that physical act still remained somewhat problematic. Repeatedly and accurately duplicating that action under battle conditions with multitudinous targets was not self-evident despite optimistic projections. This schism over technical feasibility was not readily resolvable despite test results. As a consequence, the debate became almost theological in tone; one took a particular point of view and defended it against heretics. For technologically ignorant individuals such as many members of Congress, there were aggressive proponents on both sides, vocally and authoritatively proclaiming the answer. Their judgments, once formed, became fairly rigid although others did often espouse conflicting views at different times based upon various considerations, usually budget and technology, as those variables were understood. The issue had not yet acquired the partisan tinge common today. In the 1960s, both Democrats and Republicans were comparative hawks on military matters but split on domestic questions. That began to shift across the decade as the Vietnam War impacted national life.

Second, the DoD under Secretary Robert S. McNamara was convinced that continually enhanced offensive penetration aids could be deployed that were capable of overwhelming any possible defensive configuration. Pursuit of penetration aids ultimately leads to multiple warheads capable of maneuvering during flight—a fact that enhanced evasion of ABM attacks and improved accuracy. This was technological optimism with a twist, one technology defeating another and at much less total cost than deploying a national missile defense infrastructure. In a DoD led by McNamara, cost factors were critical, and so such a cost-efficient solution was particularly persuasive.[32] The political implications of multiple warheads were not fully understood by the technologists since their tunnel vision focused only upon achieving the "sweetest" possible technological solution.

ABM proponents argued vigorously that this cost-driven view was too simplistic, underestimating the difficulties inherent in acquiring such sophisticated decoy technologies. Their larger argument focused upon the vulnerability of U.S. Minutemen forces to a Soviet first strike. Advances in Soviet missiles, notably the SS-9, suggested an approaching capacity to blast the Minutemen out of their silos, effectively obliterating much of the U.S. strategic missile forces. ABM deployment from this perspective became critical for preserving a U.S. mutually assured destruction capability since in their judgment ABM's effectiveness was sufficiently high to accomplish this mission. Both sides argued vociferously but essentially past each other since their different opening premises led inexorably to completely different conclusions. Given the tensions existing globally, the debate from 1965 to 1968 was intense and at times emotional. During the later secret congressional debate over the second ABM deployment, Senator Richard Russell was reported to have stated that "if only two human beings were to survive a nuclear war, he wanted them to be Americans."[33] In effect, the new Adam and Eve would be Americans, rebuilding a shattered world. ..

The cost factor also was considered debilitating for implementing ABM deployment. Depending upon the deployment configuration, the cost estimates ranged up to $50 billion (in 1967 dollars). Those costs made the ABM the equivalent to Egyptian pyramids or the sum total of the entire DoD budget minus Vietnam costs. Given the economic strains imposed by the "guns and butter" approach of the Johnson administration to Vietnam War funding, budget constraints were growing tighter. Deficit spending was not considered politically respectable over the long haul in 1966–1967. Vietnam War costs appeared to be escalating with no immediate end in sight since the United States was still looking for the "light at the end of the tunnel" while hoping it was not an onrushing train.

On the other side of the ledger, the upcoming 1968 presidential election made the Johnson administration particularly sensitive to possible accusations of national military weakness. This sensitivity reflected President Johnson's earlier senatorial crusade against what was labeled in 1960 as the "missile gap," the product of alleged Republican military policy blunders. The gap disappeared upon further review of Soviet missile deployment after the Democrats under John Kennedy assumed office.[34] Much of the Eisenhower administrations confidence that there, in fact, was no missile gap reflected intelligence collected through satellite observation, a totally secret program at least to the American public. Republicans claimed that John Kennedy was fully informed of this reality but never-the-less during the electoral season the charges kept flowing. Mindful of the earlier facts, President Johnson was particularly sensitive to such charges being levied against his watch. This was the era in which presidential candidates spoke of their "toughness" vis-à-vis the Chinese and Soviets. Republican and conservative Southern Democrats (both factions not particularly enamoured of the Great Society or the limited nature of the Vietnam War) pushed the issue, arguing that ABM deployment was critical for ensuring national population survival in the event of a nuclear war. Embedded in this conversation was the assumption that protection also was essential for preserving U.S. strategic forces for retaliation purposes.

Secretary McNamara argued that any ABM system technically deployable in the short term would be overwhelmed by the sheer volume of incoming missiles, combined with the proliferation of increasingly sophisticated penetration aids. U.S. missile developers had constructed devices that mimicked incoming warheads or confused detectors sufficiently to allow evasion of any feasible defensive system. The Soviets were developing or possessed similar deception devices. McNamara pursued the position that these alternatives made ABM an ineffectual choice whose costs were projected as too high and likely to grow worse. From a cost-benefit analysis perspective, offensive improvements were much more valuable and reliable, as well as cheaper than any foreseeable defensive technology advances.  In addition, McNamara saw ABM usage as demanding an extensive population shelter program due to radiation and other leakage from the battle space.

However, by 1967 McNamara's tenure was clearly growing short since he had antagonized Congress repeatedly, along with most of the uniformed services' leadership.  His policy choices, based upon stringent cost analyses combined with personal arrogance, further fueled this antagonism.  The Vietnam War was widely perceived as one direct product of his poor policy advice to two presidents.[35]  Thus, the secretary who had dominated earlier defense debates in the 1960s was no longer credible and would leave office shortly after the ABM decision announcement he was succeeded by Clark Clifford, a more adroit politician.

Clearly, the pressure was mounting on the administration to respond positively.  The choice became the usual incrementalism common in democratic politics.  Given the technical issues that still plagued ABM technologies that employed a limited area defense modality, the decision was to deploy a "light" ABM system.  The Sentinel (the renamed Nike X program) was capable of defending the general American population against a nuclear attack by a minor missile power—a choice obviously excluding the Soviet Union at least initially. The hope was that this restraint would help reduce any pressures to further accelerate the arms race.  In fact, the bureaucratic imperatives within the Soviet military meant that the decision had only minimal impact—their programs being implemented at that time had been initiated in prior years.  Turning entrenched bureaucracies in new directions is the work of years.  Temporary changes such as a small American ABM deployment would not alter that dynamic since it was unrelated to such events.  The only logical candidate at that point was China, whose nuclear missile forces were comparatively mysterious but were assumed to be small in number and primitive technologically speaking, lagging far behind the superpowers.  The earlier Soviet-Sino split had denied China continued access to higher quality ICBM technologies.  Their internally driven missile program was advancing despite some initial problems.[36]  ABM deployment would initially cover fifteen cities; each with thirty interceptors, meaning the actual ABM sites would be located near cities since this was a terminal defense arrangement.  The actual placement was "700 interceptors (480 Spartans and 200 Sprints) to provide an area defense of CONUS (continental United States) and parts of Alaska and Hawaii against the projected Peoples' Republic of China missile threat."[37]  These urban locations aroused public opposition, which was fueled by ABM opponents in order to stop deployment.  ABM policy was largely argued in the abstract in terms of scenarios and simulations that the public largely ignored.  Placement of actual ABM facilities in the neighborhood suddenly made the question both real and immediate, engaging public attention. That public attention often took the form of protests to local and federal elected officials showing that they were unhappy.  Missile defense was wonderful, just not in their locale.

By splitting the differences between those opposed to any deployment and those demanding a heavy or thick ABM system while pursuing a negotiated end to ABM, the budget parameters were controlled by the Johnson administration in the short run.  More critically, the administration inoculated itself against the political charge that there existed any failure to adequately protect the United States.  For BMD proponents, the decision was clearly perceived as the down payment on a steadily expanding national system soon to be rendered capable of stopping any Soviet missile attack.  This building block or modular approach runs through the entire ABM and NMD debates due to technological issues and cost.  One buys missile defense on the installment plan, allowing for program acceleration or deceleration based on available budget and technical progress. In the proponents' view, any technology deficits could be overcome given an enhanced developmental effort, to be funded in their judgment with enthusiasm now.  That enthusiasm was not widely shared given other political issues—the arms control community saw the ABM deployment as an accelerator further aggravating the nuclear arms race.

When the new Nixon administration entered office in January 1969, the ABM system's future development still remained a question.  Secretary of Defense Melvin Laird, in one of his first official actions, stopped Sentinel deployment while the administration decided what to do.  This stoppage was a short-term response to public outcry over initial site selection and proposed construction.  In March 1969, the deployment decision was reaffirmed, renamed Safeguard, but changed in potential coverage geographically.  Safeguard would now be oriented to protect ICBM fields rather than the cities, with twelve sites the maximum number; the first two were initiated immediately in Montana and North Dakota.  Such a revised approach reduced political controversy and delayed the need to choose which specific cities would be protected.  In 1970, six new ABM sites were proposed for development but rejected by Congress.[38] Whether this earlier public reaction could have been overcome was unclear since other factors intervened to terminate the expanded deployment option.

An uncontrolled technological imperative ironically proved to be the ultimate undoing for this initial ABM effort.  Intense research and development efforts were underway for further enhancement of the offensive side of the ledger.  The race for offensive nuclear superiority entered a new era with the development and subsequent deployment of the Multiple Independently Targeted Reentry Vehicle or MIRV.  MIRV-tipped missiles meant that several warheads, in some cases up to ten or more although usually—fewer, could be mounted on a single ICBM.  In effect, the U.S. Minuteman force already capped at 1,054 could be easily increased by a multiple of three to six.  Similar growth occurred in the submarine-launched ballistic missile fleet, the Poseidon at this point.  The Soviets moved to match this innovation with even larger boosters, meaning heavier warheads.  Furthermore, later technological development produced the Maneuvering Reentry Vehicle or MARV.  Overall, such weapons exponentially increased the interception problems encountered by the defense. The effect was to saturate the ABM system by sheer numbers of attacking vehicles.  The number of warheads on board reflected judgments as to the nuclear blast yield necessary to accomplish the specific mission assigned to a particular missile.  Larger warheads meant bigger nuclear blasts although greater accuracy in hitting the target meant the size of individual warheads could be shrunk, trading increased accuracy for weapon size but multiplying numbers. The weapons builders proved to be enormously productive developers of new innovations; each advance drove another nail in the ABM system's coffin. The two most immediate responses became thickening the ABM system dramatically to cope with the larger number of warheads or exponentially increasing the accuracy and reliability of each interception attempt. The first made the cost parameters politically unwieldy while the second was technologically suspect at that point.

Politically, the effect was perceived to escalate dramatically the dangers of nuclear war rather than reduce them. Preemptive strikes now had a reality that previous nuclear weapon delivery systems did not possess. Each warhead on the bus (the weapons carrier for the missile) was now independently targetable, further increasing the number of locations possibly threatened by a single missile. This increased the probability for a successful surprise attack, using several warheads to dig ICBMs out of their silos. The Soviet program lagged behind the U.S. missile one by several years, but was clearly capable of "catching up" with an equivalent or even larger numbers in its MIRV-equipped strategic missile force. At the same time, each side's accuracy was growing meaning a single warhead could now possibly do the work of several. The Circular Error Probable (CEP) shrank from a five-mile radius to 600 feet. That greater targeting efficiency meant more targets could be struck in the first wave instead of allotting several warheads to a single target in order to ensure destruction.

The inaccuracy inherent in most missile and bomb delivery systems was not always publicly well understood given the military rhetoric dating back to World War II and the Norton bombsight.[39] The Strategic Air Command (SAC) had recurringly described their practice, exercises as dropping the bomb down the old pickle barrel. Such accuracy was never achieved in practice but nuclear weapons provided a larger margin of error. Reducing that error (the CEP) dramatically altered the strategic balance by enhancing the efficiency of fielded forces. Even if surprised, their retaliation would be so much more effective, as nullifying some of the initial losses.

As a side proposition, the U.S.-deployed ABM force, the Safeguard, was rendered effectively marginal if not obsolete. The system when attacked by the Soviet Union could now quickly be saturated and overwhelmed. This terminal phase point (limited area) defense was particularly susceptible to such a new numbers effect. The radar was also especially vulnerable to disruption if not destruction. Given that the original assigned mission was dealing with a light attack, or an accidental launch, the MIRV did not totally destroy the ABM's rationale. Unfortunately, the projected cost of an expanded ABM system became an even larger deterrent as the domestic economy continued to erode. Imposition of wage and price controls in August 1971 was one symptom of that economic crisis.

The Safeguard system, therefore, became just another pawn in the larger game of strategic arms limitations negotiations. The Nixon administration actively pursued the finalization of agreements aimed at limiting strategic arms competition. Compliance verification would come through satellite surveillance of Soviet missile fields rather than on-site physical inspection. Controlling ABM deployment became part of that arms control package. The Strategic Arms Limitations Talks (SALT) had been initiated in 1967 as one political alternative to pursuing ABM deployment but failed at first due to Soviet disinterest. The Soviets were not initially persuaded that their security would be enhanced by such weapon's restrictions, especially given their strong national military traditions emphasizing defensive measures. In 1968, formal SALT talks began, which were continued by the new Nixon administration in 1969 after it assumed office in January.

In 1972, the Anti-Ballistic Missile (ABM) treaty was signed along with interim executive agreements implementing the decisions. The treaty represented the first bilateral disarmament agreement between the two superpowers; earlier multilateral treaties had been proliferation and testing related and did not prohibit specific weapons systems. The ABM treaty allowed for continued limited deployment but prevented expansion to additional land-based sites or space- or sea-based ABM systems while implicitly there were limits upon testing (those limits were somewhat looser depending upon the perspective of the parties). What remained unclear were the limits on theater level missile defense systems since those options did not yet exist. Those weapons were later grandfathered into the treaty in 1997 in terms of qualitative limits based on their capabilities, especially the speed of the interceptor. In the Treaty on the Limitation of Anti-Ballistic Missile Systems, the United States and the Soviet Union both agreed that each could have a maximum of two ABM deployment areas, so restricted and so located that they could not provide a nationwide ABM defense or become the basis for developing such a deployment. Each country also left unchallenged the penetration capability of the other's retaliatory missile forces. Precise quantitative and qualitative limits were imposed on the ABM systems that could be deployed. Both parties agreed to limit further qualitative improvements of their ABM technology

Clearly, the most immediate programmatic effect was to freeze deployment to a maximum of two ABM sites for each signatory. One ABM site was designed to protect the national capital, the locus of the national command authority, while the other protected an ICBM field. These dispositions graphically illustrated the essence of a mutually assured destruction (MAD) perspective. One ABM site effectively ensured that each signatory remained fully capable of destroying the other, even if completely surprised—the 1960s version of two scorpions in a bottle scenario was played out in a new, more deadly context. In addition, the national political leadership was to be maintained as functional in order to command during the conflict and to be able to terminate military actions when deemed appropriate. War, even nuclear war was to remain a rational exercise with the application of calculated force in pursuit of national political priorities as the method. Within a MAD context, politics clearly did not end with the first nuclear exchange; it just became infinitely more difficult to execute. Nuclear escalation was not a mindless spasm as was portrayed by massive retaliation in its original primitive form but was the controlled application of violence to achieve national objectives.[40]

The United States never built its second ABM site, running into the NIMBY (not in my backyard) syndrome in the Washington, D.C. coverage area. This public resistance was also fed by persistent doubts articulated by well-qualified scientists and engineers regarding ABM effectiveness. This was a question thought unresolvable in the absence of experience, a situation that no one particularly desired to witness—ignorance here was bliss. The Grand Forks, North Dakota, site was positioned to protect ICBM fields from Soviet attack. In 1974, the Soviet Union and the United States agreed to limit ABM deployment to a single site, meaning only Grand Forks for the United States. The Soviets chose to defend Moscow with their existing Galosh complex. Shortly after becoming operational, Congress subsequently mandated Grand Forks' closure when the House of Representatives terminated funding on October 2, 1975. This decision was not reversed when Congress became aware that the DoD in fact planned to deactivate the site on July 1, 1976.[41] Thus, the original American ABM deployment was unilaterally terminated although the authorization remained in effect. The sole Soviet site, authorized under the 1972 treaty and protocol, remained a worry for defense planners, despite intense skepticism regarding its actual effectiveness. In time, most analysts assumed that the system would be overwhelmed by the increasingly sophisticated missile attacks mounted by the United States. Eventually, its continuation was considered another symptom of incipient Soviet decline in that bureaucratic inertia froze programs in place regardless of their usefulness. The system was upgraded subsequently within the parameters of the ABM treaty, but its ultimate effectiveness remained in question.

Program termination by the United States occurred for several reasons. Cost grew clearly more important, especially given the perceived deficiencies in the ABM system's capabilities. Offensive technologies were outstripping the capacity of any terminal point or limited area defenses to cope with the sheer numbers being thrown at the defender. For the dollars expended, the expected improvement in defensive capabilities did not match the outgo. In a very real sense, the ABM system became destabilized on the theory that if it were thought to work effectively, the Soviets would launch as early as possible in the understandable fear that the United States might be completely sheltered, thus immune to their counterattack. That result, if true, totally undermines the foundations of mutually assured destruction in terms of its deterrent value. The United States did not hold that view, having come to an understanding that ABM deployment may have occurred too early, given the state of the technology.

The view was that the technology worked or could be tweaked to work effectively enough to provide some additional security benefit but not likely well enough to justify the added expenditures. Thus, the Democratic-controlled Congress increasingly defined the ABM as a bargaining chip, disposable at the right price. Also, since the SALT talks were continuing into the SALT II phase, the hope was that the arms race might be moderating enough to sacrifice

Safeguard. Sacrificing ABM for this larger goal of nuclear arms reductions was seen as a trade that was very acceptable in terms of achieving world peace. This convergence between domestic priorities (hopefully freeing up moneys for other purposes) and international ones (sustaining the strategic balance) made cancellation comparatively painless, especially when its sacrifice might facilitate the larger and more important strategic arms negotiations process.

Militarily speaking, the Safeguard system relied upon nuclear detonations to obliterate incoming warheads and their decoys. That usage severely degraded any·existing sensor capacity as the battle-space environment became polluted across the light spectrum. Sensors were either overwhelmed, unable to function effectively, or destroyed. The actual margin of security provided degraded severely under such battle-space conditions. From one perspective, the original ABM deployment, even though ultimately discontinued, provided critical operational experience in constructing and operating the system. The lengthy time span, however, between this earlier cancellation and any possible new deployment has largely nullified that experience. That activity moved NMD from the realm of paper or computer simulation to the next level where problems could be more fully identified. Nuclear warheads and their side effects remained one of those issues to be resolved, a factor that could have nullified any protective value provided by Safeguard.

## AFTER THE FALL

In response to this nuclear spillover problem, the army in 1976 renewed an intensified developmental effort (in reality, developmental efforts were continuous, but they just became more the focus since deployment was impossible). This developmental effort was centered upon greatly improved computers (faster, with significantly larger data capacity), improved and more robust sensors, especially phased array radars to handle more targets, and kinetic energy or hit-to-kill (HTK) weapons. These latter devices physically strike the warhead or its bus destroying the MIRVs prior to dispensing them. Work was also pursued regarding direct energy weapons (DEW) including lasers and particle beams. In effect, the Army was laying the foundation for much of what later becomes publicly known as the Strategic Defense Initiative (SDI) in the 1980s.

BMD now entered from 1975–1976 onward a prolonged period of technology development with deployment continually being urged by some but generally rejected as premature. The effective counterresponse to these persistent deployment demands was the defensive technology's immaturity compared to the offensive side's growing sophistication. The Soviet ABM site, for example, was caught in the same cul-de-sac, rendered effectively obsolete by offensive improvements. Its continued existence, however, fueled constant suspicions that the Soviets were somehow stealing a march on the United States. Their continued deployment was continually interpreted as strong evidence supporting an American counterpart. The most likely explanation, as suggested earlier, was basically bureaucratic in that the Soviet military's doctrines and traditions argued for such a defensive deployment if at all technically possible. Costs were not irrelevant but less pressing within the Soviet political apparatus. In time, costs did become relevant since the Soviet Union ultimately lacked the resources to dramatically upgrade its capabilities. That situation has only worsened in the post-Soviet era; replacements are not economically feasible. As a consequence, this situation has made the Russians adamant about freezing the status quo, meaning the 1972 ABM Treaty, and thus preventing a new arms race. One to which many doubt Russia could immediately respond but would be forced to do so in the future.

By the late 1970s, arms controllers, on the other hand, were dominating the debate in Washington; their efforts were inadvertently assisted by the worsening federal budget deficit. Deficit spending was, by the 1970s, part and parcel of the American political scene despite implementing a series of congressionally mandated budget gimmicks and devices to end them.[42] There existed a great reluctance to add another weapons program with unknown cost projections and even more uncertain military value. The reality is that weapons programs consistently run over budget projections and schedules. Across the 1970s, military spending also remained in decline relative to the Vietnam War–era build up, a situation not reversed until the last years of the Carter administration in response to the Soviet invasion of Afghanistan and a general worsening of relations. The United States had entered the age of limits and growing perceptions of national decline, a situation psychologically hostile to bold new endeavors, the age of malaise in President Carter's words.[43]

As a political question, NMD also receded amid intense debates during a continual litany of strategic weapons issues, especially the question of the growing vulnerability of American strategic forces. Deployment of the Pershing 2 to Europe and MX basing modes, for example, dominated the strategic weapons debate with NMD clearly located at a lower level below with regard to elite attention. The Soviet missile buildup initiated in the 1960s in response to the Cuban debacle was altering the strategic landscape through its sheer numbers, heightened accuracy, and increased throw weight. Questions arose regarding U.S. capacity to respond directly both after a Soviet attack and in the event of a crisis. Europeans, for example, increasingly questioned U.S. willingness to respond to an attack upon Europe, undermining the central premise of NATO, because of growing U.S. vulnerability to a Soviet missile attack. These questions are endemic to a political-military strategy premised upon responding to a serious attack at any conventional level primarily with nuclear means. U.S. efforts to significantly expand the conventional or subnuclear options were resisted because the Europeans perceived themselves as becoming the battlefield across which the United States would attempt to fight while remaining comparatively unscathed itself. Those questions were not new; in fact, the French have raised them since the 1950s. Fighting to the last European did not strike the Europeans as being to their advantage.

Regardless, between the demise of the first NMD deployment and the subsequent public announcement of SDI in 1983, the field became even more complicated. The army had continued to pursue its traditional air defense function across the period with the emphasis focusing upon tactical or theater-level air defense. Manned bombers no longer represented a serious threat to the continental United States, compared to that posed by growing Soviet ICBM and SLBM capabilities. The continental Nike air defense systems were phased out of operation. From a MAD perspective, defense of the continental United States was no longer an issue since population vulnerability, in fact, lay at the heart of this strategy. Effective population defense became counterproductive to fully implementing the MAD approach. Protecting troops in the field from all possible threats came to incorporate the question of using short- and intermediate-range missiles for air and missile defense. The initial assumption was that such short-range missiles should in fact be easier to intercept, an assumption not totally accurate, given the drastic shrinkage that occurs in the time and distance available for achieving effective interception. The offsetting factor is the decrease in missile speed and altitude compared to ICBMs.

Although, the concept of theater missile defense (TMD) proved harder to implement effectively than many had imagined, continuing advances in sensors, computers, and missile launch technologies made that effort worth pursuing given the troops' growing vulnerability to missile attack otherwise. Initial target identification would come from the Defense Support Program (DSP) satellites although their primary surveillance missions remained Soviet and Chinese missile forces. Initially, TMD was simply an extension of traditional air defense with no weapons fully capable of reliably achieving interception. The early Patriot system, PAC-2, already under development, was reconfigured to incorporate the potential, albeit a weak one, for TMD.[44] As a practical matter, the technology needed significant and expensive research and development, something unlikely to occur, given the unresolved technical issues generally.

The emergence of TMD as a realistic proposition regardless of the short-term technical problems had the consequence of smoothing out potential DoD organizational difficulties. Ultimately, developmental activities were centralized in a single organization (the SDIO first, now the BMDO) while the Army was assigned TMD as its primary focus and the air force focused on NMD with the navy handling any ship-borne systems. As an organization, the army had become increasing disengaged from NMD as an activity it desired to pursue as compared to earlier in 1967 with the Sentinel. Budgetarily, NMD did not support programs the army considered critical for its missions and the public outcry in the 1960s regarding ABM siting in local neighborhood's had further eroded the service's public image, one already under attack due to Vietnam.

Such a logrolling approach reduced potential interservice strife, especially entering a period of technology development of unknown duration. This arrangement in fact mirrored an earlier set of 1950s presidential decisions apportioning ballistic missiles and military space activities in which the air force took the lead strategically while the others focused upon particular facets. This reduced duplication and wasteful program competition that was critical, given the intense animosity BMD, especially at the national level, aroused in certain political circles. In the 1950s, for example, individual service-based programs had generated congressional coalitions that sharpened the attacks upon specific elements. BMD, if rent by interservice rivalries, would have further undermined its already nebulous political support especially regarding the national-level effort.

## STARTING OVER

The ballistic missile defense world dramatically shifted on its axis on March 23, 1983, when President Ronald Reagan announced what he hailed as the Strategic Defense Initiative (SDI), or Star Wars to its critics. Labeling the program "Star Wars" after the movie series was an unsuccessful effort at ridiculing the idea as so fantastic as to be only a movie plot, not real. In the end, Star Wars became merely a label denoting the futurist aspects of the concept but one thought truly possible, if not immediately at least in the not too distant future. Reagan's original announcement, while vague on the specifics, delineated a ballistic missile defense program national in scope with profoundly disruptive international policy implications. Reagan's focus was upon something other than "the specter of retaliation...Wouldn't it be better to save lives than to avenge them... I am directing a comprehensive intensive effort to define a long-term research and development program to begin to achieve our ultimate goal of eliminating the threat posed by strategic nuclear missiles."[45] This new twist held out the hope that a shield against ballistic missiles could be erected over the United States.[46]

The SDI program, by explicit intent and design, attacked the basic MAD precepts by undermining the central understanding of mutual population vulnerability. The United States, if truly successful, would alone possess the capacity to strike the Soviet Union first and then decisively defeat any possible counterresponse. In effect, the United States would become invulnerable to Soviet or any other state's nuclear coercion, at least in the form of missile attack. The old Soviet ABM system, the Galosh, was perceived as obsolete while their economic capacity to engage in a new arms race in NMD was already deemed suspect. More critically, the Soviets ironically had bought into the MAD perspective as restraining U.S. aggressive tendencies. In that sense, the world had changed, U.S. efforts to "educate" the Soviet leadership into accepting certain perspectives regarding nuclear weapons had succeeded, and now the United States was arbitrarily changing the script. Earlier in the 1960s, Secretary of Defense McNamara engaged the Soviets in a dialogue aimed at convincing them that nuclear weapons were not extensions of conventional munitions but represented a new order of violence, difficult to control once unleashed. Over time, Soviet nuclear weapons behavior came closer to U.S. understandings, allowing a mutual caution in their use and threatened use. Now, the United States appeared to be moving in directions that discard those hard-won distinctions.

SDI, so baldly stated, assumed that the technological imperative and its twin must have full rein in order to succeed. Success was presumed to be guaranteed if sufficient effort and resources were poured into the endeavor. In fact, only the most optimistic early scenarios envisioned almost total defensive success. Even those rosy pictures quickly receded to the status of political hyperbole as the defense bureaucracy and its technologists grappled with the realities of successfully implementing SDI.  Conceptually, the original announcement, despite its vagueness on specifics, bought into the basic concepts already being developed by the BMD community.  Edward Teller, progenitor of the hydrogen bomb, was an active and aggressive lobbyist, one who reportedly found a receptive listener in President Reagan.  The bases for SDI were the technology development efforts initiated in the 1970s after earlier deployment termination and continuing into the 1980s.  SDI concentrated additional resources and accelerated that already existing development program.  The key change became the enthusiastic presidential leadership and advocacy that now permeated the field, an enthusiasm not universally shared, especially in Congress, most strongly in the House of Representatives, which remained skeptical.

There are many claimants to the role of presidential advisor regarding SDI's initiation.  The key is that Ronald Reagan for reasons of his own choosing bought into the concept of NMD.[47]  Others provided information, often greatly simplified, but the key fact was that the president firmly believed in its possibility and was willing to pursue his belief as far as politically possible. That vision, while unnerving to others was a great comfort to the president since it changed the debate from how many Americans would die in a nuclear exchange to how many people would live as a result of his efforts.  Such a dream was powerful although it was widely believed by others to be disconnected from technological realities.  Surviving nuclear war was the dream embedded in SDI.

Subsequently, in April 1984, the Strategic Defense Initiative Organization (SDIO) was established as the lead DoD agency to conduct the research necessary to implement a successful NMD system.  Initially, SDI was an accelerated technology development effort.  The overall operational concept quickly evolved into a layered defensive schema in which incoming missiles would be attacked successively at different stages during their flight to the target.  No longer would the defenders engage the attacker only during the final stages of flight when the time parameters are most compressed and hurried with failure highly probable.  Once missed there, warheads were unlikely to be re-engaged.  The new approach presented a gauntlet of attacking defensive systems.

Those developmental efforts, even their prospect, were disruptive internationally as can be seen in the "dust up" over the subsequent 1985 effort by the Reagan administration to reinterpret the ABM treaty.[48]  The intent there was to interpret the ABM treaty as placing no restrictions upon the testing of space-based and other mobile BMD systems in the absence of actual deployment.  This "permissive" or "broad" interpretation was widely perceived as effectively negating the treaty, both overturning the existing understandings with the Soviets and those with the U.S. Senate during treaty ratification. Ultimately, this move failed in part because technological progress lagged somewhat while the Soviet threat visibly declined in intensity.  The point of political confrontation with the Soviets was never approached for several reasons. First, the technology proved more intractable than expected. Second, the Soviets came to the conclusion that NMD technology would not work so they moved on to other issues—that is: they could override any projected defensive arrangements.

Toward the end of the Reagan tenure and the early Bush administration, a new approach was formulated that was ultimately labeled "Brilliant Pebbles." It was planned to be a 100-kilogram interceptor orbiting the earth in large numbers (5,000 at a minimum, depending on capabilities). The concept was to intercept the missile during the boost phase when it was most vulnerable to such efforts. The interceptor would act through direct kill methods, that is, physically striking the target. This program represented a revitalization of the SDI effort in part because it moved away from the laser-based concepts that had animated the early program.[49]   Critics of the program suggested that Brilliant Pebbles was readily subjected to interception and destruction by anti-satellite weapons (ASAT).[50]   Regardless of the purported technical merits, the program was delayed and then cancelled during the last years of the Bush administration and the early days of the Clinton administration.[51]   In time, the concept became Brilliant Eyes, a global surveillance system that would immediately identify any launches and provide other benefits, including global monitoring. None of these permutations saved the program from cancellation.

By 1988, toward the end of the Reagan tenure in office, SDI was clearly in political trouble, given its budget demands, which were beginning to escalate in an era when federal budget deficits appeared unending and ever increasing. Those efforts had ballooned due to the earlier Reagan-driven tax cuts along with the concurrent failure to reduce other government expenditures. Even more debilitating for SDI's future prospects was the gradual but steady public deterioration in viewing the Soviet Union as a direct military threat to the United States. Mikhail Gorbachev with his efforts at internal economic and political reforms and willingness to initiate negotiations on virtually all strategic issues was reducing tensions. Or, at least, Gorbachev's gestures undermined any sense of urgency regarding NMD. The two nuclear forces still glared at each other, but the decline in tension was palpable, especially when compared with the worst days of the Cold War. Those Soviet internal changes gradually led to the final dissolution of the Soviet Union in early 1991, ending the Cold War and further undermining any immediate rationale for NMD. If there was no major missile threat, why continue such an expensive program at a high level of intensity. Threat perceptions among government leaders did not dissipate immediately, a fact that kept existing programs in place for a time. Continued disintegration of the Soviet bloc undermined the credibility of such drastic evaluations especially when the Russian Federation also encountered hard times both politically and economically.

Ballistic missile defense as a program quickly reflected those international political changes as the Bush administration publicly repositioned the national-level BMD effort in January 1991. Its earlier budget choices had already slowed SDI development. The new program, Global Protection against Limited Strikes (GPALS) was structured into three components:  (1) ground-based NMD, (2) ground-based TMD, and (3) space-based Global Defense.[52] The stated goal was to deal with isolated attacks by minor powers or accidental attacks by rogue former Soviet units, an effective scaling back of the entire effort. Russia was officially no longer the enemy although GPALS obviously had implications for deterring its decaying nuclear forces, still powerful even in their state of decline. The fear was that as missile technologies proliferated across the world, the United States might be subject to attack by unknown or unexpected actors. This particular program was aborted by the unexpected defeat of President George Bush in his bid for reelection in November 1992. In one sense, Bush's intention was to bridge the transition from the previous highly intense Cold War bipolar nuclear confrontation to a diverse multiple-threat environment. Space-based technologies would become particularly critical because of their presumed capacity to react worldwide to unforeseen events. These technologies, however, lay in the distant future, ensuring that a continued developmental effort was required in the short term.

The GPALS program clearly lost its political momentum with the Bush administration's demise, but the concepts embodied in that effort continued on. This was especially true regarding the heightened emphasis placed upon the threat of proliferation globally. The Soviet Union's disintegration had not only created almost immediately several additional nuclear powers in the Ukraine and Belarus, but the great power restraints upon dissemination of missile technology and the technical skills to successfully build such artifacts were also gone. Sale of existing missile stocks and other technologies became an issue, one that continues into the present. Earlier and continuing efforts at controlling such proliferation through the Missile Technology Control Regime (MTCR) were proving more problematic than many assumed (this will be dealt with in greater detail in chapter 4).

Also, in August 1990, Saddam Hussein led an Iraqi invasion of Kuwait, seizing control of its oil fields. The United States responded militarily within several days of that takeover along with its allies, deploying ultimately a half-million personnel in the region. From August 1990 until January 1991, the United States along with its coalition allies built its military force in order to recapture Kuwait, while punishing the aggressor for his transgressions in the process. The military engagement turned into an Iraqi rout as high-tech U.S. forces assisted by the coalition partners overwhelmed their formations, employing weaponry designed for NATO use against Soviet divisions.

During that military confrontation, a subplot arose concerning the question of ballistic missile defense and its purported effectiveness. Iraq launched Scud missiles against targets located in both Saudi Arabia and Israel. The latter attacks represented an effort to force an Israeli counterresponse against Iraq since Israeli security policy has traditionally followed the principle of almost automatically retaliating against any Arab attacks. The Iraqi hope was that the Israelis would respond to these unprovoked missile attacks by striking back at Iraq, Israel not being formally engaged in the conflict. The attacks required the Israeli government to provide their civilian population with protective masks and other equipment against possible Scud-delivered gas attacks. Iraqi use of weapons of mass destruction (WMD) was widely feared and expected throughout the conflict. These strikes constituted a direct challenge to the Israeli government's ability to control public opinion while not retaliating. Any Israeli retaliation, it was assumed, would generate intense public pressures upon the Arab allies of the United States to withdraw from the coalition. This situation possessed the potential to unravel the war effort, undermining the public rationale supporting the coalition that diverse but outraged states, including Arab ones, were responding to unprovoked Iraqi aggression. Instead, the military effort would be painted as yet another neocolonial effort to suppress Arab nationalism as represented by Iraq. In response to this potential military and political threat, the United States deployed Patriot missile batteries both in Israel and in Saudi Arabia to deal with the Scud attacks. Militarily, the Scuds posed a minimal threat to coalition forces, especially after the bulk of the forces had entered Saudi Arabia and were dispersed across the desert.[53]

The Patriot-Scud duels in the desert, while providing dramatic television imagery, proved entirely a wash militarily although not politically. The evidence appears fairly persuasive that the Patriots did not, in fact, intercept any incoming Scuds. To the contrary, some evidence suggests that a Patriot near miss may have led to a Scud strike on a U.S. troop barracks, causing twenty-eight deaths. Scuds were generally ineffectual due to their obsolescence and poor quality, being very inaccurate weapons. The Al Hussein Scud missiles moved more quickly than Soviet Scuds but tended to break up during reentry, in effect creating decoys that hampered Patriot operations.[54] The Scuds were essentially terror weapons, not militarily relevant. Politically speaking, the Patriots provided sufficient political cover for the Israeli government not to intervene to punish Iraq, allowing the coalition to continue its operations until Iraq was defeated and driven out of Kuwait. The Israeli government apparently thought the Patriots totally ineffectual although politically critical to the defeat of Iraq.

The terrorist aspect of Scud attacks upon helpless civilian populations was made crystal clear through global television coverage. For weaker states, the message was clear—mere possession of such weapons made a more substantial threat than their objective military value merited. Defensive efforts still appeared futile or at least incomplete whether one hunted the missiles prior to launch or attacked them during flight. The political effects were twofold: reasserted political interest in theater-level defense and rejuvenated attempts to control proliferation at the source, the technology producing states. The Scud hunts by coalition ground and air units started late and were primarily a response to the political necessities; they proved ineffectual. Media reports of great coalition success in destroying Scuds did not survive close post-war scrutiny. On both sides, the focus was upon propaganda rather than substantive results since there were none. Missiles flew despite the best efforts of the coalition but did comparatively little damage although civilian life was disrupted.

Within the realm of BMD, the Gulf War politically validated the concept of theater missile defense as a necessary adjunct for pursuing any future U.S. intervention overseas. More critically, the ambiguous interception results meant that further developmental work became essential to ensure greater success the next time. In a world grown increasingly fragmented with the Cold War's end, those intervention opportunities were perceived as very likely. President Bush for a time verbally asserted America's expanded role as the world's policeman—a position abandoned in its broadest terms but emblematic of an expectation that the United States would continue as a world player of consequence (see chapter 1 regarding this elite expectation concerning the U.S. role in world affairs).

The new Clinton administration entered office in January 1993 generally hostile to NMD because of both its budget and international ramifications. One sign of that hostility was the reorganization and transforming of the SDIO into the BMDO in May 1993. TMD, however reflecting its new stature after the Gulf War, was now secured programmatically and especially developmentally. The BMD program now entered into a period labeled "Technology Readiness," meaning the focus shifted to developing fundamental technologies with no thought of immediate NMD deployment. The Department of Defense under Secretary Les Aspin conducted the Bottom-Up Review (BUR), aimed at restructuring the American military for the post–Cold War environment. The Soviet Union's disappearance and the success of the Strategic Arms Reduction Talks (START) agreements mandated a re-evaluation of the composition and cost of future forces since START I mandated significant reductions in Russian and U.S. strategic forces. The decline in U.S. strategic forces was highlighted by the removal of nuclear weapons from aircraft carriers and bombers. Only land-based ballistic missiles and submarine ballistic missiles remained on standby, but they were reduced in numbers and not immediately targeted at the Russian Federation. In 1990, the United States had 10,563 warheads, a total reduced to 7,982 by 1998 with reductions to 3,500 expected by 2007 as a result of START II.[55]

Given the administration's general hostility to NMD, the BUR reduced the expected future expenditures from $39 billion to $18 billion with the bulk of the reductions occurring in NMD. The first priority became theater level, principally the PAC-3—the Patriot upgrade, THAAD, and Navy Theater BMD. Technology development, the third leg of the program components, was refocused upon the more difficult fundamental issues inherent in BMD. By 1994, NMD was effectively cancelled, being reduced to solely a technology demonstration effort. All BMD activities whether national or theater level were now to be totally treaty compliant, a major shift from SDI in its larger manifestations where space-based weapons constituted a major future component for securing interception success. In a sense, the entire BMD effort reverted part way back to its pre-SDI status and outlook except that TMD was now clearly a national priority. This heightened priority for the latter reflected political necessity if an activist foreign policy was to be sustained and there were to be projected improvements in the technologies.

The budget implications of NMD also represented a major factor in shaping Clinton administration policy choices. Already skeptical concerning the likely effectiveness of any NMD system, the cruel budget choices confronting the administration in January 1993 further drove the president's decisions. Earlier, in the fall of 1990, President George Bush and the Democratic congressional leadership had concluded a now infamous (in Republican circles) budget agreement. Two major components stood out among several, a tax increase and a strict budget cap on discretionary spending. The tax increase inflamed conservative Republicans, especially after the president's earlier pronouncement at the 1988 Republican convention of "Read my lips, no new taxes." By 1990, that hard-line position shifted as federal budget deficits grew in size. The compromise became an agreement to raise revenues (e.g., taxes) while concomitantly restricting discretionary expenditure growth in order to preserve the inviolability of the entitlement programs, notably Medicare and Social Security. For BMD generally, the most immediately pressing question became these budget caps which severely limited growth in discretionary spending. The U.S. government has an obligation to defend its population but how that specific function actually occurs remains a policy choice made by elected officials. That reality translates into different program emphases from year to year, as perceived national security needs change in response to events. Therefore, BMD is not guaranteed any particular amount of money or even continuation from year to year although inertia and incrementalism shelter most programs from excessive change normally. Often a program does not get rich, but neither does it starve to death.

The Defense Department represents the largest single discretionary federal budget entry, directly competing with social programs, veterans' benefits, farm subsidies, and other, important—at least to their recipients—programs. The budget cap effectively limited their total future growth (without regard for projected need) with the result that there arose intensified competition across all programs while their constituents struggled to acquire any new funding. Given the diminishing foreign military threat, reductions in DoD funding became the major source from which new and existing programs could be handled. For example, breast cancer research was funded through the DoD because that was where the money was, not in the National Institutes of Health, which fell under the budget cap. Such budget devices were pursued because otherwise the new Clinton administration would have had no major opportunities to create its own initiatives. That circumstance is especially debilitating for any newly elected president who has promised voters programs aimed at meeting their specific needs.

Overall, defense spending fell about 30 percent from earlier budget totals and even more dramatically against DoD spending projections made prior to the end of the Cold War. The speeding up and deploying of a NMD program were also an obvious no-go, given the prevailing political optimism regarding the START process. Reductions in nuclear forces along with de-escalating confrontational tactics by the two major nuclear parties (now the United States and the Russian Federation) undermined the perceived urgency for NMD. Pursuing lower intensity technology development from this perspective met the political exigencies of the day. Also, the Democratic Congress was clearly aware of the budget linkage existing between this potentially expensive program and others more critical to its priorities, and thus was strongly resistant to further BMD program growth. In one sense, the Democrats in Congress, especially the liberals, were repeating their earlier experience with the original ABM deployments.

The congressional elections in November 1994 shifted the ground rules when the Republicans assumed control of both houses of Congress for the first time in decades. Their election manifesto, the "Contract with America," included increased national defense as one item among ten. NMD was included as a gesture toward the earlier, now much revered, Reagan era. On any intensity scale, however, defense as a public issue ranked well below the other items, which were more directly related to Republican domestic priorities—including tax cuts and reductions in government regulations and programs.[56] Adherents argued that the general Republican stance that defense spending needed to increase significantly included NMD as a major priority. Their extrapolation, based on the "Contract" was interesting as an expression of their fervor but was disconnected from political reality. In fact, NMD stalled due to presidential reluctance to proceed.

Congress despite its often-strident rhetoric was unable to impose an NMD solution upon an obviously reluctant administration. But, the Clinton administration in response (the triangulation strategy pursued to achieve Clinton's reelection) adjusted its rhetoric and approach to the extent that a "three plus three" approach was agreed upon as the new NMD deployment strategy, ending the technology readiness developmental approach. This new arrangement essentially politically protected the administration from any successful accusations of a failure to be militarily strong. As a matter of practical politics, Democratic tactical adjustments were driven by the recent Jimmy Carter difficulties in securing reelection in 1980 plus earlier episodes involving the missile gap in 1960 and the 1967 Johnson administration ABM gap debate response. Later Republican intentions to force a great debate in 1996 over the NMD issue floundered during the unsuccessful Bob Dole presidential candidacy. Senator Dole was not able to overcome voter economic contentment despite their visible uneasiness with President Clinton personally. In the absence of an external security threat and presidential leadership, the public was unmoved by future hypothetical threats.

The "three plus three" meant that at any particular point in time final deployment remained six years away at a minimum. The Republicans assumed that it meant a go decision in 1997 and deployment in 2003. From the president's perspective, the answer that if the decision were to accelerate NMD deployment, three years of development would elapse prior to when a definite deployment decision would be made with actual physical deployment completed three years later. The developmental decision became, in essence, a choice being driven by continually updated threat evaluations. If the threat potential remained sufficiently low, then that decision could be deferred indefinitely. For the Republicans, the implications were that a deployment decision could be forced at some point even if the administration in office remained reluctant. Their surface acquiescence in this stratagem reflected their strongly held view that a Republican would be in the presidency by January 1997. Failure to win the presidency left them frustrated but locked in, given the Clinton administration objections. Even a weakened president has the power to impede and block those programs he opposes. The veto is a blunt instrument, much like a nuclear weapon, but its presence does facilitate the compromise process.

For the administration, "three plus three" had the sublime virtue of rolling any heavy deployment expenditures into the future, quickly becoming another president's problem. A similar scenario, for example, occurred regarding the original Space Shuttle decision in January 1972. President Nixon effectively rolled the heavier costs forward to successor administrations. Similarly, Ronald Reagan despite his strong support would never have confronted the ultimate SDI costs if development had been successfully completed. In addition, the Clinton administration at first was reasonably confident that the ballistic missile threat profile would not shift quickly since the most likely rogue states were still thought to be a decade to fifteen years away from posing a direct security threat to the United States. In fact, more immediate security threats were thought to be nonstate actors, especially terrorist groups of different ideological and religious persuasions. Against these looming domestic threats, BMD was irrelevant.

Terrorists were thought the more realistic threat in part due to demonstrated American military superiority over any likely opponent.[57] The Gulf War experience for Americans loomed large in evaluating the world militarily. Despite their rhetoric, U.S. policy makers have tended to underestimate other states' willingness, despite their obvious military inferiority, to challenge the United States and suffer adverse consequences. What was not really grasped clearly was the terrorist aspect of ballistic missiles despite the Gulf War experience. One can still strike from afar without warning or any likely successful defense. In fact, other forms of terrorism by small groups proved more difficult to implement than many expected since most states, even poor ones, are not indifferent to possible internal security threats, including the United States.[58] Missiles have become a substitute coercive device for those states otherwise militarily inferior to the United States. As will be discussed in chapter 3, states and their elites are often driven by domestic political agendas for which ballistic missiles possess maximum political value regardless of their objective military worth. Missiles have military value, but barring use of nuclear weapons, their usefulness is more limited than is often thought. Delivery of biological or chemical agents is not an easy task. But, their terroristic implications, however, can be profound and disruptive to a society under threat of such attack.

## CONCLUSION

By 1997, U.S. BMD policy had essentially been driven into a cul-de-sac in which both facets of BMD, national and theater were still being pursued but deployment of the former remained illusive. The technologists were steadily solving problems but at a rate insufficient to generate political momentum. The 1996 presidential election had come and gone with no "great debate" on the topic. Instead, domestic issues especially the state of the economy, dominated all considerations. Foreign policy remained a marginal issue during the election while NMD policy generally was basically irrelevant. Republican success in retaining control in Congress, however, kept the issue alive in Washington. Effectively, NMD proponents hunkered down to await the 2000 presidential election. As indicated, presidents even when severely politically weakened as Bill Clinton became in 1998–1999, remain capable of structuring the flow of policy especially on issues clearly marginal to the public. Barring a credible military threat made against the United States, NMD was clearly of minimal public interest. Presidents by virtue of their office can dominate public discussions of such esoteric issues. By ignoring and downplaying the question (in the absence of credible threat), Clinton forced NMD as an issue to the margins of the political agenda. However, the issue did not expire but rather returned to the nether land of policy debate without closure.

## NOTES

1. As examples for the prior period through SDI, see Donald R. Baucom, *The Origins of SDI, 1944–1983* (Lawrence: University Press of Kansas, 1992); Steven E. Miller and Stephen Van Evera, eds., *The Star Wars Controversy* (Princeton, NJ: Princeton University Press, 1986); Fred Kaplan, *The Wizards of Armageddon* (New York: Simon & Schuster, 1983); Ernest J. Yanarella, *The Missile Defense Controversy: Strategy, Technology, and Politics, 1955–1972* (Lexington: University Press of Kentucky, 1977); Benson D. Adams, *Ballistic Missile Defense* (New York: Elsevier, 1971); K. Scott McMahon, *Pursuit of the Shield: The U.S. Quest for Limited Ballistic Missile Defense* (Lanham, MD: University Press of America, 1997). Other works provide historical insights and are referenced where appropriate.

2. Frank H. Winter, *The First Golden Age of Rocketry* (Washington, DC: Smithsonian Institution Press, 1990), 26.

3. James Harford, *Korolev: How One Man Masterminded the Soviet Drive to Beat America to the Moon* (New York: Wiley, 1997).

4. William E. Burrows, *This New Ocean: The Story of the First Space Age* (New York: Random House, 1998), 83–93.

5. McGeorge Bundy, *Danger and Survival* (New York: Random House, 1988).

6. Baucom, *Origins of SDI*, 4.

7. Dennis R. Jenkins, *Space Shuttle: The History of Developing the National Space Transportation System* (Marceline, MO: Walsworth Publishing Company, 1992), 1–2.

8. Roger Handberg, Joan Johnson-Freese and David Webb, "Hype or Hypersonic: Policy Development At the Frontiers of High Technology." (Paper presented at the Annual Meeting of the American Political Science Association, Washington, DC, August 1991).

9. T.A. Heppeenheimer, *The Space Shuttle Decision: NASA's Search for a Reusable Space Vehicle* (Washington, DC: NASA History Office, 1999).

10. Charles Gunn, "Failures Are Not an Option," *Launchspace* (January/February 1999): 24–29.

11. Dwayne A. Day, John M. Logsdon, and Brian Latell, eds., *Eye in the Sky: The Story of the Corona Spy Satellites* (Washington, DC: Smithsonian Institution Press, 1998).

12. Bruce G. Blair, John E. Pike, and Stephen I. Schwartz, "Targeting and Controlling the Bomb," in Stephen I. Schwartz, ed., *Atomic Audit: The Costs and Consequences of U.S. Nuclear Weapons since 1940* (Washington, DC: Brookings Institution Press, 1998), 197–199.

13. Jeffrey T. Richelson, *America's Space Sentinels: DSP Satellites and National Security* (Lawrence: University Press of Kansas, 1999).

14. Ballistic Missile Defense Organization, *BMDO Timeline* (Washington, DC: BMDO, 2000).

15. Department of Defense, *Conduct of the Persian Gulf War: Final Report to Congress* (Washington, DC: Department of Defense, 1992).

16. For a positive though realistic overview of the Patriot's performance, see McMahon, *Pursuit of the Shield*, Appendix A.

17. Morton H. Halperin, "The Gaither Committee and the Policy Process," *World Politics* 13 (April 1961): 365–367; David L. Snead, *The Gaither Committee, Eisenhower, and the Cold War* (Columbus: Ohio State University Press, 1999), 122–128.

18. George Friedman and Meridith Friedman, *The Future of War* (New York: Crown Books, 1996), 181–203.

19. Roger Handberg, *New World Vistas: Militarization of Space* (Westport, CT: Praeger Books, 2000), chapter 2.

20. Sylvia K. Kraemer, "Organizing for Exploration," in John M. Logsdon, ed., *Exploring the Unknown*: Vol. I: *Organizing for Exploration* (Washington, DC: Government Printing Office, 1995), 611.

21. Baucom, *Origins of SDI,* 11.

22. Ibid., 7–14.

23. Walter A. McDougall, *The Heavens and the Earth: A Political History of the Space* Age (New York: Basic Books, 1985), 191.

24. Richelson, *America's Space Sentinels*, 11–32.

25. SBIRS appears to be a linear descendant of ARPA's late-1950s Project Defender-Project Bambi satellite configuration, aimed at achieving boost phase detection and interception. Baucom, *Origins of SDI,* 16.

26. *Ballistic Missile Defense Organization, Timeline.*

27. Arthur T. Hadley, *The Straw Giant, Triumph and Failure: America's Armed Forces* (New York: Random House, 1986), 220–222. In 1986, Hadley wrote of the excessive age of the existing ICBM arsenal, an issue that grows with the passage of time with the probability of a high failure rate if weapons were fired. The Russian missile forces are presumed to be in worse shape, given their budget issues over the past decade.

28. Desmond Ball, *Politics and Force Levels: The Strategic Missile Program of the Kennedy Administration* (Berkeley: University of California Press, 1980), 143–162; William W. Kaufman, *The McNamara Strategy* (New York: Harper & Row, 1964).

29. Brian Harvey, *The New Russian Space Programme: From Competition to Collaboration* (New York: John Wiley, 1996), 27–46.

30. In the early discussions, missile defense was called anti-ballistic missile or ABM. Over time, the generic usage became ballistic missile defense or BMD with NMD for national level and TMD for theater level (or theater ballistic missile defense or TBMD even more recently). All deal with the same question, just different time frames and levels of defensive coverage.

31. Morton H. Halperin, "The Decision to Deploy the ABM: Bureaucratic and Domestic Politics in the Johnson Administration," *World Politics* 15 (October 1972): 69–95.

32. Cf. Charles J. Hitch, *Decision Making for Defense* (Berkeley: University of California Press, 1965). Charles Hitch was one of the architects of the budgetary reforms associated with McNamara's tenure in office as secretary of defense.

33. Halperin, "The Decision," 74.

34. Ball, *Politics and Force Levels*, 88–105.

35. McNamara's views shifted over the years. The longer he was out of office, the sense of certainty that drove him while in office was modified by time and reflection. Cf. Robert S. McNamara, The *Essence of Security, Reflection in Office* (New York: Harper & Row, 1968); idem *Blundering into Disaster: Surviving the First Century of the Nuclear Age* (New York: Pantheon Books, 1986).

36. Iris Chang, *Thread of the Silkworm* (New York: Basic Books, 1995), 208–230.

37. McMahon, *Pursuit of the Shield*, 84.

38. Baucom, *Origins of SDI*, 40–58.

39. Robert A. Pape, *Bombing to Win: Air Power and Coercion in War* (Ithaca, NY: Cornell University Press, 1996), 92–96.

40. Herman Kahn, *On Escalation: Metaphors and Scenarios* (New York: John Wiley, 1965).

41. Baucom, 96.

42. Aaron Wildavsky, *The New Politics of the Budgetary Process*, 2d ed. (New York: HarperCollins, 1992), 150–162.

43. Paul Kennedy, *The Rise and Fall of the Great Powers: Economic Change and Military Conflict from 1500 to 2000* (New York: Vintage Books, 1989).

44. McMahon, *Pursuit of the Shield*, Appendix A.

45. *Department of State Bulletin* 83, no. 2073 (Washington, DC: Government Printing Office, 1983), 8, 13–14.

46. Francis Fitzgerald, *Way Out There in the Blue: Star Wars and the End of the Cold War* (New York: Simon and Schuster, 2000), 208-212.

47. Kerry L. Hunter, *The Reign of Fantasy: The Political Roots of Reagan's Star Wars Policy* (New York: Peter Lang, 1992), 19–24; Fitzgerald, *Way Out There in the Blue*, 202–209.

48. Kevin C. Kennedy, "Treaty Interpretation by the Executive Branch: The ABM Treaty and Star Wars Testing and Development," *American Journal of International Law* 80 (October 1986): 854–877.

49. Baker Spring, "Brilliant Pebbles: The Revolutionary Idea for Strategic Defense," *Heritage Foundation Backgrounder,* no. 748 (January 25, 1990).

50. Richard L. Garwin, "Theater Missile Defense, National ABM Systems, and the Future of Deterrence," http://www.nationalacademies.org/cpsma/nsb/dt-h.htm.

51. Government Accounting Office, *Strategic Defense System: Stable Design and Adequate Testing Must Precede Decision to Deploy* (Washington, DC: Government Accounting Office, July 1990).

52. Baker Spring, "For Strategic Defense: A New Strategy for the New Global Situation," *Heritage Foundation Backgrounder* no. 824 (April 18, 1991).

53. General Donald J. Kutyna, "Indispensable: Space Systems in the Persian Gulf War," in R. Cargill Hall and Jacob Neufeld eds., *The U.S. Air Force in Space, 1945 to the Twenty-first Century* (Washington, DC: USAF History and Museums Program, USAF, 1998), 118–120.

54. McMahon, *Pursuit of Shield,* Appendix A.

55. Walter Pincus, "Nuclear Expert Challenges U.S. Thinking on Warheads," *Washington Post* October 24, 2000, A3.

56. Michael W. Traugott and Elizabeth C. Powers, "Did Public Opinion Support the Contract with America?" in Paul J. Lavrakas and Michael W. Traugott, eds., *Election Polls, the News Media, and Democracy* (New York: Chatham House Publishers, 2000), 105–107. Traugott and Powers found that only about 25 percent of the electorate supported the Republican view that defense spending was too low.

57. This perception was widely shared, even impacting the public. In a CNN/USA Today/Gallup Poll reported in November 1997, 65 percent of the population saw an attack upon the United States by terrorists employing chemical or biological weaponry as very or somewhat likely. Forty-six percent saw such an attack employing nuclear weaponry similarly. *The Gallup Poll: 1997*, Appendix 256.

58. For an interesting commentary upon U.S. policy regarding terrorism and the difficulties of organizing an effective response, see Andrew D. Grossman and Thomas J. Raven, "The Past as Prologue: Policy Planning, Civil Liberties, and Civil Defense in the Age of Super-Terrorism" (Paper presented at the Annual Meeting of the American Political Science Association, Washington, DC, September 2000).

# 3
# Breakdown of the Old Verities

## INTRODUCTION

Pursuit by the United States of ballistic missile defense (BMD), at least in the present era, reflects the realization that certain verities or truths that have long informed international politics no longer appear to have the same weight. Simply put, deterrence, it appears, has broken down as an effective tool for managing international relations at least from the perspective of the United States. This reported breakdown reflects both objective changes in the scope and nature of American military power and in the psychological aspects inherent in the concept of deterrence. The latter, it is argued, have changed dramatically, always however in the direction of steadily declining threat credibility. Why all this is occurring lies somewhat outside our focus, but the political effect has been to further fuel the drive for BMD deployment especially at the national level. Such massive uncertainty increases the political drive to seek out other avenues for maximizing national security. National Missile Defense (NMD) becomes a refuge against the avoidable storms of a constantly changing and ever more threatening world according to its proponents. Opponents argue that other more traditional means are preferable because they are both effective and flexible while NMD handles only one aspect, the worst-case scenario, a missile attack upon the United States. This disagreement concerning BMD's ultimate effectiveness fuels the debate. Here, however, the focus, hones in upon the changing world and its impact upon U.S. fears. Clearly, other methods for insuring American security notably the diplomatic route, have not been totally abandoned. Rather, the attitude expressed becomes one in which diplomatic options are either more perfunctorily applied or readily discarded if instant gratification does not occur. Gratification in this context is defined as agreement with U.S. objectives.

## DETERRENCE AND ITS DIFFICULTIES[1]

Deterrence in both theory and practice represents a straightforward exercise in the explicit calculation of comparative costs versus benefits by several parties operating from their independent perspectives. Each player influences the other's calculations. Essentially, the problem boils down to the situation in which one actor, the reactor or defender, informs (threatens) a second actor, the initiator, that if a certain action(s) by the latter occurs, some form of punishment or retribution will result as a matter of course. The punishment inflicted will in principle be calibrated to such a precise level that a higher (often much higher) cost (injury) is from the offending party than the benefit received from completing the action. Effectively, the costs exceed the benefits received or C > B. The metric for cost or benefit can prove murkier than one might suppose since the benefit or reward received may be psychological rather than material in nature. That caveat (a large one to be sure) to the side, such calculations are assumed to be routinely computed by both parties in order to assess one's future course of action. Clearly, these unknowns make the calculations more nebulous than appears on the surface. Regardless, this simple yet complex relationship remains central to the deterrence concept.

In the meaning being ascribed here, the purpose being pursued involves stopping the undesirable action from occurring. This response is not equivalent to compliance because sufficient pain is threatened or inflicted in order to force some action otherwise not desired by the party being compelled to conform. The forms of coercion being applied range along a spectrum from verbally aggressive diplomatic actions to economic measures to military responses calibrated at different levels of threatened or applied violence. The argument being made politically in the United States is that deterrence at all levels increasingly fails to work against certain states. American views can be crudely summarized in the label attached to several states as being "rogue states" or, more recently, "states of concern," a class of national players apparently perceived as outside the normal rules of international decorum. As a result, coercion operating in the form of deterrence is defined as the only bulwark standing between these states with their illegitimate claims and international anarchy. Though this fear is possibly exaggerated, it in part, motivates the concern with sustaining a large American military budget even with the Cold War's end and the dispersion of possible threats by lesser and militarily much weaker states. Despite the Cold War's demise, U.S. defense spending (controlling for inflation) remains 90 percent or more of what it was just prior to the end of the Cold War. And, in fact, defense expenditures are likely to increase further over the next decade as obsolete equipment is retired and new military technologies are brought on board, probably including NMD.

Deterrence in action comes in two general forms, denial and punishment.[2] The first involves denying the other party's access to whatever objective (political or physical) is being closed off to it. For example, military forces intervene to prevent a territorial incursion, driving the other military off either through superior force (defeat) or by increasing the probability of a military confrontation (displaying sufficient forces in exposed positions). The party being deterred may have assumed prior to the actual counterresponse that there would be no outside intervention as, for example, occurred in Korea in 1950. During the Cold War, American forces in isolated West Berlin were kept large enough to create sufficient disturbance to trigger a larger confrontation, but were themselves clearly insufficient to defeat a Soviet attack.

Punishment, on the other hand, is basically reactive, inflicting extraordinary damage upon the violator after its transgression. The costs imposed must be made extreme compared to the benefits received, including the very real possibility of military defeat and government overthrow. Punishment is in a sense more difficult to successfully implement because the party being punished will likely strenuously resist. In practice, the deterring state may suffer great damage even while achieving success in its policy of deterrence. That also means that success may prove difficult to achieve, especially where the states are asymmetric in their power relationship. For example, a sea-based power may lack leverage against a land-based power or vice versa. Or, one state may be unable to apply its power swiftly enough to make a real difference. Empires historically were often extraordinarily dominant militarily but powerless in particular settings due to terrain and distance. Tribes would retreat into the forests or deserts beyond effective pursuit. The United States has discovered some of those limits, even in the present high-tech military age. Distance and terrain have not vanished from the military equation although their effects may be less debilitating than previously. For example, in 1999, the weather and terrain in Serbia hampered air operations. Target identification was difficult, meaning many were missed, a fact graphically evident when Serbian forces left Kosovo after the fighting ceased.[3]

Underlying all of these calculations is the assumption of rationality by both parties especially the one being deterred. As used here, rationality simply assumes that one is capable of accurately assessing the likely responses to one's actions, but, even more critically, one does so before reaching any decision as to what to do. This perspective is often very inaccurate in reality, but deterrence in a sense hangs upon this expectation. Irrationality means the threat is not heeded or, more likely, not understood and the requisite calculations of cost-benefit are not applied. Or, of greater likelihood, the resulting calculations are erroneous usually due to misinformation but also due to the willful manipulation of reality by the decision maker that is, the persistent reinterpretation of events to fit one's preconceived judgment.

Obviously, calculating this relative cost-benefit ratio becomes complicated by the continual intrusion of emotional-psychological factors, including political variables, into the equation. For example, a state that succumbs to such an overt threat without resistance may feel that such a loss of national prestige results that suffering severe physical damage may be completely acceptable in order to establish conclusively one's likely resistance to being intimidated. To the superior power, this choice represents irrationality, but that is merely a reflection of one's dominant position in the relationship. Becoming the victim, despite the expected physical losses imposed may prove a positive gain in terms of the weaker player's long-term objectives. In fact, the international political fallout may be so high that one of the parties involved may become unwilling to engage in such actions the second time. Democracies often confront this dilemma in part due to their extreme sensitivity to expected public reactions. For example, the continual infliction of damage upon Iraq since the Gulf War has not deterred the Iraqi leadership from pursuing the forbidden policies while public support in the United States and abroad for such coercive action wanes. Larger issues get washed out in the immediate reality of human suffering. Such idiosyncratic calculations become almost infinite in their variety with deleterious effects upon the central pain versus gain calculation embodied in deterrence. In fact, a threat that deters one state may not affect another state's cost-benefit calculations at all. Tailoring deterrence threats to match a particular situation in order to maximize overall effectiveness makes deterrence a more difficult and problematic event than most expect. One threat size or type does not fit all.

In fact, deterrence often fails because states attempt to extrapolate directly from an earlier success to the immediate context. For example, NATO success in Bosnia using air power to stop Serbian actions was extended to Kosovo. The situational dynamics unfortunately may be totally different, undermining the likelihood of success.[4] The infatuation, for example, with air power due to the potential for minimizing or even eliminating U.S. casualties can lead to solutions inappropriate to solving the problem on the ground. This argument was made vehemently by critics of the U.S. intervention in Kosovo. They argued that the policy failed due to the expulsion of Albanians from the area by Serbian forces. Air power was unable to affect those actions in the short term. Counterarguments suggested that the question was one of degree—mass extermination was prevented at the cost of great social upheaval.[5] The point is that air power as a coercive tool contains great limitations, a fact not always recognized by its adherents who are enamored by its high-tech qualities, especially the killing at a distance.

In form, during a deterrence situation, a verbal and/or physical and/or behavioral line is often drawn with adverse consequences predicted for the initiator if that line is crossed. The linkage between violating these established expectations and the damages inflicted must be made crystal clear with no ambiguity suggested on the enforcer's part as to the probability that immediate retaliation will in fact occur. Avoiding that ambiguity often proves difficult in practice, given the slipperiness of language. The major difficulty comes from the reality that the state defending some territorial aspect or principle against aggression may not have thought through clearly what exactly it is defending and, in fact, how far it wishes to pursue the matter. Crises often arise because the assertive state has found what it perceives as a point of weakness in the deterring state's perimeter. For example, as Alexander George and Richard Smoke discuss, the 1948 Berlin Airlift, the 1950 Korean invasion, and the 1962 Cuban Missile Crisis all arose in the context of surprise for U.S. policy makers. The exploited vulnerabilities clearly existed prior to the crisis, but the actual U.S. response was not transparent, so the other party perceived a target of opportunity.  The ultimate surprise became the U.S. willingness to respond as assertively as it did in each situation.[6]

There exists an extensive literature regarding the process of detailing a credible threat line that must not be violated.  All identify the many difficulties inherent in transmitting with total clarity exactly what is the absolute final boundary separating the parties.  The difficulty remains in establishing at what point the situation has deteriorated so badly that only coercion is sufficient to restore both sides' relative positions or stop further deterioration.  Diplomacy by its nature often garbles that essential clarity since such threats are not routinely exchanged, except in more extreme situations.   Even the threats that are transmitted are often dismissed as merely fodder generated for domestic consumption.  The caricature would be Mussolini strutting upon the balcony haranguing the crowd.   Separating out the real from merely the rhetorical becomes almost an art form.  In addition, diplomatic messages are usually simultaneously aimed at several audiences—rallying allies, informing neutrals, and deterring adversaries.   Unfortunately, messages are not earmarked with which specific section is applicable to which particular audience.  In the global communications era, such compartmentalization is infinitely more difficult to sustain.  Diplomatic messages are exchanged, but can be supplemented by literally thousands of communications adding purported insight or analyses of what was said.  Many allege to be reporting the beliefs of significant domestic and international players whose views, if true, would impact how the state will actually respond.

Plus, the most important message remains one's actions—for example, mobilizing military forces or in the modern era putting one's strategic forces on heightened alert status.  Nonactions such as no military movements are also critical indicators.   But, certain military forces such as solid-fueled intercontinental ballistic missile (ICBMs) or submarine-launched ballistic missile (SLBMs) do not visibly change even though they now operate at a higher alert level.  For example, detargeting one's ballistic missiles is a task quickly reversed and an ominous event during a crisis.  Detargeting refers to removing the target coordinates and other necessary instructions from the missile's guidance system.  To reload those instructions becomes a deliberate act, signaling a important step in the seriousness of the situation.  The United States and Russia have engaged in such a deescalating act but both clearly recognized its largely symbolic character.  Moving military units closer to a potential crisis location has not lost its significance politically, but that gesture may not be the most important one for a nuclear power.

The tendency therefore becomes one of fixating on certain geographic features (either natural or humanmade) that appear to physically delineate or separate the conflicting parties.   Principles of international law such as free passage for shipping are more slippery constructs because there exist well-established exceptions that allow interference with that principle.  Regardless, crossing over the boundary, however defined, becomes the triggering event initiating the threatened retaliatory response.  In fact, since the 1960s, in a strategic nuclear weapons context, the mere act of launching the missiles, even prior to their physically entering U.S. airspace, was deemed sufficient justification to mobilize an immediate and overwhelming counterresponse. Failure to immediately respond could expose the United States to the possibility of total nuclear devastation with no effective counterstrike. As a consequence, part of the U.S. strategic nuclear response process became the development of the technical means to detect all possible missile or bomber attacks earlier and earlier in the flight process. In addition, by forewarning the Soviets of this enhanced detection potential, future attacks could, in principle, be deflected because there now existed no reasonable possibility for achieving effective surprise.

More interestingly, this capability moved the nuclear arms competition back a step toward the testing phase. Both states assiduously observed and evaluated each other's missile- and nuclear-testing programs in order to assess the military characteristics of their present and future weaponry, for example. How many warheads did a new generation ICBM carry and with what footprint or impact on target pattern? Knowledge regarding these questions was critical for assessing potential U.S. vulnerability to attack. Those calculations remained somewhat abstract since the data assessed was experimental in nature, meaning the weapon system received extraordinary attention prior to launch. In service equipment might prove less reliable or accurate, given the normal deterioration in an operational environment. Calculating precisely how many weapons would be lost as a result of enemy action and how many lost as wastage due to mechanical and system failures became a guessing game. The outcome was usually to overbuild weapons to provide sufficient redundancy to survive such losses. The result was arsenals that grew much larger over time.

Previously, militaries had engaged in "live" demonstrations of their weapons' effectiveness—nuclear weapons have made that option impractical although testing could obviously take place. Nuclear warhead testing also occurred both above and below ground, providing indirect information to the other side as to the size and effectiveness of a state's respective nuclear arsenal. The other effect of this intense monitoring was to deter rash actions, especially as nuclear weapons grew more powerful. These became the nuclear equivalent to the threat display engaged in by fighting cocks in order to intimidate their rivals. For example, in 1998, India and Pakistan tested what they vigorously asserted were militarily useful nuclear devices. American intelligence estimates were generally more modest regarding the yields achieved, implying less success than claimed.[7] The technologies used to monitor their testing were developed during the Cold War. In fact, these monitors' continuance and expansion to assist in test ban compliance monitoring has become controversial in part because any evidence of violation might demand action by the United States, a choice resisted by isolationists who reject opportunities to engage in such activities.

Regardless, the "firewall" of no nuclear weapons use since World War II has proven to be one boundary no nuclear-capable state has been willing to breach up to this time. The nuclear weapons used against the Japanese are still, as of this date, the only two used against an enemy state. Crossing over into that unknown land of actual nuclear weapons exchanges has proven too troubling because of its escalation potential. The fear is that the first instance of nuclear weapon use, even if only tactical, will spiral out of control into a cataclysmic annihilation of civilization. That represents a rejection in practice of the earlier posture of tactical nuclear weapon use as an immediate option. The concern about escalation continues despite the dramatic reductions in nuclear arsenal sizes since 1991. The fear exists that a nuclear exchange could explode into a war of all against all since even the "winner" will be prostrate at the end. A nuclear state under attack would attempt to take down all potential rivals at once in order to level the field after the war.

The Indian-Pakistani border confrontation in the Kargil Mountains, for that reason, is considered by outsiders the conflict most likely to break that psychological barrier, given their intense military clashes with an active escalation potential. If one party or the other (likely Pakistan) feels it is losing the conflict, the temptation will be to raise the military exchange to the next level in pursuit of victory or, at least, stalemate. Both parties vehemently reject this view, seeing themselves as fully capable of controlling any escalation process as the superpowers did for nearly forty years. Outsiders, mostly established nuclear states, attribute that viewpoint to their inexperience with such weapons and their implications. Regardless, the potential for nuclear escalation poses a distinct threat to U.S. ability to control such regional events. Whether such control was possible even earlier is unclear, but now powers possessing nuclear weapons are thought even less controllable. Almost by definition, new proliferation states have already moved partially outside the control of the international regime.

What further complicates the global situation is the precipitous decline in Russian conventional military capabilities. There is some suggestion that Russian policy makers are now defining tactical nuclear weapons as their fall back position in some circumstances.[8] Earlier, in the 1950s, the United States implemented the New Look strategy, which explicitly incorporated nuclear weapons as a substitute for weakness in conventional forces. Russia is apparently pursuing the same route due to budget and military shortfalls. The viability of those plans is obviously suspect, given the taboo against such use except in extreme circumstances. However, Russian security needs may demand such expedients as crutches for their country's declining military force structure. For the United States, this move, if it occurs, will complicate deterrence calculations, particularly if Russia is overtly involved as the partner of rogue state. The question remains hypothetical in the short term, but may be an early harbinger of a more complicated international military environment. Since the Cold War's end, most scenarios have defined nuclear weapons as a persistent but declining feature. This perspective reflects the fact that the rogue states lack those weapons or else possesses only a few nuclear weapons. By contrast, even in decline, Russia represents a significant nuclear power. That fact does not translate automatically into a return to nuclear confrontation or anything close to that situation. Rather, it points out how fragile the assumptions are that underlie the concept of deterrence as practiced.

What further complicates U.S. efforts at deterrence is the fact that deployment of weapons of mass destruction (WMD) no longer represents a credible first option at least for the United States. Deterrence now generally involves employing conventional albeit, high-tech weaponry. WMD especially nuclear weapons are clearly reserved for what one might term last resort situations in which national survival is at stake. Conventional weapons by their characteristics are more limited in their effectiveness and lethality. This, however, does not mean they cannot devastate wide areas. Iron bombs are disparaged as crude devices but their cumulative effects are disruptive and deadly. Nuclear weapons by contrast possess an instant finality that conventional weapons do not. Such devices both deny and punish simultaneously. Usage of conventional weapons may be extremely damaging as illustrated by the spring 1999 NATO air campaign against Serbia, but the effects are most likely slow acting or inconclusive in asserting dominance over the situation. Nuclear weapons are blunt instruments, but their effects are so devastating that their threatened use could be persuasive. The Eisenhower administration engaged in such threats in Korea and Indo China in the early 1950s–but that option is now much more restricted if, practically speaking, available at all. Whether conventional weaponry provides the same brutal disincentives for possible violators is clearly in question, further undermining the credibility of deterrence.

A factor further complicating deterrence in practice, threat credibility also is not as easily established as one might have expected. Table 3.1 lays out the components of threat credibility. Most deterrent threats are too ambiguous, being hedged as they are by various contingencies—the import of these caveats being to create some doubt as to the exact threat being made, that is, exactly what interests are being put at risk and how seriously is the threat perceived. Humans often demonstrate an amazing capacity for misinterpreting even very clear statements articulating possible acts of deterrence. As discussed earlier, some leaders and their governments twist everything to fit their preconceptions. In one cruel sense, an action can be clearly more effective in message transmittal than the most carefully crafted verbal or written warning. In addition, words and phrases may be translated into very different, although related, concepts when rendered in other languages. What appears as forceful to the threat maker may lack that feel for the receiver hearing or reading the message in a different language. Absolute threats are often, practically speaking, impossible to definitively establish because circumstances constantly arise that subtly change the situation. Plus, professional diplomacy like common law decision-making is often hobbled by its obsessive concern for anticipating future consequences. Therefore, diplomats word their statements so carefully that the import of the message becomes obscured or is so hedged by multiple and often-implausible contingencies that it becomes unclear what exactly is being forbidden. Threat ambiguity is endemic to the process of human communications, especially during situations of high stress, such as a crisis with the possibility of war hovering over the horizon.

**Table 3.1**
**Components of Threat Credibility[9]**

- Perceived interests at stake
- The estimated military costs of counterretaliation
- General reputation
- Legitimacy
- The reputation costs of not following through on threats

The credibility of the threat itself also becomes subject to a tenuous process of negotiations between the defender and the initiator. Both sides are struggling to make their threat both obvious and credible to the other. Over time, a message with its understandings (both explicit and implicit) must be reinforced or reiterated to refresh its credibility. Otherwise, the threat appears to be an isolated, almost random, utterance of little consequence. Reiteration reenforces the exact nature of the rule being announced. Conversely, the deterring state's actions or nonactions in other geographic regions of the world may have negative effects upon its threat credibility in the present crisis. The failure by the defender to respond in an earlier situation in what is thought to be an appropriate fashion lends psychological support to others challenging the status quo elsewhere. In their minds, at least, the two situations are closely linked, even though the state doing the deterring in both contexts does not perceive or necessarily accept that linkage. Thus, creating and sustaining threat credibility remains a recurring sore point between the involved parties and onlookers. In American foreign policy debates, this linking of administration choices in one area to subsequent problems is endemic. This perspective was argued between the Bay of Pigs debacle in 1961 and the subsequent Cuban Missile Crisis a year or so later. Similarly, Vietnam in the mid-1960s was defined as a test case for American resolve globally. One may dispute the linkages but they are potent attacks restricting presidential choices.

Threat credibility also is enhanced or diminished by whether the threat being made is consistent with earlier behaviors. Simply put, a state whose leadership has not previously employed military force to preserve or pursue its interests may lack credibility when finally uttering such threats. The offending party may calculate that the latest threat will not be effectuated or else it will lack sufficient follow through to be effective. Adolf Hitler from all reports did not perceive the democracies, France and Great Britain, as credible when they announced their military support for Poland. Several earlier events, the 1936 Rhineland seizure and the Munich debacle in 1938, had undermined any sense that effective counteractions would occur especially given the enormous military disparities regarding Poland versus Germany as well as with the Allies' inability to directly intervene. However, the Allies by August 1939 felt their political credibility had been so undermined that only a declaration of war could adequately demonstrate their resolve despite their military unpreparedness. The "phony" war period however further undermined that resolve when the time of decision arrived in the spring of 1940. In any case, Germany was not deterred from pursuing further action even assuming that its leadership was sensitive to such considerations. His military advisors were more cautious although not in principle hostile to a war, just the question of when. Hitler is personally thought to have desired such a confrontation given the correlation of forces, as he understood them, in September 1939. His view was that the opposing powers would only be strengthened by delay—mobilization of their resources was already underway. In fact, the allies possessed large forces in the field; they were just poorly organized and deployed relative to German forces. Intervention came because the British and French lacked credibility in the eyes of the aggressor.

Later, similar calculations led the United States to intervene first in Korea in June 1950 and then in Vietnam in order to establish concrete evidence regarding U.S. credibility with regard to its verbal threats of deterring communist expansion. In both situations, unchecked communist expansion was perceived as the primary issue. In Korea, the triggering event involved blatant armed aggression (an invasion of South Korea by North Korea) that force a response especially after the events leading up to World War II and the lessons learned from them. While in South Vietnam, the local response was conditioned by broader concerns about "wars of national liberation." Both situations became self-defined as major tests of U.S. credibility. Whether deterrence in reality demanded that degree of engagement is unclear, but elites clearly operated upon the assumption that such exertions were thought essential. That self-imposed description effectively made each conflict an explicit test of general U.S. deterrence posture across the globe. Universalistic rhetoric by the United States raised the ante so that failure had larger consequences. Whether those situations should have been considered failures of credibility is unclear. However, once the United States intervened militarily on a large scale, its actions changed the respective situations into tests of national resolve imbued with long-term international consequences. Their ripple effects still impact U.S. policy. The doubts, one might argue, are mostly self-doubts since, from the perspective of other states; the United States has been consistently willing—even eager—to employ military force in pursuit of its policies. The 1989 invasion of Panama, the 1991 Gulf War, the continuing air operations over the Iraqi no-flight zones, and the 1999 Serbian air campaign have all involved U.S. forces being aggressively employed against other states. The justifications here varied but all involved an American willingness to employ force.

Even during the Cold War, the United States remained very prone to commit military forces at least symbolically to bolster allies in resisting what was perceived as communist aggression. If credibility is measured by one's willingness to intervene or threaten to do so by employing military forces repeatedly, the United States consistently ranks high on any scale of effort at least since the Korean War. Containment as a political strategy was articulated prior to the Korean conflict, but that action symbolically cemented apparent U.S. willingness to consider and employ military force if deemed necessary. What often lessens U.S. credibility is the fact, that as a democracy with a comparatively speaking open political process, the United States engages in often-acrimonious debates over whether it should intervene originally or persist once actions have begun. The result is to cast some doubt upon American firmness in pursuing such deterrence activities over the long haul. The question perennially raised is, Which specific issues or questions represent such fundamental challenges to American interests that such extreme measures must be pursued?

Threat credibility is also impacted by the existing military capabilities (whether defensive or offensive) wielded by both parties. Modern military technologies including the possible use of WMD, have undermined the earlier conception of military potential—that is mobilization of one's industrial and technological base may produce enormous military power but likely much too late to be influential during the actual crisis. Instead, military forces already in place become the basis for whatever military leverage can be quickly applied to the situation. A state may transport its existing forces to the scene, but those will not include any newly raised from scratch organizations. Developing such military assets takes time, a commodity possibly in short supply during a crisis, especially one involving the threat of nuclear weapons use.

After the initial deployment and/or clash, forces must be built up to continue the action or to increase the coercion applied. However, an initial defeat may make any subsequent action problematic unless the stakes are perceived as so high that quitting is considered unacceptable. Iraq's failure to push further south into Saudi Arabia in 1990 allowed the United States and the coalition to regroup and then improve their forces' position prior to mounting a counter offensive. Apparently, the Iraqi leadership thought the United States was so paralyzed by its earlier Vietnam experience that no effective response would be forthcoming. Given the decade long Reagan administration military force buildup, that expectation was puzzling but clearly signaled a perception that U.S. military forces in themselves did not constitute a credible deterrent. That impression had apparently been reinforced by ambiguous messages conveyed by the Bush administration prior to the 1990 incursion.[10]   What was ignored or not understood was President Bush's personal history of serving during World War II. The Munich analogy, much maligned after Vietnam, was not an abstraction but a reality to him, aggression cannot go unchecked. As a result, the unyielding nature of the initial American response came as a surprise but not one sufficiently credible to compel Iraq to initiate withdrawal in advance of military action, a situation that continues into the present regarding other issues, such as resisting UN weapons inspections. There is an intransigence likely reinforced by American statements clearly demarcating the limits of military force to be applied against Iraq and the growing international criticism of the economic embargo and flight restrictions.

Capabilities are measured in several ways. First, they may be largely offensive or defensive in nature. The offensive aspect must be sufficiently powerful to overcome any possible resistance and be capable of inflicting a level of damage commensurate with the threat made and subsequent violation. This means that the force being applied must be germane or relevant to the issues raised between the two parties. Striking in a random manner undermines the threat, becoming just crude violence for the sake of violence. Conversely, one can employ defensive capabilities sufficiently powerful to stymie any feasible attack by the other party. Effectively, one party cannot be coerced by the other, frustrating the attacker. This is the essence of one argument (among others) for implementing BMD, especially at the national level.

Inability to wield sufficient force may undermine threat credibility because the damage inflicted may not be perceived as linked to the violation. The ability to tailor one's threat to the level and type of provocation suffered is critical. For example, nuclear weapons ultimately proved to be muscle bound in that their threatened use was not truly credible for most crisis situations. Destroying societies over a small territorial incursion was not thought reasonable or was so grossly disproportionate as to offend any sense of credibility. As a result, the United States has oscillated over the years between building up assets to handle those lesser incursions while subsequently reducing its conventional forces for budget reasons. Threatening nuclear holocaust has truly not been credible under most ·conceivable circumstances. Limited or tactical nuclear war was not a realistic option since escalation loomed in the background given American and Soviet capabilities. Whether tactical nuclear weapon use is more credible presently remains unclear since such use dramatically breaks with the past. A bright line runs through international politics regarding the first use of nuclear weapons, a line crossed only under extreme duress.

Nuclear attacks upon states not possessing such capabilities or not capable of resisting would be difficult to justify in the absence of strong evidence of dire national peril. Retaliating to a nuclear attack clearly falls outside these restrictive parameters. This latter context provides the only credible political justification for nuclear weapons use at the present time. In a peculiar way, war has become more deadly because energies are now largely focused upon enhancing conventional weapon capabilities (which can be used). Nuclear weapons become the shotgun behind the door protecting the home against burglars but only after failure of other means.

Conversely, inflicting disproportionate damage upon another society through conventional means may undermine future threats by eliminating the political possibility of that application of force to future situations. Excessive force may not teach potential adversaries the lesson of restraint. Instead but the message learned becomes, if confronted, escalate immediately in order to forestall the punishment or at least minimize its impact. Extreme aggressiveness becomes a protection for the state being deterred. By raising the costs of deterrence significantly, one may be able to effectively forestall such counteractions being taken. One forces negotiations or concessions since the threat maker is unwilling to endure the heightened costs associated with maintaining deterrence. Here, the threat has truly lost its credibility.

Thus, agreements such as the North Atlantic Treaty Organization (NATO) are structured in the so that an attack on one member state becomes an attack on all members. This ensures the triggering of an immediate counterresponse by all especially the United States. American nuclear strategy during the Cold War strove to expand that deterrence pattern through out the nuclear realm. The

United States repeatedly assured the Soviet Union and, by extension, its allies that any direct attack on the United States and its allies would initiate a counter response up to and including employment of nuclear weapons. From this fundamental premise, nearly two generations of American foreign policy has flowed.

The critical question remains one of keeping up the military and political credibility of that deterrence posture. For example, since World War II, the United States has long maintained significant troop commitments in many of the areas being protected. Those forces, usually insufficient in themselves locally to defeat aggression, were unequivocal symbols of the purported intensity of the American commitment. U.S. forces stationed overseas would actively resist any intrusions by the Soviets and/or their proxies. Their casualties, along with their dependents, would constitute the blood price of guaranteeing a larger American engagement. The Berlin garrison during the Cold War was probably the clearest example of this symbolic though largely sacrificial military force. Clearly, too small to effectively resist a Soviet or East German invasion and in a physical environment where retreat was impossible, the troops were stationed there as tokens of U.S. seriousness. Their physical isolation inside East Germany meant military relief was impossible except through NATO military incursions through the Soviet controlled sector. The Berlin Airlift was an earlier manifestation and reaffirmation of that geographic isolation but also of U.S. commitment. The Soviets could have stopped the airlift, but were constrained by the U.S. nuclear monopoly and other considerations within Europe. Failure to respond would have resulted in elimination of the Western forces; whose their position would have been untenable.

In the twenty-first century, the steady decline in American troop commitments overseas further undermines threat credibility. In most situations, the conscious choice will now have to be made in favor of military engagement—there exist no American forces on the ground effectively forcing the issue. There may exist strategic interests justifying intervention but all of those reflect less than directly threatening situations. The United States may be uncomfortable and unhappy with the flow of events but its security is not so directly threatened as to constitute a clear and present danger. The danger is likely more long term and debilitating rather than directly militarily challenging. All of these factors are ones that make an assertive response difficult to sustain politically since significant domestic groups oppose an extensive U.S. overseas intervention. Quick in-and-out interventions are still possible, but longer running affairs become more difficult although inertia and events may lengthen U.S. troop involvement.

Additionally, earlier on, extensive and expensive efforts were continually made to sustain the military credibility and survivability of the U.S. nuclear arsenal. Whether the arsenal would be used as advertised politically was beside the point, however, if the weapons could not survive an initial surprise attack. The triad of bomber, submarine-launched missiles, and land-based ICBMs was developed and sustained so that the United States could guarantee its capacity to inflict unacceptable damage upon any possible attacker. Acrimonious debates ensued over the often arcane and ultimately unknowable (in the absence of experience) questions regarding missile and bomber survivability in the event of a total surprise attack.  Constant adjustments were made or debated at length regarding changing missile-basing modes and improving weapon capabilities. The perception was that effective nuclear deterrence demanded constant vigilance if the Soviets were to be effectively deterred from mounting a nuclear Pearl Harbor.  The endless MX controversy illustrated this question as several administrations struggled with the destabilizing nature of the missile, complicated by its vulnerability to Soviet attack.  Extraordinary political efforts were expended on the question of the MX's basing mode with inconclusive results because public opinion in the affected Western states rejected the original preferred options, including the "race track."[11]

Retrospectively, arguments have been suggested that the Soviets never pursued an agenda as aggressive or threatening as U.S. policy makers assumed or feared.  In the world of deterrence, however, images are as real as actions in generating counter-responses since the actions being threatened or deterred are often based upon impressions of impending decisions or attitudes.  Rarely does one state know for certain how the other state is actually going to proceed and under what conditions.  In fact, often the resultant outcome is significantly different than that assumed most likely prior to the crisis.  Altering already existing impressions is the gist of the situation, one fraught with uncertainty and misunderstandings

On a less dramatic level, deterrence as an intellectual construct has informed U.S. efforts at influencing other states' behaviors across the entire spectrum of possible circumstances.  As indicated earlier, the damages or injuries threatened need not be only military but can also take other forms including economic embargoes or seizing another state's assets.  For example, Iranian assets within the United States were frozen in response to the embassy hostage situation.  In fact the actual application of military force normally marks dramatic evidence of a breakdown in the original threat's credibility.  The other side's willingness to continue challenging the state making the deterrence threat indicates its judgment that the threat made is either not serious or the deterrer lacks sufficient means to carry out their threat.

Either situation forces the deterring state to respond or withdraw from the situation.  Once defeated on an issue, the responding state's concern becomes that the aggressive state not be emboldened to push the line even further, the much maligned domino theory in action.  Thus, the argument repeatedly arises whether an automatic reaction should result for any violation, given its otherwise deleterious long-term impact upon threat credibility if no effective response occurs. When can a state selectively choose not to respond and still be credible later becomes the issue.  Once credibility is lost, recovery becomes difficult and may require extraordinary exertions, although not necessarily the initiation of armed conflict.  This situation ironically increases the instability and conflict potential in future crises since the use of force becomes even more probable because the deterring party no longer has any leverage.

Perversely, however, deterrence as a policy works best when nothing, at least on the surface, appears to happen—that is the party being deterred apparently accepts the threat and therefore simply does nothing. Voila! Success has been achieved. Such an outcome, while highly desirable, proves politically frustrating in the sense that those leaders can only point to the status quo's continuation as evidence for their success, which is a deflating outcome and possibly a self-deceptive one.

The other side of the coin is that deterrence may only appear to work because the other side is in fact uninterested in the question. The state's gestures are simply annoying but not actually threatening since there exists no intention to push harder. Some national leaders, because of their domestic political weakness, employ such episodes to divert attention from pressing domestic or international questions for which they have no solution. Therefore, the threat being articulated has no actual bearing upon their subsequent behavior. Thus, the absence of war may reflect successful deterrence or simply the generally peaceful intentions of all involved parties. For example, the U.S. nuclear arsenal can be employed globally but Great Britain is not normally perceived as a state that it is thought necessary for the United States to deter. Disputes may and do arise between the two governments, but the behavioral expectation is one of negotiating a solution rather than mobilizing for war. Other states may be actively hostile but are too weak to engage in sufficiently provocative behaviors. Cuban-American relations have long operated in this mode. Cuba's hostility was not backed by sufficient power while the United States was constrained at first by its strategic relationship with the former Soviet Union, Cuba's patron. Over time, an uneasy détente arose at least officially while unofficial actors were never allowed to get too out of control, despite rhetorical flourishes on both sides that could possibly provoke an armed confrontation. This relationship persists into the present even after the demise of Cuba's earlier guarantor, the Soviet Union. The exchanges that do occur are kept below the level of the provocation necessary to mobilize further U.S. coercive power although existing sanctions (e.g., the economic embargo) remain in place. For the United States, the constraints upon its behavior are as much domestic as international.

Deterrence therefore does not mean "rolling back the Iron Curtain" or liberating enslaved peoples; rather the purpose becomes more mundane (but likely achievable), stopping the other party from doing what it desire's to do. Further territorial expansion is denied but the status quo becomes the framework within which future policy evolves. One can clothe this basic concept in elaborate terminology and scenarios, but at its heart, deterrence has only been measured by its failure. Once the status quo was established, if not to each side's satisfaction, at least with their concurrence, events become routine. Crises may arise but their effects were contained because neither party wished to upset the equilibrium sufficiently to justify the risk of doing more.

George and Smoke, writing in 1974, offered an analysis of conventional deterrence use as the centerpiece for American foreign policy that is germane to the present discussion. They observed that containment as originally conceived and executed in Europe "worked" due to certain structural conditions related to the states being supported and the physical circumstances under which American actions would take place. That initial success in Europe then supposedly provided an intellectual framework that could be applied elsewhere. First, containment was applied within Asia and along the Pacific Rim, effectively attempting to freeze the status quo although with clearly mixed success. Later, the same deterrence approach, fundamentally based upon employment of military means, was applied in the Middle East. At each point, the United States sought to structure the overall situation in terms of military coercion in order to limit if not prevent communist expansion. Other foreign policy instruments became secondary or supportive of that basically military approach to deterrence. Flexible military response, for example, expanded the options available. It continued the basic containment framework but with a strengthened capacity to deal with lower level military incursions by those actors perceived of as supportive of Soviet and Chinese expansion

The argument made in 1974 was that such an approach was much too narrow and possibly counter productive because it placed the United States in the situation of having to respond in regions where its interests were minimal at best and the threat to U.S. national security minor or nonexistent. From the perspective of thirty years later, the counterargument is that containment in fact worked—validating the use of deterrence in a basically military framework. By frustrating the Soviet Union militarily and, by implication, China, the internal contradictions inherent in their economic and political systems brought one state to ruin and another to dramatic reform (a process still underway and not clearly successful). The fact that the Soviets, in fact, lost the economic competition is obscured by the sense of triumph pervading American political circles. Military-oriented deterrence therefore becomes the answer for protecting the United States from a world characterized by unstable regimes capable of severely damaging American society.

Dating from the end of the Cold War and especially with the subsequent restructuring of international politics, there has arisen even more concern that for the United States deterrence is becoming less potent in discouraging unacceptable behaviors by other states. That is a disturbing prospect if deterrence was the linchpin around which the U.S. security was premised. These impressions of heightened uncertainty appear to align into three broad categories. First, there is the physical reality that deterrence, as the United States perceives it, becomes less workable when the available instruments of military coercion decline in size and effectiveness. Second, it is argued, changes occurring within other international actors have led to greater resistance to being coerced by the United States or any first-world power. Finally, domestic American political realities have drastically altered, severely reducing the military credibility of any U.S. intervention threats. Each of these factors contributes, it is often suggested, to the aggregate decline in overall deterrent threat effectiveness, necessitating NMD as a last—resort providing the protection necessary due to the likely failure of deterrents to work effectively. NMD becomes the ultimate backstop when and if deterrence fails. This becomes especially true when WMD and ballistic missiles can be melded together into nearly unstoppable terror weapons. This conception is somewhat simplistic but underlies much of the fervor underpinning the debate over NMD. The search for the perfect defense becomes an obsession rather than a topic for discussion.

**Table 3.2**
**Changing Size and Composition of U.S. Military Forces[12]**
**(Selected Fiscal Years, 1989–1999)**

| | 1989 | 1993 | 1997 | 1999 | Percent Change 1989–1999 |
|---|---|---|---|---|---|
| **Strategic Forces[a]** | | | | | |
| Land-Based ICBMS | 1,000 | 787 | 580 | 550 | -45 |
| Heavy Bombers[b] | 310 | 194 | 126 | 143 | -54 |
| SLBMs | 576 | 408 | 408 | 432 | -25 |
| **Conventional Forces[c]** | | | | | |
| Land Forces: | | | | | |
| Army divisions active[d] | 18 | 14 | 10 | 10 | -44 |
| Marine Corps expeditionary forces[e] | 3 | 3 | 3 | 3 | 0 |
| Naval Forces: | | | | | |
| Battle force ships[f] | 566 | 435 | 354 | 317 | -44 |
| Aircraft carriers active | 15 | 13 | 11 | 11 | -27 |
| Carrier air wings active | 13 | 13 | 10 | 10 | -23 |
| Air Forces: | | | | | |
| Tactical fighter wings | 25 | 16 | 13 | 13 | -48 |
| Airlift aircraft: | | | | | |
| Intertheater | 401 | 382 | 345 | 331 | -17 |
| Intratheater | 468 | 380 | 430 | 425 | -9 |

[a] Forces with basically nuclear missions.
[b] Includes some long-range bombers that do not have strategic missions.
[c] Forces with largely non-nuclear missions.
[d] Excludes separate brigades that are not part of a division.
[e] A marine expeditionary force includes a division, an air wing, and supporting forces for those combat elements.
[f] Includes all Navy ships involved in combat—for example, ballistic missile submarines, surface combat ships, aircraft carriers, and amphibious craft—as well as some other vessels.

## DECLINE IN THREAT RESPONSE FLEXIBILITY

Bluntly speaking, the U.S. capacity to threaten (i.e. deter) others has severely declined simply because its existing operational military forces have dramatically shrunk since 1991. The military forces that crushed Iraq on the battlefield represented the last hurrah of the Cold War. Much of the equipment and units engaged in Desert Storm largely disappeared within three years of the conflict. Continued personnel recruitment issues have made sustaining even current reduced force levels at times somewhat problematic. As can be readily seen in Table 3.2, the active American military forces have shrunk dramatically. The declines in strategic forces are considered part of the general reduction of the nuclear confrontation that characterized the Cold War. Sufficient nuclear forces remain in place to deter any attacks by emergent nuclear powers. The only peer remains the Russian Federation although its strategic forces are also in decline due to a combination of arms reduction agreements and economic difficulties.

As can be readily seen in Table 3.2, the active American military forces have shrunk dramatically. The declines in strategic forces are considered part of the general reduction of the nuclear confrontation that characterized the Cold Wars. Sufficient nuclear forces remain in place to deter any attacks by emergent nuclear powers. The only peer remains the Russian Federation although their strategic forces are also in decline due to a combination of arms reduction agreements and economic difficulties.

What have declined are the large-scale conventional military forces, which provided operational flexibility, allowing for interventions of overwhelming force to be mounted. Those days are gone. For the discussion here, the decline in conventional capabilities especially in the army and the air force is the most striking. Deployments overseas increasingly stress existing forces while the capability to, in fact, fight two-and-a-half wars concurrently is coming into serious question. Regardless, the reality is that the United States no longer possesses the capacities that existed during Desert Storm , meaning its conventional threats become less credible regardless of whether the national will exists to in fact intervene. Globally, the United States remains dominant but in specific regional contexts, its capabilities may be matched by area powers. The United States could likely dominate but at the cost of stripping its force structure. Where that leaves deterrence credibility is an unanswered question. Congress has not shown a willingness to commit to some form of national service that would be necessary to re-expand the conventional forces. The counter argument has been made that U.S. forces are now so high tech and professional that their combat efficiency is greatly enhanced, and therefore one is able to do much more with less people and equipment—in terms of numbers. The difficulty comes when multiple crises arise—ones in which the United States feels morally obligated to participate for a combination of strategic and moral reasons. Numbers are not irrelevant if multiple crises arise since deployment of military formation of some fighting power takes time.

One sign of this is the extraordinarily high reliance upon active reserve forces to deploy overseas. For example, the 10th Mountain Division (an active duty formation) was relieved of its mission in Bosnia by replacements who were commanded by a reserve general called to active duty for that specific assignment. In fact, the DoD has had to develop overseas deployment rotation policies that explicitly incorporate reserve units. This is being done to reduce the disruption imposed on both active and reserve units to sustain morale. Prolonged and indefinite separations from their families were driving both groups to leave the military whenever their terms of service ended. Effectively, the DoD is coping with two distinct pressures. First, the decline in aggregate force size puts more pressure on those present and, second, the pursuit of a deterrence approach to foreign policy has led to an extraordinarily high engagement rate, meaning units are continually being deployed overseas to back U.S. commitments. Those commitments are not necessarily military in nature; humanitarian and peace-keeping missions have in fact become more prevalent.

The existing U.S. military force structure, based upon the *Quadrennial Defense Review* (QDR) completed in mid-1997 (the next QDR is scheduled for 2001 with another administration in office) calls for the United States to continue its capacity to fight a nuclear war if necessary plus several conventional-type conflicts.[13]    The 2001 QDR will likely change direction slightly in that conventional capabilities may be emphasized more. How much change in the military's structure will occur depends upon the budget and the willingness to innovate. This emphasis reflects an effort to rebuild more traditional forces, albeit ones equipped with high-tech weaponry and more mobile than they currently are. The slowness of the ground force deployment during the Kosovo situation helps fuel some of these changes.

The nuclear component, through the Strategic Arms Reduction Talks (START), has been significantly downsized although sufficient residual force remains to devastate any probable adversaries. The nuclear arsenal is concentrated into land-based ICBMs and sea-based SLBMs although the bomber force remains an option. The ICBMs consist of 500 Minutemen III (each carrying a single warhead) and fifty Peacemakers, formerly the MX, (each with ten warheads). One issue not loudly discussed is the possible obsolescence of these systems. Minutemen III production ended in 1978 with the Peacemaker production line closing in 1988. Upgrading and modernizing these systems remains a critical priority in order to maintain credibility of U.S. response. The SLBMs are housed on Ohio-class Trident submarines with older vessels being scraped. Future treaties will likely see elimination of MIRV (Multiple Independently Targeted Reentry Vehicles) missile systems. In 1990, the United States had 10,563 warheads on strategic weapons, but the number had declined by 1998 to 7,982. By 2007, under START II, the total will fall to 3,500 warheads. The START negotiation process represents a step-by-step minimization of the likelihood of nuclear war. Continuation of the overall treaty process, as will be discussed, may be negatively impacted by the BMD choices made by the United States. In the spring of 2000, the Russian Duma finally ratified the START II treaty (albeit with several restrictions). One important caveat was that the United States not deploy a NMD: if this happens, the Russians will cancel their missile drawdown.

Policy regarding conventional conflicts has proven even more difficult to conceptualize and implement in this new operational environment. Officially, U.S. policy now pursues a 2½-war concept. This translates roughly into the conventional military capability for fighting two major high-intensity regional conflicts, hopefully sequentially but in principle simultaneously, along with an ongoing insurgency situation. The proposed hypothetical situations are a conflict in the Persian Gulf region and another in East Asia with the insurgency action likely located in South America. This scenario assumes a well equipped, highly mobile, and qualitatively superior force structure is in place for use by the national command authority.

All of those factors are thought to be in severe question in part due to ongoing extensive U.S. military commitments across the globe. Those commitments grow as the United States pursues the role of being the pole in a unipolar world—providing a de facto world police force if deterrence as a strategy is to work in practice. The United States is the critical participant in ensuring that many international interventions can in fact happen. Other states are reluctant to lead or else are incapable of providing all the requisite military necessities, especially logistical ones. Such excursions demand on-call flexible military capabilities, the capabilities that are proving most difficult to sustain. Equipment inventory depletion and personnel losses in critical military occupation specialties (MOS) have rendered some units unable to function. In the fall of 1999, two army divisions, the 10th Mountain and the 1st Infantry, were categorized as unfit for immediate deployment. Significant division elements had been deployed to Bosnia and Kosovo, reducing the remaining state-side units below the standards necessary for immediate operational use. Similar force readiness issues exist within the air force and navy in terms of personnel and equipment shortages in critical specialties. For example, continued civilian economic growth has depleted pilot ranks due to booming airline pilot job prospects. Personnel losses significantly reduce operational flexibility due to such shortages. In fact, recruitment issues threaten to totally undermine any continued deterrent potential.

The United States remains fully capable of defending itself from attack but may lack the surplus military capacity to intervene globally in support of its foreign policy objectives. Simply put, the United States may be discovering the limits of its power, a lesson already confronted earlier in a very different fashion in Vietnam. The alternative perspective is that the United States must more carefully ration its scarce military resources, meaning that very explicit and hard choices must be made regarding the relative priority of different events and regions. Policy choices should no longer be driven by short-term factors or else one is rendered ineffectual everywhere. The Bush presidential campaign in 2000 argued that U.S. responsibilities should be pared back, reducing the necessity for U.S. deployments. Whether that is sustainable in a world where the United States wishes to be the critical player is unclear. Under pressure, the United States may find itself forced to be more proactive than expected.

This latter point is often cloaked in expressions of dismay that CNN (as the prime surrogate example), with its graphic news coverage of atrocities, creates public pressures to intervene to stop the killing. The intervention during the fall of 1999 in East Timor illustrates the issue. Other states, led by Australia, committed the necessary combat troops, but the U.S. forces provided a significant portion of the logistical support. Such commitments further strain capabilities as personnel and equipment wear down. But, for the United States, the crisis was deemed important, given its internal consequences for Indonesia. Instability in that location was deemed a major security concern, even though East Timor itself was not, but the conflict, if unresolved, could destabilize the entire region given Indonesia's importance.

Military inadequacies across a broad spectrum of possible responses to potential crises undermine threat credibility in a more subtle manner. The issue becomes one of establishing the proportionality of response to a specific violation, the military version of tailoring the punishment to fit the crime. Declines in operational flexibility drive one to invoke high-tech solutions, especially employing various forms of air power. Potential opponents become ever more aware that the United States lacks the capacity or will to insert ground troops into the conflict. By their presence, troops occupy territory—either seizing it from the aggressor or denying access to their forces. Through such actions, a physical presence can directly undermine the indigenous government or limit its behavior presence. Instead, air power has become the first option employed. That scenario played out in Serbia, where the regime only acquiesced as the threat (not in reality the possibility) of ground troops entering the conflict grew closer. Those forces were sent in to police affairs afterward but not to push their way in over armed resistance. In fact, a troop commitment would have come just as the weather in combination with the terrain, would have made effective action difficult. The uncertainties inherent in such situations were magnified by an inability to quickly mount such an operation.

The difficulties in employing air power for coercion purposes are clear.[14] One can obviously inflict immense damages upon the enemy, but air power by itself does not secure territory held by the other side or, barring nuclear weapons, force permanent changes in behavior. If the air attacks are constrained for whatever reasons, which they increasingly are, their use becomes counterproductive since there exists no logical next step. This scenario appears to be playing out with respect to Iraq. Continued air attacks have not ended Saddam Hussein's defiance or unified political opposition to his regime, quite the contrary. Given the clear political constraints placed upon implementing expanded air operations, its limitations become clear. In addition, not all targets are equally susceptible to such attacks even using precise guided munitions and GPS-directed standoff weapons. There exist very real physical constraints regarding proper target identification as events in Serbia amply demonstrated yet again. Targets were missed completely due to use of camouflage and decoys were destroyed.[15] In addition, presidents have been sensitive to the United States appearing a bully, wantonly inflicting harm on others. That concern, for example, helped shorten the Gulf War in 1991 prior to the destruction of the Iraqi Republican Guard, cornerstone of the Saddam Hussein regime.[16]

More potent constraints are the inability to accurately identify the perpetrators if terrorists or non-state actors strike the United States. The suicide bombing of the USS *Cole* in Yemen points out the difficulties of such identification, especially in a state whose support for U.S. activities in the Persian Gulf is ambiguous at best. There may not exist suitable targets for which the weaponry available is appropriate or proportionate. Terrorist bases are often so intermingled with the local population that striking from the air only increases their support, or at least inflames opposition to the local parties who are supporting the United States. The delicacy of the situation limits action. In addition, after the attacks have ended, there is nothing to prevent the terrorists from starting up operations again, creating an escalating cycle of violence.

Even more challenging for implementing a successful deterrence approach is the difficulty in sustaining control over the escalation process. Infliction of violence either personally or through surrogates such as the military creates psychological pressures to expand or intensify the violence imposed in order to quickly end the confrontation and, by extension, the suffering. Modern industrial states too often indulge their proclivity for inflicting violence upon the weaker states; so control over force application remains an issue. In doing so, proportionality often gets lost, undermining the deterrence concept especially if the message is also aimed at impressing other parties not presently involved. Violence may not have an inner logic but it does have a momentum to it. When lesser levels of violence fail to achieve one's goals, escalating the pain level inflicted becomes attractive since obviously rational people will quit—an understanding held by the dominant power that too often fails the test of experience.

American military actions historically tend to be pursued aggressively with great resistance to any politically imposed force constraints.[17] Administrations often run great domestic political risk by arguing for only a small application of force to achieve limited political objectives. More traditional views argue for "victory" and total defeat of the other party.[18] Thus, properly executed deterrence at its core contains substantial political risk for the president and his party. Moderation in war has not been an outstanding American trait. Successful deterrence demands both finesse and self-control by the United States, a more difficult proposition than most assume to sustain in the face of domestic criticism. American traditions strongly argue for escalation and rapid termination of the conflict.

Deterrence has been more sustainable in the nuclear realm because its expected use came only at the highest level of national danger, nuclear attack. Such weaponry provides ultimate protection but its first use would likely constitute a worldwide catastrophe. This explains why the concept of limited or theater nuclear war largely faded out from the lexicon of nuclear strategy despite its logic as propounded in the 1950s and 1960s.[19] Igniting the nuclear fires has no obvious breakpoint except continuing escalation toward total nuclear conflagration. As a consequence, nuclear weapons lack credibility in most crises, as the price extracted is too gross for the infraction committed.  This partially explains the concerns expressed concerning India and Pakistan and their acquisition of nuclear weapons.  Given their ongoing history of active military confrontation, the potential for escalation becomes sizable if one party perceives itself as losing the conflict.

Thus, the most useful tools for deterrence in the military realm remain largely conventional in form and substance.  These, however, are the capabilities the United States is having the most difficulty sustaining organizationally. Substituting technology is consistent with American historical practice, but such devices are still limited as to their usefulness in many situations.  Those limitations are not always well understood or recognized by those wielding authority.   Too often, expressions of concern about military or political effectiveness are treated as unfortunate expressions of personal softness.  That situation arose during the Vietnam War and the disputes over the efficacy of the escalation strategy.  The effect was to intimidate dissent or, more prosaically, alternative views regarding the policies being pursued.  Instead, the race was to be tough.   Overall, the military weapons most readily available for decisionmakers remain blunt instruments for what are often thought surgical or delicate political operations.

## "NO BEAR, BUT MANY SNAKES"[20]

To beat a proverbial horse to death, the Cold War's end dramatically reshaped international political dynamics and all the attendant linkages that for nearly a half-century had structured the international security system.  These changes have occurred at several levels with the consequences rippling through every point in the international system.  The overarching result ironically was to liberate both the United States but also all other states to more fully pursue their particularistic national agendas.

Too often, it is forgotten that all international parties benefited from the disappearance of the great power rivalry that had so long dominated events.  The threat of nuclear war receded although it did not totally disappear.  In truth, the United States has encountered its greatest emotional and intellectual difficulties shifting gears since the Soviet Union and its actions constituted the central reference point for so long.  Other states were freer of that concern unless they became the focus of the superpowers' attentions at a particular moment.  For those states, regional and internal issues remained more salient except when thrown into the maw of the central disturbances of the Cold War such as Korea, the Congo, Vietnam, Angola, and Central America at different historical points. Those states orbited the black hole that was the Cold War, on occasion being sucked in against their will.

Whatever sense of externally imposed constraint existed previously has now largely dissipated as long as no overt threat is made against the United States or its direct interests.  Iraq discovered that harsh reality when it seized Kuwait, activating American fears concerning Middle East oil supplies.  The unknown future constraint for most disruptive states is the long-term implications of the

Kosovo and East Timor international military incursions for the exercise of national sovereignty regarding internal matters. If those particular precedents stand or expand, then purely local events will possibly subject to external intervention, especially under conditions of threatened or actual genocide and ethnic cleansing.[21] That caveat to the side, the limitations formerly imposed by the two superpowers in order to reduce their potential conflicts are gone. Thus, regional and internal factors that were formerly suppressed now obtain fuller play in the new situation.

From the U.S. perspective, every regional or internal conflict no longer is automatically perceived as part and parcel of some larger global conflict. East Timor and Rwanda are examples. This argument can be seen in the often-emotional congressional debates over possible U.S. troop commitments in Bosnia, Kosovo, and, most recently, Colombia. The arguments are essentially that the problems there are not the U.S. concern and, more pragmatically, that the United States cannot affect events. Whatever the merits of those analyses, for many clearly the United States no longer expects or desires to go everywhere in defense of freedom, democracy, and human rights. The interventionist sentiments expressed by John F. Kennedy in his inaugural address no longer hold.

Some argue that the relevant overlay now is no longer the superpower rivalry as before, but a larger conflict based upon civilizational differences.[22] Those differences represent conflicts in fundamental values and aspirations, ones made especially divisive because they often correlate to disparities in economic development, further inflaming the situation. The economic differences between the First World and other states grow each larger year, but those states provide a reality toward which other states can strive. Failure to be able to do so is often attributed, the machinations of the First World and the desire to keep the poorer states in their place. Therefore, societies based upon some larger vision become attractive. Islamic states are the most obvious manifestation of this pattern where the state and religion are brought together in harmony (at least in principle). Religion, often reinforced by ethnic and national separatism, fuels the dynamic character of these states.

The argument put forth is that societies organized upon such particular worldviews, especially those based upon common religious premises will come together in larger political and economic blocs. In a sense, a global conflict arises, based on values reminiscent of the Christian crusades or the period of Islamic expansion. Not all societies in a particular bloc will be as equally fervent in their views but the cultural parameters will predispose certain states to affiliate particular states rather than others. The crosscutting pressure is economic in that not all states within a civilization operate at the same economic level. Therefore, elite perceptions evaluating the world, while colored by certain common assumptions, will differ fundamentally as to their interests. The argument of this approach is that despite the caveats serious conflict will occur and even intensify with these cleavages structuring the competition.

Previously, such local flare-ups (civilizational or otherwise) were generally suppressed or if possible ignored in order to reduce the potential for a great power dust-up. The Soviet Union or the United States was often invited to intervene in order to solidify the position of whichever faction was presently in authority. Usually the situation involved some internal threat to their continuation in power. In effect, those local disputes got absorbed into the framework of Cold War rivalry with each side becoming identified with a superpower. However, some disputes drew no overt intervention because each superpower perceived the conflict as lying within the other's sphere of influence. Covert operations often occurred in the other's sphere of influence, but plausible deniability was the usual rule. With the removal of that great power overlay, the United States, in principle, can become much more selective in its interventions. There are some disputes where the United States is frankly not interested. There are no obvious national or strategic interests implicated or those implicated are thought insufficiently important to merit military intervention. Therefore, other options become possible, including indifference. Diplomatic options can run the gamut of publicity regarding an unacceptable activity to breaking diplomatic relations. Or, alternatively, economic sanctions of varying degrees can be applied, including an economic embargo. The latter is likely long term but can be effective in dealing with those states most immersed in the international economic system. Selective embargoes are common in order to deny militarily relevant technologies or supplies to such powers.[23]

As an immediate outcome, many regional and internal conflicts are becoming in more likely to play out without direct U.S. military intervention. The United States, in principle, may desire to secure world peace and stability, but it is clearly unwilling to pursue those goals beyond a certain rhetorical level. Under certain circumstances, sanctions of various types might be imposed. Those, however, are usually imposed multilaterally, meaning the United States is joining or is joined by other states. How vigorously the particular sanctions are enforced becomes another issue.

The wild card comes in those situations where humanitarian issues surface, especially in the glare of global media coverage. The random element becomes whether the problems (e.g., war refugees, starving children, genocide) being televised into American homes elicit an emotional public response. Otherwise, the administration can, politically speaking, ignore the problem since it remains just below the national political horizon. This reluctance to intervene often reflects the judgment that U.S. intervention is unlikely to materially change the situation. The end game (how the United States withdraws) has become a more explicit calculation in these minor disputes. The disputes are deemed minor because their linkages to more critical issues are tenuous. However, when the linkage is made, as in Bosnia, the United States increases its proclivity to intervene.

The other side of this, comparatively speaking, noninterventionist U.S. posture, is that state leaderships are even more likely to rise to power based upon narrow nationalist and ethnic agendas. Such views are not intrinsically threatening to other states but can in many circumstances increase conflicts with outsiders. Irredentist claims can drag adjacent states into serious conflict since the goals sought are irreconcilable—that is territorial claims, as part of a national homeland mean the affected land must be seized from another state. Such disputes are not easily resolved given the often-mixed historical record of the controversy; goodness and evil may be a more evenly distributed fact than acknowledged by the aggrieved parties. From the U.S. perspective, this reality makes the parties even more intransigent since the elites' political base is predicated upon their strident advocacy of national pride and an often well-developed sense of historical injustice.

In fact, many leaders come to power in direct verbal opposition to the United States and the developed states in general, seeing their societies as repressed by the First World's overwhelming economic dominance. Earlier, these economic grievances were often presumed to reflect adherence to communist proclivities since the arguments were usually articulated using Marxist or Maoist terminologies. Those cues often obscured the parties' fundamentally nationalist orientation. As a result, the United States was often persuaded that the dissidents were adherents of the Soviet bloc, demanding a U.S. response. Now, the economic and other grievances are more visible (although still intellectually framed in often quasi Marxist or-religious terminology). The United States has become more tolerant of alternative views provided the challenges posed remain internal to the society and do not violate humanitarian values (whatever those values may be at a particular point in time). For the governments, however, this tolerance or indifference may prove only a further source of irritation, graphically illustrating their comparative political and economic unimportance. Thus, more verbally—at least—violent attacks may ensue. This rejectionist attitude is further inflamed by earlier historic experiences with European colonialism, a situation in which U.S. dominance is perceived as a historical extension. Any economic shortfalls and other current domestic issues including ethnic strife are attributed to the residues or poisons lingering from that earlier period. This absolves the present government from any responsibility; a view not necessarily shared by the First World states, especially the United States. National pride is therefore placed on the line during any confrontation with the United States, and compromise becomes unacceptable possibly treasonous. Insult is readily perceived and sought out. Political leaders are fully aware that others are clamoring to replace them at the first sign of apparent weakness. Even successful leaders often confront major internal challenges, all of which further undermine any willingness to be agreeable in the eyes of the industrial states or regional rivals.

Within the context of these reinvigorated regional disputes, quarreling states seize whatever advantage possible. Therefore, possession of ballistic missiles, regardless of their actual military effectiveness, becomes a major coercive asset, given their opponent's clear inability to defend itself. Any American intervention to protect the other party (if it occurs) produces resistance to U.S. demands, in theory placing the United States itself at risk from missile attack. This scenario has become very prominent in the discussions justifying the necessity for theater missile defense and, by extension, national efforts. The leaderships being confronted are in principle presumed undeterrable, not due to insanity, but based on their completely different set of domestic political calculations. For these leaders, to appear less than defiant regarding the United States is too often tantamount to political and personal suicide.

Extensions from this perspective heavily emphasize the instabilities inherent in the post–Cold War period. More alarmist accounts perceive such states as sliding into chaos, emphasizing the viciousness and apparent helplessness of these situations.[24] Those events do occur but reflect internal pathologies and disabilities due to the breakdown in internal control and often the difficulties in mobilizing outside intervention.[25] Globalization has proven extremely disruptive for many societies whether economically involved or more peripheral within the larger world economy. Markets have disappeared or become subject to drastic upheavals. The most unstable situations involve states already fairly marginal to the world economy but also often geographically adjacent to more economically critical states. When the states are so physically isolated that their internal disruption does not disturb states of economic importance, the problem is often ignored. Rwanda and Burundi come to mind. The rise of various isms including religiously based reactions to modernization fuels many of these efforts, providing an emotional fervor not susceptible to either threat or reason, at least from the U.S. perspective. The latter situation may be exaggerated, but clearly the political discipline formerly loosely enforced by the superpowers no longer exists. One party has disappeared while the survivor lacks the requisite will and possibly the means to discipline disruptive states.

Implicit in this perspective is a conception of the world as divided into haves and have-nots or, in other terminologies, First World versus Third World or First Tier versus Second Tier.[26] From the perspective of the former, the haves, the latter are extremely disgruntled states, often trapped in vicious cycles of poverty with all its attendant problems.[27] These states are perceived (erroneously usually) as having nothing to lose. Such states may possess much less than the wealthy but that which is held is of great value to them. All of this further inflames their emotional intensity when confronting the United States as prime representative of the dominant global order. One method by which these states can damage or, more realistically, psychologically terrorize the United States or other advanced states is through the threat, if not use, of ballistic missiles. As their missile ranges lengthen, that possibility grows more real, a prime weapon for the weak. Given already negative American perceptions of their national leadership's hostility and stability (both politically and personally), deterrence becomes problematic. Demonology becomes an important factor in threat perception on both sides. Therefore, BMD in whatever form becomes an insurance policy, protecting the United States against such blatant coercion by the weak. Otherwise, the United States becomes less powerful and more constrained in its freedom of action globally. BMD at both the theater and national level becomes the method by which the United States retains that freedom of action.

## CHANGING DOMESTIC POLITICAL IMPERATIVE

A more subtle but very real and growing inhibitor regarding U.S. ability to engage in credible deterrence behavior comes not from external factors but from internal ones. Crudely put, there exists strong doubt internationally (and shared domestically) concerning the U.S. "will to respond" to threats located below the level of direct attack. From World War II onward until the Cold War's demise, the United States consistently espoused publicly, usually with fairly substantial political support, a position of a national willingness to respond externally, at least in selected situations. Such responses, below the level of an overt attack, were not mindless, but the span of potential scenarios deemed worthy of evoking a military response was thought to be fairly broad. Some situations saw surrogates and covert actions employed but the United States was clearly identified as the action's author (even if formal plausible deniability existed on paper).

The essence of American foreign policy remained that there existed an assumed willingness to intervene in direct support of U.S. policy objectives. That willingness at times placed the United States in awkward situations, as the ramifications grew wider than recognized originally. The Vietnam War grew well beyond the expectations of those deciding upon the initial U.S. escalations. The rhetoric of deterrence drew the United States deeper into a quagmire, which ironically became more difficult to escape without a commensurate loss in national prestige and credibility. Eventually, that price was paid after intense domestic turmoil and badly frayed relations with other international players including putative U.S. allies. American emotional exhaustion after Vietnam led to much discussion of whether a "Vietnam Syndrome" existed as an effective inhibitor upon any future U.S. military action. The situation in fact became subtler than that. The United States still possessed the instincts of an aging prizefighter, just no longer the willingness to absorb the punishment.

Since the Gulf War ended in 1991, U.S. readiness to intervene in other states to support U.S. deterrence objectives has become even more problematic. The Bush administration intervention in 1990 was almost reflexive in the sense that the administration perceived the Iraqi invasion of Kuwait as the moral equivalent to the acts leading up to World War II, the "Munich analogy." President George Bush's formative political experiences had been caught up in that war so the association was at one level easily made. However, the success of the Gulf War in punishing aggression with minimal loss of American personnel has heightened the political pressures not to intervene in the future except under the most extremely favorable conditions. In fact, Munich as an analogy is more ambiguous than often realized—by delaying war for a year, the Allies bought time to rearm. Their efforts were initially in vain (witness the fall of France in 1940) but for the United Kingdom its survival chances were enhanced through delay.

American policy makers have become obsessed with intervening with minimal, preferably no, American casualties and few deaths on all sides although the latter position is fungible. Deterrence at its core contains the brutal reality that not all coercive threats are successful, action must follow if long-term credibility is to be sustained. Casualties, in a crude sense, have become the new "third rail" of American domestic politics replacing Social Security and Medicare. Any possibility of Americans being killed is thought sufficient in some critics' view's to nullify any prospect for immediate U.S. intervention. Whether there is anything in the end valuable enough to defend becomes a very real and contentious issue since direct action against the United States still remains remote. The larger question becomes whether such delays create an even more dangerous future situation as the other party becomes emboldened by American inaction. Also, initial delay allows entrenchment, significantly raising the difficulty of expulsion if that subsequently becomes the goal sought. The difficulty is that deciding what is most important once you move past the question of defending the United States directly becomes divisive. The Cold War period was not as simple or easy as it seems in retrospect, but the existence of the Soviet Union provided a clarity that is now presently lacking. Obviously, there are states that are hostile to the United States but that in itself does not demand military intervention. Threats are now more likely to be economic in nature than overtly military—in a sense, outside the range of deterrence in a military sense. The other nonmilitary tools of deterrence become much more germane.

The irony comes in the realization at the same time that the U.S. military has engaged in more different interventions over the past decade than in any comparable earlier period.[28] In fact, the rate of such activity is now so high as to adversely affect the readiness of U.S. forces through dispersion of their personnel and equipment in a myriad of situations. But, such interventions have normally been carefully structured to be either largely humanitarian in nature or minimizing the exposure of U.S. forces to hostile action. The latter provides political cover against partisan attack. For example, Republican congressional resistance to such activities has become extremely visceral in nature. The intervention in Kosovo generated intense backing when the House of Representatives voted to support American troops but explicitly rejected supporting the intervention there once American forces were committed. The political point being made was that interventions over there were not within the realm of strategic interests as the House defined that slippery concept. The separate votes allowed House Republicans to reaffirm their distaste for the Clinton administration and the larger role the United States was called upon to fill. The attitudes were not truly isolationist rather they wanted to assume the role of selective hegemon.

As a consequence, a generally shared perception has arisen that the United States is no longer to be feared in the sense that any military action—outside the context of direct confrontation—will be taken as a routine matter of course. The United States, it is argued, appears psychologically incapable of sustaining its role as a hegemonic unless technology can always be substituted for personnel or provide perfect protection when troops are engaged. The consequences flowing from Somalia, for example, adversely affected the Clinton administration in deciding what to do in the Balkans.

**Table 3.3**
**Comparing Levels of Deterrence**

|  | **Strategic** | **Other** |
|---|---|---|
| 1. Own Objectives: | | |
| Number | one | many |
| Are they in conflict with each other? | --- | usually |
| 2. Opponent's objectives: | | |
| Number | one | many |
| Are they clear? | yes | rarely |
| 3. Own means: | | |
| Number of kinds appropriate | basically one | many |
| Criteria for selection among | --- | unclear |
| Criteria for selection of quantity | clear | unclear |
| 4. Opponent's means: | | |
| Number of kinds | basically one | many |
| Difficulty in estimating which means or how much he will use | none | usually considerable |
| 5. Degrees of polarization of actual or potential conflict | absolute | variable and mixed |
| 6. Difficulty in estimating whether deterrence is succeeding or not | none | often considerable |
| 7. General ambiguity in the situation | very little | usually very great |
| 8. Number of other national policies that intersect with the deterrence policy | very few | many |
| 9. Likelihood of conflicts among these policies that will be difficult to resolve | no | usually |
| 10. How many possible outcomes are there to the situation | very few | a great many |
| 11. Does a crisis in deterrence last long enough to alter many of the above-listed variables and considerations | no | yes |
| 12. Is the nature of "rationality" in dealing with the crisis problematic | no | considerably |

*Source*: Alexander L. George and Richard Smoke, *Deterrence In American Foreign Policy* (New York: Columbia University Press, 1974), 52–53.

## DIFFICULTIES IN PRACTICING DETERRENCE

The central tenets of deterrence as practiced were largely structured by the bipolar nuclear rivalry that existed from 1950 until 1990 or so. Attention primarily focused upon the deterrence of a possible nuclear strike against the United States. That scenario possessed a stark simplicity about it that no longer exists. One way to consider this change is displayed in Table 3.3. The table is a reworking of an earlier checklist set up by Alexander George and Richard Smoke. That checklist was their attempt to compare various aspects of deterrence across three distinct levels of engagement. The three case levels were strategic, limited war, plus crisis, and crisis preventive diplomacy. Those levels translate into a full scale nuclear exchange based upon an attack against the United States; a nuclear and/or conventional conflict limited by geography or objective but less than total; and a conflict, possibly involving conventional but not nuclear weapons at any level. Their argument was that the nuclear case was so clear and unequivocal that deterrence was at an intellectual level very easy to conceptualize for that situation. Operationalizing the concept more broadly remains difficult. Conflict below that nuclear confrontation level becomes more ambiguous and confusing because there exist multiple pathways to deterrence. Table 3.3 lays out in a very abridged form the difference between the two deterrent situations. The middle case of limited war possibly including nuclear war, has been excluded here because it has become a less likely option. Also, initiation of a nuclear exchange will very probably escalate into a full-blown nuclear exchange, or at least one at the level the states involved can reach. Decreasing national nuclear arsenals have reduced significantly the damage possible using existing arsenals, but for Russia and the United States, overkill is still the situation. A new arms race could, however, dramatically change those numbers and increase the number and power of new participants. That latter question remains central to the NMD debate and what consequences will flow if the decision is made to deploy.

The intent of Table 3.3 is not to delineate all those factors that differentiate deterrence at the nuclear level from less deadly quarrels. Twelve table items are laid out, and several include subcategories. Scanning the table, the uniqueness of the nuclear case becomes blatantly obvious. Objectives are grossly simplified into national survival or not. The means available also become essentially a zero-sum choice of nuclear weapons use or not. However, once a state enters into a general deterrence relationship, the "other" category becomes extraordinarily difficult to simplify. Possible outcomes proliferate while crises drag out, creating even more sweeping problems of deciding what should be done or can be done given the alternatives available. Simple solutions or formulas become misleading and deceptive because their final result may further inflame the crisis. When one adds up the above factors seen as moving against the United States, the fear of possible catastrophe becomes an issue. NMD becomes one vehicle to escape these dilemmas since it simplifies the national protection question at one level of threat. The uncertainties are magnified enormously by the multidimensional nature of the problem.

For example, the objectives (item 1) of the United States with regard to southeast Europe—former Yugoslavia—were multifaceted, making response to the Bosnian situation and then Kosovo more problematic. One important objective at least rhetorically was encouraging Europe to take charge of its security needs within the region. But, the United States also desired to remain politically dominant within Europe, preventing the rise of an independent European security policy outside NATO and so the United States was ultimately drawn into both situations.[29] Policy therefore appeared, muddle along, allowing further deterioration of each situation prior to intervention.

Ironically, U.S. policy in the region had been clear during the Bush administration, no intervention. That stance however was compromised by European efforts, led by Germany, to assume a more proactive role. Such actions forced a U.S. response if its control over NATO and by extension the direction of European security was to be maintained. Further complicating issues were widely held American perceptions that the region was a cauldron of religious and ethnic hatreds unresolvable by outsiders.[30] Immersion into the situation likely meant a long engagement—a position that American presidents have grown leery of pursuing in recent years. All in all, decision making from this perspective becomes complicated.

A subtler and more effective weapon may be economic sanctions since they quietly inflict pain upon others without the dramatic pictures of human deaths or injuries directly attributable to U.S. action—"wash their hands" of guilt. This argument has been made regarding UN economic sanctions against Iraq. The civilian population has suffered immensely without moving the Iraqi leadership to comply.[31] That slowness in response, however, is why military solutions have been preferred. Compliance if military force is successfully applied comes more swiftly because choices are removed.

## CONCLUSION

Given these general issues, the argument for NMD is that deterrence becomes more difficult to sustain as an adjunct to a national strategy or, at least, an effective one. For policy makers, the central dilemma is that their intention is to remain fully engaged in world affairs while domestic opinion grows in their view more skeptical. Unlike Japan, the United States has not foresworn a continuing possibly military role in world affairs. Even Japan is encountering difficulties sustaining its, militarily speaking disengaged role—neighboring states are not allowing that situation to continue due to their actions.[32] For the United States, there exists no philosophical commitment to pursuing such a non-coercive international role. Rather, the national intention is to engage in whatever actions best suit the immediate situation at hand, possibly but not necessarily including the employment of coercive military force. The question becomes in principle what actions are in the best interests of the United States, taking into account those diverse domestic and international factors. The difficulties arise due to the deterioration of the national instruments of deterrence and changes in both the international environment and domestic political context. Enter national ballistic missile defense as a partial solution for these problems that are otherwise beyond remediation at least in the short term. Others argue for diplomacy as the first line of defense while NMD proponents push the argument that paper guarantees are only paper. Therefore, one must pursue BMD in order to protect U.S. forces abroad and the homeland simultaneously.

## NOTES

1. The discussion in this chapter draws heavily from several works, none of whose authors are responsible for the conclusions drawn. Robert Jervis, *Perception and Misperception in International Politics* (Princeton, NJ:  Princeton University Press, 1976); Glenn H. Snyder, *Deterrence and Defense: Toward a Theory of National Security* (Princeton, NJ:  Princeton University Press, 1961); Patrick M. Morgan, *Deterrence: A Conceptual Analysis* (Beverly Hills, CA:  Sage Publications, 1977), Keith B. Payne, *Deterrence in the Second Nuclear Age* (Lexington, KY:  University Press of Kentucky, 1996).

2. For a perspective on deterrence prior to the advent of nuclear weapons, see George H. Quester, *Deterrence before Hiroshima* (New York: Wiley, 1966), 1–5.

3. Michael O'Hanlon, *Technological Change and the Future of Warfare* (Washington, DC: Brookings Institution Press 2000), 120.

4. Barry R. Posen, "The War for Kosovo: Serbia's Political-Military Strategy," *International Security* 24 (Spring, 2000): 39–84.

5. Ivo Daalder and Michael O'Hanlon, "Unlearning the Lessons of Kosovo," *Foreign Policy* 116 (Fall 1999): 131–132.

6. Alexander L. George and Richard Smoke, *Deterrence in American Foreign Policy* (New York: Columbia University Press, 1974).

7. Paul Mann, "India Blasts Upend Nuclear Status Quo," *Aviation Week & Space Technology* (May 18, 1998): 28–30, "Subcontinent's Nuclear Duel Raises Miscalculation Risk," *Aviation Week & Space Technology* (June 8, 1998), 58-59.

8. Paul Mann, "Russia Waxes Assertive, Fearing 'Encirclement,'" *Aviation Week & Space Technology* (May 8, 2000): 54–55.

9. Scott D. Sagan, "The Commitment Trap:  Why the United States Should Not Use Nuclear Threats to Deter Biological and Chemical Weapons Attacks," *International Security* 24 (Spring 2000): 85–115. Table 3.1 is a modified version of the table found on page 98.

10. Michael R. Gordon and Bernard E. Trainor, *The Generals' War: The Inside Story of the Conflict in the Gulf* (Boston: Little, Brown, 1996). The early chapters provide a perspective, based upon American sources, of their surprise at Iraq's action.

11. Lauren H. Holland and Robert A. Hoover, *The MX Decision: A New Direction in U.S. Weapons Procurement Policy* (Boulder, CO: Westview Press, 1985), 215–229.

12. Table 3.2 is drawn with some minor modifications from Congressional Budget Office, *Budgeting for Defense:  Maintaining Today's Forces* (Washington, DC: Congressional Budget Office, September 2000), 9, Table 2.

13. William S. Cohen, *Quadrennial Defense Review* (Washington, DC:  Government Printing Office, 1997).

14.  Cf. Robert A. Pape, *Bombing to Win: Air Power and Coercion in War* (Ithaca, NY: Cornell University Press, 1996), 55–86.

15.  Daniel A. Byman and Matthew C. Waxman, "Kosovo and the Great Air Power Debate," *International Security* 24 (Spring 2000): 5–38.

16.  Frank N. Schubert and Theresa L. Kraus, *The Whirlwind War: The United States Army in Operations DESERT SHIELD and DESERT STORM* (Washington, DC: Center for Military History, 1995), chapter 8.

17.  Russell F. Weigerly, *The American Way of War: A History of United States Military Strategy and Policy* (New York: Macmillan, 1973), chapters 7, 16.

18.  Walter Russell Mead, "The Jacksonian Tradition," *The National Interest* 58 (1999/2000): 5–29.

19.  Herman Kahn, *On Escalation.*

20.  The section heading is drawn from a quoted statement by army Lieutenant. General Patrick M. Hughes (ret.).  Paul Mann, "Fathoming a Strategic World of 'No Bear, But Many Snakes,'" *Aviation Week & Space Technology* (December 6, 1999): 61–64.

21.  Strobe Talbot, "Self-Determination in an Interdependent World," *Foreign Policy* 118 (2000): 152–163.

22.  Samuel P. Huntington, *The Clash of Civilizations and the Remaking of World Order* (New York: Simon & Schuster, 1996), 183–206.

23.  Donald M. Snow, *National Security* 4th edition (New York: St. Martin's, 1998), 180–188.

24.  Robert D. Kaplan, *Balkan Ghosts: A Journey Through History* (New York: St. Martin's, 1993); idem, "The Coming Anarchy," *Atlantic Monthly*, February 1994, 44–76.

25.  John Mueller, "The Banality of 'Ethnic,'" *International Security* 25 (Summer, 2000): 63–70.

26.  Cf. Max Singer and Aaron Wildavsky, *The Real World Order: Zones of Peace, Zones of Turmoil* (Chatham, NJ: Chatham House, 1993); Robert D. Kaplan, *The Coming Anarchy* (New York: Random House, 2000).

27.  The sense that such states are acted upon rather than being actors can be seen especially in the Balkans.  But often when the states did act, their actions were such as to increase further their difficulties both domestically and internationally.  Cf. Misha Glenny, *The Balkans, Nationalism, War and the Great Powers*, 1804–1999 (New York: Viking Press, 2000).

28.  Disputes exist over how much should be done and for what goal.  Andrew J. Bacevich, "Policing Utopia," *The National Interest* 56 (1999): 5–15.

29.  Kenneth N. Waltz, "Structural Realism after the Cold War?" *International Security* 25 (Summer 2000): 20–25.

30.  Cf. Warren Zimmerman, *Origins of a Catastrophe: Yugoslavia and its Destroyers* (New York: Basic Books, 1996); Christopher Bennett, *Yugoslavia's Bloody Collapse* (New York: New York University Press, 1995); Tim Judah, *The Serbs: History, Myth, and the Destruction of Yugoslavia* (New Haven, CT: Yale University Press, 1997).

31.  John Mueller and Karl Mueller, "Sanctions of Mass Destruction," *Foreign Affairs* 78 (May/June, 1999), 43–53.

32.  Roger Handberg, "Changing Parameters of Japanese Security Policy: The Advent of Military Space in the Post Cold War Environment." (Paper presented at the Annual Meeting of the Southern Political Science Association, Savannah, November 1999.)

# 4

# Why Missile Defense?

## INTRODUCTION

Why missile defense? That would appear to be a question for which a definitive and easy answer should already be available, given the intensity and length of the ballistic missile defense (BMD) debate. In fact, the justifications put forth have shifted widely over time, reflecting the continuing interaction between the specific political concerns of the day and the existing state of the relevant anti-ballistic missile (ABM) technologies. Technological capability by itself, as will be discussed in chapter 5, has never been fully definitive in resolving the vexing question of whether national missile defense (NMD) works reliably. Rather, BMD technology, its capabilities, and results become merely fodder fueling the continuing discussion while the actual meaning assigned at any particular time has been much less clear than one might assume. For example, the Department of Defense (DoD) earlier touted its October 2, 1999, interception of a test warhead by a hit-to-kill (HTK) vehicle as an unequivocal success. Subsequent analyses pointed out that the success was in fact more qualified and, in some more skeptical eyes, was defined as a failure in reality. Both sides argued the same facts but drew diametrically opposite conclusions.[1] In that sense, the debate has not been entirely rational but rather quasi-rational with preexisting psychological predispositions central to explaining the evaluation process.

Here, for purposes of this discussion, however, acceptable levels of successful interception are assumed to have been achieved or are likely to occur shortly, and the focus becomes the "why" or justification question. The answers provided for that question hopefully make clear the broad purposes that ballistic missile defense at both the national and theater levels are presumed to advance. These purposes are clearly distinct but are linked—merging over into a unitary system in the distant future. Four purposes will engage our attention in this chapter and provide an entry point into evaluating the ongoing debate in Washington. As presently articulated, the purposes range from ones essentially moral in character and tone to those resolutely politically realistic in their approach.  Their advocates as will be described in chapter 5, often passionately hold the justifications expressed in support of NMD.

## ALTERNATIVES TO NATIONAL BALLISTIC MISSILE DEFENSE

Before reviewing the various rationales suggested for implementing ballistic missile defense especially at the national level, some consideration must be extended to consider the other policy options or alternatives suggested in place of implementing an NMD deployment.  These alternatives, in a manner equivalent to BMD generally, do not guarantee perfect success in protecting the United States.  There exist no guarantees whichever approach is chosen—a fact that leaves the choice up to the decision makers' judgments.  The primary virtue of these alternative approaches in the minds of their advocates is that they represent more traditional remedies, not greatly upsetting existing international and domestic political and military relationships as NMD is alleged to do.  In their view, those relationships have, generally speaking, maintained the peace for over fifty years especially in regard to the possibility of nuclear war, a not inconsiderable accomplishment.  This attitude does not represent any blind adherence to the past but rather reflects judgments regarding the long-term implications of change.  NMD proponents especially do not share these judgments since failures do occur when using every approach.

As a general statement, U.S. policy up to this point has been to concurrently pursue each of these alternatives, including BMD, at both levels, albeit with different degrees of intensity and enthusiasm depending upon circumstances. This pattern renders the policy environment extraordinarily complex since different emphases become the primary focus. depending upon a rapidly shifting international context. Such continual moving back and forth across the range of possible avenues has made policy a constantly shifting mosaic. All approaches, however, are ultimately aimed at enhancing if not ensuring American security from any external attack by ballistic missiles bearing weapons of mass destruction (WMD), especially since those attacks are the most difficult to stop militarily.

For BMD adherents, this constant merry-go-round of considering and implementing various policy alternatives produces extreme frustration because (from their perspective), just when the conversation hones in on the essence of the question of NMD deployment now; the opponents shift the grounds of the debate.  This changing of parameters reflects the uncertainties inherent in BMD technologies and the twists and turns of international politics.  The international system is affected by the actions and non-actions of all the parties—many of whom are not completely or, in some instances, even partially responsive to U.S. desires.  Even as a historically temporary hegemon, the United States is still often the prisoner of others' actions.  Those uncertainties therefore allow full play for other approaches since NMD even if deployed cannot guarantee total national security.   Total security is no longer a certainty although it is rhetorically suggested to be one by some advocates.

Regardless of the NMD advocates' frustration, these other alternatives are being seriously pursued, and this could negate the requirement or necessity for BMD deployment at the national level.  As will be discussed, theater level ballistic missile defense over the past decade has been raised to the status of a political icon.  Regardless, the major policy inhibitor there remains the technical difficulty of accomplishing successful missile interceptions under almost all reasonable attack scenarios.  The overall debate has advanced at least in the political sense to the point that no one seriously suggests establishing a perfect defense against all ballistic missiles.  The Strategic Defense Initiative (SDI) at first blush held out that promise—but it was quickly quashed by the physical and political realities.  However, weapons of mass destruction (WMD) raise the perceived stakes even higher if some "leakage" or interception failure is presumed to occur.  Even in the theater missile defense (TMD) arena, the technical parameters for successful interception still remain daunting although their advocates argue success is high.

The policy alternatives suggested here are generally considered less relevant to TMD because of the wider diversity and number of potential participants in that arena.  The Missile Technology Control Regime (MTCR) has helped delay diffusion of the more advanced technologies, but knowledge that they exist means that others can duplicate their parameters.[2]  On the other hand, intercontinental-range missiles are not simply a scaling up of shorter-range weapons but pose a different order of magnitude in difficulty given their flight path and speed.  That reality explains why the threats posed by the states of concern are perceived as still lying in the future.

As a result, several policy alternatives (including BMD) suggest themselves with multiple variations possible within each.  U.S. policy has pursued all these avenues with varying degrees of vigor since before the inception of ballistic missiles as a realistic military threat.  Among the most prominent alternatives are (1) maintaining an assured nuclear retaliation capability; (2) international agreements, including strategic arms reductions and nuclear test bans; (3) nonproliferation agreements regarding missile technology and nuclear weapons; (4) efforts at fostering peaceful political and economic change; and (5) national ballistic missile defense.  The latter will be the subject of our analysis in chapters 5 and 6, so only the first four will be briefly recapitulated here.

### Assured Nuclear Retaliation

The first option, maintaining assured nuclear retaliation, has constituted the bedrock of American national security policy since immediately after the end of World War II.  In fact, its mere existence has been often asserted as rendering NMD unnecessary.  In the beginning, the atomic bomb, first used in World War II was considered simply a bigger bang for the buck (this misimpression in part reflected the widespread lack of knowledge of such power due to secrecy surrounding it), but rather quickly its potential as a deterrence weapon was recognized.  The societal damage inflicted would be so horrible that enemies would hesitate before striking since they were guaranteed to be counter-attacked with horrific results for their society. Nuclear threats were an exercise in terror. The United States, through its bomber wings at first and later ballistic missiles, both land and sea based, has aggressively pursued sustaining the physical capability to destroy any enemy whether surprised or not by their onslaught. In fact, at times, the United States seriously contemplated employing first-strike scenarios if necessary to protect its military capacity to severely damage or destroy any potential foe. Preemptive and preventive war was rejected as an explicit policy option in the late 1940s but its implications have lingered on to this day.[3] Even in the present reduced state of the U.S. nuclear arsenal, a larger capacity has been retained relative to other states' nuclear forces and their delivery capabilities. To attack the United States with weapons of mass destruction is presently to suffer devastating retaliation.

The key variable here becomes ensuring the survivability of current nuclear weapons systems and guaranteeing their robustness in striking back. Survivability means the capacity for riding out, through use of hardened missile sites, concealment, or a combination of both, the initial nuclear onslaught. Robustness refers to remaining capable of inflicting sufficient damage to punish the attacker heavily despite possible losses due to the enemy's actions and defenses. These questions have led to long and effectively interminable debates over scenarios whose outcomes can vary dramatically based upon the preliminary assumptions made. The arguments in the 1950s over "finite deterrent" illustrate the problem since the Eisenhower administration and its critics never agreed upon the probability of either condition being met. Effectively, the question becomes what constitutes "enough" to guarantee a successful counterattack, thus deterring any potential attacker. Robert McNamara proposed the concept of "assured destruction" as the policy mechanism for ensuring the survivability of the U.S. strategic forces. That concept allowed the Kennedy administration to effectively freeze the number of land-based intercontinental ballistic missiles (ICBMs) and submarine-launched ballistic missiles (SLBMs) thought necessary. The policy focus then shifted in essence to the perennial problem of keeping pace with possible Soviet offensive improvements and remaining capable of negating their anti-ballistic missile (ABM) efforts. From that concern flowed the Multiple Independently Targeted Reentry Vehicle (MIRV) with its attendant penetration aids, all in the never-ending quest for certainty.

The MIRV represented two solutions to the problem. First, each ICBM now carried more than one warhead—a fact that translated into an increased likelihood of targets being destroyed. Second, a MIRV-equipped force allowed a single missile to hit multiple targets. The result was an enhanced capacity both to attack targets and to override the capacity of any BMD system to cope with the numbers.

Earlier deterrence debates, spanning the 1950 until the late 1980 also operated in a context in which new weapons were presumed to be actively under development—a constant race to keep ahead. For example, the Minutemen missiles progressed from the first through the third versions to be succeeded partially by the MX (now Peacemaker) while the original Polaris SLBM was replaced by the Poseidon followed by the Trident, all in the quest for maintaining an assured destruction capability. Now, the focus shifts to keeping the existing ICBM and SLBM inventory operational despite its increasing age. As mentioned earlier, the land leg of the American strategic capability is aging with no replacement system projected or new copies of old missiles being built. In time, the reliability of those Minutemen and Peacemaker systems will become truly problematic.

Their survival as the aging backbone of the American strategic weapons inventory is probably the best symbol that the arms race spiral, if not broken has at least been severely bent. For the United States, there exists presently no immediate competitor sufficiently threatening to drive a new round of offensive weapons development. In one sense, BMD becomes the only game in town. Proponents of economic explanations could argue that the arms industry is pushing this aspect as a replacement for lost markets. The ideological fervor with which NMD is advocated makes that perspective less persuasive given that other areas within the DoD budget hold out prospects for greater rewards—the Joint Strike Fighter for one—with less political difficulties.[4] The Joint Strike Fighter could total $200 billion or more if built in its presently conceived three distinct designs. NMD also has a history of erratic funding that discourages corporations. One can measure that understanding informally by contrasting the amount of advertising in the trade press for various fighter configurations compared to those for NMD. The former, jet fighters, are seen as a field of opportunity with BMD generally a closed site with too few program opportunities of, comparatively speaking, limited value. Boeing heads the NMD team while Lockheed Martin leads the largest TMD program. This general decline in program urgency is bitterly contested by defense preparedness proponents, but the threat context remains too nebulous to return to earlier levels of developmental activity. That international context is obviously subject to change, but as long as U.S. nuclear forces appear as overwhelming as they are currently, the situation will not change suddenly. By contrast, conventional weaponry remains an active field, especially when the export potential is factored into the economic equation.

### Arms Limitations

The other side of that assured destruction coin has been a consistent pattern of striving to reduce the potential for nuclear war through the construction of strategic and other arms limitations and nuclear test bans. The latter ban acts to diminish future nuclear weapon development by limiting data collection. Nuclear test bans also reduce the ability to ensure that one's nuclear weapons have not deteriorated badly. Without actual test data, the weapons designers are forced to rely upon simulations that always contain an element of artificiality and possible error, undiscoverable unless actual use occurs.

The process has been a cumulative one in that the first treaties established the general principles, which were gradually extended geographically and by weapon category.  Table 4.1 briefly lists various treaties and agreements not as a complete enumeration but to provide a context.   Clearly, until 1999, the expectation was that the spread of such agreements would continue, reflecting the decline in global tensions.  That incremental process ran into a roadblock when in October 1999 the United States Senate rejected the Comprehensive Nuclear Test Ban Treaty.  The ramifications of that decision are both immediate and short term.  Several states on the verge of ratification have delayed action while U.S. leverage in the larger arms control process has been stunted.  With a new administration taking office in 2001, the process would have slowed in any case but the new Bush administration is even more skeptical.

Rolling back previous understandings (the ABM treaty to the side) is not a priority but momentum has been forfeited.  The Senate's rejection was a combination of a slap at the Clinton administration and the desire by the Republican Senate majority to assert their independent role in the arms negotiation process.  The latter aspect will continue for the foreseeable future simply because of the narrowness of the Republican margin in Congress.  Regardless, the logic underlying such negotiations has not disappeared, but the process has become more fragile.

**Table 4.1**
**Arms Control Agreements**

**Bilateral – Nuclear and Other WMD:**
 Anti Ballistic Missile Treaty—1972
 Strategic Arms Limitations Treaty I  (SALT 1)—1972
 Strategic Arms Limitations Treaty II (SALT II)—1979
 Intermediate Range Nuclear Forces—1987
 Strategic Arms Reductions Treaty I (START I)—1991
 Strategic Arms Reductions Treaty II (START II)—1993-2000
**Multilateral:**
 Limited Test Ban Treaty—1963
 Outer Space Treaty—1967
 Non-Proliferation Treaty—1968
 Seabed's Arms Control Treaty—1970
 Biological Weapons Convention—1972
 Threshold Test Ban Treaty—1990
 Chemical Weapons Convention—1997
 Comprehensive Nuclear Test Ban Treaty—unratified
**Bilateral Risk Reduction:**
 Accidents Measures Agreement—1971
 Hot Line Agreements—1972
 Incidents at Sea Agreements—1972
 Prevention of Nuclear War Agreement—1973
 Ballistic Missile Launch Notification—1980
 Cooperative Threat Reduction—1991
 Mutual Detargeting—1994
 Joint Data Exchange Center—2000

Strategic arms reductions represent one avenue through which war, if it occurs, becomes less devastating—by limiting the destructive potential possible. The reality of nuclear weapons is that their destructiveness is so immense, especially against "soft" (i.e., civilian) targets that the loss of life will still remain enormous. The "nuclear winter" scenario described by scientists in the 1980s further amplifies the long-term destructive potential of such devices—a human version of multiple catastrophic asteroids or comets striking the Earth. These agreements tend to be heavily numbers driven since that is easily measurable.   The naval treaties of the 1920s and 1930s were an earlier expression of that quantitative methodology. Qualitative improvements such as MIRVs are more difficult to verify but simply reducing the aggregate number of launchers does have an impact although it is less direct than previously.

In addition, accidental nuclear exchanges are minimized.  Accidents can be deliberate or truly accidental.  By deliberate, we refer to rogue or rebellious military units firing missiles without government authorization.  This issue was raised during the early years after the Soviet Union's fall.  Questions of political loyalty were significant issues in a newly established political system.  By significantly reducing their numbers, that likelihood could be reduced.  Truly accidental launches may still occur due to equipment or system breakdown.  As the Russian military deteriorated because of economic shortfalls, questions regarding equipment reliability became urgent since inaccurate attack alerts can be  sounded  or  launch  controls  can  misfunction  during  training.    By consolidating their forces, the Russians were able to maintain political control over their units.   This has been especially important since the understanding between the United States and Russia is that their nuclear forces are left "on constant alert."  The latter refers to the fact that Russian missile forces are kept in an operational status allowing virtually instant retaliation if an attack occurs.[5] The quoted phrase comes from the official document presented to the Russian government with regard to changes in the 1972 ABM Treaty to allow U.S. development (discussed in chapter 6).  The official document was obtained by the *Bulletin of the Atomic Scientists* and passed to the *New York Times* for publication.

Furthermore, as discussed earlier, maintaining a state's assured retaliatory capability was ironically one important factor in stopping the original NMD deployment.   The 1972 ABM treaty represented an explicit attempt to slow the nuclear arms race by in effect guaranteeing for each side a successful nuclear attack. The Safeguard system in its largest configuration was seen as potentially disrupting that relationship; therefore, the deployment was first reduced in scope and subsequently shut down completely.   On that basis, the Strategic Arms Limitations  Talks  (SALT)  first  began  their  odyssey  across  the  political landscape, followed by the START series.  The SALT I treaty signed in 1972 initiated the arms reduction process but bore no immediate fruit after the Soviet invasion of Afghanistan and the advent of the Reagan administration in 1981. The  SALT  II  agreement  has  been  reluctantly  negated  by  the  Carter administration in response to those events. By the last years of Ronald Reagan's tenure, the process, albeit with numerous false starts, was fully underway.  The most dramatic manifestation of this process was the 1987 Treaty on the Elimination of Intermediate-Range and Shorter-Range Missiles (the INF treaty). The INF treaty was the first agreement in which actual weapons were discarded. All nuclear-armed ground-launched ballistic and cruise missiles with ranges between 500 and 5,500 kilometers were destroyed with on-site inspections conducted by both sides to verify compliance. The impending collapse of the Soviet Union added urgency to these efforts, culminating in the START I treaty in 1991. The process stalled again until 2000 due to the Russian Duma's unwillingness to ratify the START II treaty.

That logjam was broken in April 2000 when President Vladimir V. Putin pushed the treaty through the Duma. The goal was two-fold: (1) to preserve Russian strategic weapons numerical equality with the United States and (2) to further pressure the United States not to deploy an NMD system. The former refers to Russian economic issues, which are undermining their capacity to sustain their nuclear forces at current START I levels. By simultaneously going lower with the United States, through START II, Russia is better able to sustain its credibility as a major power, concentrating its limited resources on fewer systems. Ratcheting down the arms race becomes a mechanism for sustaining strategic equality, a situation otherwise unsustainable in the short term. The Russians have steadfastly rejected expanded NMD deployment as a blatant violation of the ABM treaty. By ratifying and agreeing to implement START II, their gamble is that the United States will become slower to deploy a system seen as so potentially disruptive internationally. Further pressure was exerted by their subsequent ratification of the Comprehensive Test Ban Treaty (in contrast to the United States Senate's rejection of it in October 1999). Whether this approach works or not is unclear, but both actions reinforce awareness that arms reduction agreements can be employed to manipulate the strategic arms environment in unanticipated ways. The new Bush administration will have to juggle those questions when deciding which direction to pursue regarding NMD and arms control measures.

Arms reductions had earlier been extended into conventional weapons systems also. This mirrors efforts at conventional arms reductions dating back to the post–World War I period with various naval treaties plus rules of war conventions being implemented with erratic success (cheating was common). More recent efforts operated to reduce the confrontation potential in Europe where the Soviet led Warsaw Pact directly confronted NATO. Conventional forces in Europe were significantly reduced in 1990. In an effort to lower confrontation potential, elaborate formulas were developed regarding how many and what types of weapons are in the region. These limits have proven to be less arduous than originally expected due to Russia's declining capacity to sustain its conventional forces. That decreased threat has led all other states to reduce their forces.

### Nonproliferation

Nonproliferation agreements have also been implemented in several areas but two in particular are relevant here: ballistic missile technology and nuclear nonproliferation. The latter has had stronger international interest, given the obvious stakes involved, although states sufficiently motivated are still able to produce nuclear weapons. India and Pakistan, driven by their perceived regional security needs, have developed such weaponry despite adverse international reaction. As Table 4.2 shows, the international community has structured several agreements to slow if not stop weapon proliferation by controlling the technologies.    Earlier listed in Table 4.1 were the Biological Weapons Convention and the Chemical Weapons Convention, other examples of such control efforts. Diffusion of nuclear weapons technology, however, has been much slower than many expected especially in the early 1960s, but that reflects the fact that several potential weapon states, South Africa, Argentina, and Brazil, chose to forgo pursuing their programs. All were under international pressure to do so. The persistent economic problems in the Russian Federation have continued to arouse fears of widespread proliferation since many of their weapon and missile technologists are now available for hire. The Nunn-Lugar Act has been used to accelerate nuclear weapon destruction in the Ukraine, Belarus, and Kazakhstan while other programs have pursued providing alternative employment opportunities. The point is that sustaining nuclear nonproliferation has proven more difficult in the post–Cold War era than expected. Nuclear technology in theory is now more available than ever before although the slowdown in commercial nuclear power growth has helped reduce dissemination.

The political determinants of nuclear proliferation, however, are not entirely controllable from outside a society. As was discussed in chapter 3, national leaderships are driven by domestic agendas that emphasize their independence, even defiance, of any foreign government dictates. From this perspective, seeking such weapons becomes rational as a tangible measure for acquiring international prestige and power. For example, other states, especially immediate neighbors, become more wary of directly challenging nuclear states. In fact, the mere hint of nuclear weapon possession may in itself provide a distinct measure of respect among one's enemies.

**Table 4.2**
**Selected Nonproliferation and Export Controls Agreements**

Treaty on the Non-Proliferation of Nuclear Weapons—1968
Nuclear Suppliers Group—1974
Nuclear Materials Convention—1980
Fissile Materials Cutoff Treaty—under negotiation
Wassernaar Agreement—1996 (conventional weapons & dual-use technologies)
Missile Technology Control Regime (MTCR)—1987
International Trade in Arms Regulations (U.S.)

The Israelis have long played a shell game as to whether or not they actually possess such weapons, never emphatically denying the possibility of possession but also not officially confirming it. Doing the latter would activate international sanctions as India and Pakistan discovered after their almost concurrent publicly announced nuclear tests.  U.S. ability to enforce any sanctions, however, is always bound by the willingness of other signatories to support that effort. In most strategic weapons areas, including nuclear areas, the United States is not the only possible supplier or even the primary source for many types.  This is most readily apparent regarding dual-use technologies where Japan is the leader in many high-tech areas.

Missile technology has become more widely proliferated although the Missile Technology Control Regime (MTCR) has clearly slowed movement of such technologies.  Much of that technology proliferation predated the MTCR's establishment, reflecting previous arms sales and the provision of weapons to various allies during the Cold War.  Over time, the United States especially became sensitized to the regionally destabilizing aspects of such missile technology proliferation.  The Soviets and (later the Russians) were slower to move in that direction.  Both Russia and China have constantly used sales of such missile technologies to obtain desperately needed hard currencies.  In fact, a continuing source of controversy has been Russian assistance to Iran.  North Korea has continued its activities for that same reason, having no other exportable assets of equivalent value.  The United States has reduced North Korean exports through subsidies, effectively a bribe for good behavior.

In form, the MTCR is an agreement but not a treaty among the established missile technology producers not to disseminate such technologies to states not already in possession of them.  The looseness comes from the dual-use nature of rocket or missile technologies. When is the technology for peaceful uses?  Missile technology's dual-use nature was obvious from the very beginning of the space age, but its significance got lost for a time until the first Bush administration honed in on the issue.  That obscurity reflected the tunnel vision inherent in the Cold War when the two superpowers kept their gaze fixed upon each other.  For example, under the auspices of the MTCR, Russia was actively discouraged by the United States from providing India with the technology necessary for developing the third stage for its spacelift program.  The military implications were considered destabilizing within the South Asia region.  The United States had also became aware that states such as South Korea (an ally) had converted short-range missile technologies provided them by the United States into longer range ones.  Their justification was the serious threat posed by North Korea and their growing concerns about U.S. steadfastness in defending South Korea.  Recent U.S. efforts to placate North Korea were especially interpreted as signaling a lessening U.S. commitment to the Republic of Korea.

Clearly, the states being restricted perceive the MTCR as just another mechanism by which the dominant space powers keep others out of the field.  This perspective reflects their strongly held view that the United States and the others employ the dual-use aspect to hamper their development of peaceful and especially commercial space efforts in competition with the space powers. The first Bush administration was particularly insistent that states desist from pursuing any space launch capacity due to its military applications. From those states' observations, space applications, especially communications, are absolutely essential for entering the global economy and remaining competitive. Thus, these allegedly security driven restrictions, in their view, become simply the monopolist's effort to sustain its economic position rather than a disinterested attempt at maintaining world or regional peace. The rich stay rich and the poor remain poor due to their technological backwardness. This perception grows even stronger as space-based commercial applications proliferate in type and value. Value-added processing of the products of space activities can be very lucrative, but the processor remains dependent upon the spacecraft's owner. For example, satellite communications can be encrypted or navigation satellite signals can be rendered inaccurate or launch services denied to possible competitors. All of these have been done in the past and can be done in the future. Therefore, national ownership becomes one protection against control by the already dominant states.

### Changing Values

Finally, the United States has consistently sought to foster those global economic and political changes that support U.S. values and by implication its policies. This approach is obviously very generalized, but is based on the expectation that as states become more democratic and capitalist, their hostility to the United States should moderate in tone and behavior. This position does not mean no disagreements occur between the United States and other like-minded states, just that political resolution will normally occur through peaceful means rather than through force of arms.

The concept of the "democratic peace" is controversial as the historical record is fairly thin because until recently only a few states were democracies and those were all economically advanced states. As democracy spreads as a concept and program for political reform, the likelihood for conflict between democracies will grow, posing a more difficult test of the hypothesis. In the meantime, however, U.S. policy is to encourage the development of democracy and its sibling (according to the American perspective) market economies in the hope that the result will be a more peaceful world. The counterargument is that democracies, because of their democratic character, are more able to mobilize national power since it is explicitly based upon the consent of the populace. Thus, wars fought by democracies become more terrible since the full weight of the society is brought to bear. The Clinton administration as did its predecessors pursued this goal fairly systematically although the concept of democracy loses some of its rigor in the process of accommodating real-world situations.

## FINISHING THE HISTORICAL THREAD

In chapter 2, we cut off our historical journey regarding BMD as a general policy issue with the continuation of the Clinton presidency into its second term. At that point, both Congress and the administration were locked into a relationship acceptable to neither but the best available given their relative power bases. This was political version of the 1960s scenario of two scorpions locked in a bottle together. That relationship further deteriorated into the acrimonious "Clinton Chronicles" so absorbing to Washington but of comparatively little interest to the public. Public views of both sides were generally negative but fluctuated over time depending on the issue. BMD debates tracked a similar path, absorbing in certain Washington circles but of little apparent concern to the American public. In neither case did that understanding of the public's reaction diminish the passion with which each issue was pursued.

BMD, especially theater-level efforts, benefited from these political collisions in the sense that the administration felt obligated to increase its relative budget share in a mixed effort at staving off larger Republican NMD initiatives. The larger question regarding TMD was the persistent inability to make the technology work successfully. The Theater High Altitude Area Defense (THAAD) and Patriot PAC-3 programs both lagged significantly behind schedule. The THAAD in fact failed nine times during testing before first achieving its objectives. Those failures reinvigorated already existing doubts among opponents concerning the feasibility of success for BMD even at the theater level. Failure during testing is routine but continued failure is not acceptable. Improvement is expected if a system is to move forward.

If a weapon system encounters extraordinary difficulty performing in such a structured environment, its likelihood of success in the chaos of combat is questioned. Testing supposedly identifies problems, but solutions are expected fairly routinely or else the technology is deemed premature. In the case of THAAD, one explanation suggested that the contractor, Lockheed Martin, had reassigned its best people to newer projects or to work on proposals for future work. As a result, it was argued, the BMDO became a prisoner of the corporation's desperate need to establish a pipeline of projects to sustain the company's economic performance. Lockheed Martin was encountering similar quality assurance problems across its entire program inventory, a situation that eventually led to a major shake-up of its corporate leadership.[6] Regardless, the TMD effort was held hostage to those internal problems for several years.

Additional events continued to impact the BMD policy debate. One issue that was at least temporarily resolved was whether TMD efforts impinged upon the ABM treaty. In September 1997, the Standing Consultative Commission, authorized by the ABM treaty, arrived at a consensus document allowing TMD to continue. The limitations included the following: "1. (a) the velocity of the interceptor missile not exceed 3 km/sec over any part of its flight trajectory; (b) the velocity of the ballistic target-missile does not exceed 5 km/sec over any part of its flight trajectory; and (c) the range of the ballistic target-missile does not exceed 3,500 kilometers."[7] Additional statements attached to this understanding restricted possible deployment of space-based TMD systems. By definition, this defined a space-based system as exceeding the 3-km/sec restriction. The agreement has not been submitted to Congress so that the Republicans argue that the understanding has no effect. Their larger point is that the Russian Federation has no authority to amend the ABM treaty. The Soviet Union is dead. However, the Russian Federation was agreed by the United States during the first Bush administration to be the successor state to the Soviet Union, at least in the strategic weapons realm. To deny that status would completely undermine the international security structure now in place. Revision may occur but the United States has benefited from that transition.

Domestically, BMD found itself in an intensifying competition with other military programs for, comparatively speaking, fewer dollars. This arose for two reasons. First, despite the Cold War's end, U.S. forces were being repeatedly deployed across a wide variety of international crises. This list included a continuing military confrontation with Iraq over the no-fly zones plus a later air campaign against Serbia. Both endeavors strained organizational resources, especially munitions and general readiness budgets. All this activity had the effect of depleting scarce resources to cover troop deployment expenses while procurement inventory shortages grew due to budget shortfalls. Earlier stocks of critical equipment and munitions were being expended without immediate replacement. This "holiday" in defense spending ironically facilitated reducing the budget deficit while the economy heated up, producing the projected surpluses much bandied about during the 2000 election. Readiness levels became an issue as replenishment lagged behind demand, never mind the personnel losses resulting from excessive deployments overseas. The all-volunteer military was clearly more professional and competent but also older, meaning more likely to have families—stressing personnel due to the instability caused by repeated deployments for unknown periods of time. Personnel losses in critical specialties became especially pronounced. Against these very pressing and immediate demands, BMD generally held its own but growth remained minimal compared to projected developmental needs.

Compounding these difficulties in the short term, the second factor became the renewed spending caps established in 1997 that restricted any dramatic future budget growth. Cuts would have to be made in other programs—either in DoD or other agencies in order to loosen up funds for an expanded BMD effort. The likely alternatives were not politically attractive, including busting the recently achieved balanced federal budget. This issue became symbolically important as President Clinton advocated funneling any future budget surpluses into stabilizing Social Security and reducing the national debt while Republicans passed a tax cut (vetoed by the president). The other political option was returning to the budget shell games of the recent past by rolling expenditures into future years and deferring or stretching out programs (the net effect raises costs over the long term but saves money for other uses in the short run). This latter option was increasingly pursued since the discretionary spending cap could not—symbolically at least—be broken openly. The cumulative effect was to lessen the budget potential for immediate dramatic BMD increases.

This effective budgetary logjam was partially broken in mid-1998 when several events occurred, ones that heightened the sense of an imminent ballistic missile threat. Republican NMD supporters had become increasingly disenchanted by what they perceived as overly rosy scenarios projected by the CIA about when future ballistic missile threats would become serious problems. In response to those rather optimistic CIA Threat Estimates, the congressionally mandated Rumsfeld Commission, whose report in July 1998 severely truncated the expected arrival date of the missile threat was established.[8] That report dramatically escalated the political pressures for accelerating the NMD developmental effort with deployment to follow immediately. What had been denied earlier in 1996 by the "three plus three" option as interpreted by the Clinton administration now appeared within the NMD advocates' grasp. As if on cue, in August 1998, North Korea launched a Taepo Dong-1 missile with an unexpected third stage over Japan.[9] This effort was proclaimed by North Korea to be an aborted space launch. Initial U.S. interpretation was that a missile test had occurred although eventually the United States accepted that explanation.[10] Two interpretations flowed from this crystallizing event. First, North Korea was much closer to achieving success in developing longer-range missiles—the Taepo Dong-2 being already under development with a projected range of 4,000 to 6,000 kilometers. The additional stage (the third) that extended the Taepo Dong's range proved a "surprise" in the intelligence sense: meaning no warning occurred concerning the enhanced technology. That inability to predict such events accentuated the feeling that other more deadly surprises might occur. By September 1999, National Intelligence Estimates were reflecting this sense of impending threat, though not immediately.

Second, Japan became much more interested in developing an effective BMD system. Its immediate choice was a variant on the Navy Theater Wide (NTW) system that was based on employing Aegis-equipped missile ships similar to those that Japan already possessed.[11] Such a sea-borne system provided flexibility in coverage as well as reducing the need for land bases for missile deployment, a particularly potent question in a nation with few open and undeveloped spaces. Any such joint U.S.-Japanese BMD effort increased Chinese apprehensions regarding existing and future power relationships in the East Asia region. The original Japanese-U.S. cooperative effort had begun during the earlier Bush administration, but had languished in part due to Japanese indifference. The United States was already discussing similar missile defense endeavors with Taiwan and South Korea. Taiwan's efforts became embroiled in U.S. domestic politics with Congress pressing the executive branch to do more. All of these possible BMD deployments in East Asia were perceived by China as terribly disruptive, undermining their military credibility in coercing other states in the region.[12] Chinese conventional military capabilities were more prospective than immediate, reflecting mobility and technology issues.[13] Ironically, these efforts were energized by fears raised by China and its ally,

North Korea, and their threatened use of ballistic missiles.  The 1996 Chinese terror campaign against Taiwan had made clear the credibility of such threats. North Korea's internal problems fueled concerns about that regime's stability and proclivity for verbally threatening other states including, by implication, the United States.

In addition, in 1998, Iran successfully tested a Shehab-3 missile with a 1,000-kilometers range, demonstrating a more immediate longer-range missile capability than expected.  Iran also announced that even longer-range missiles were under development.  Europe was clearly placed under the threat of Iranian missiles once they were deployed—a situation likely to inhibit their assertiveness.  European concern however remained low, reflecting their less militarily assertive role in global affairs than the United States.   Virtually overnight, American perceptions of likely ballistic missile threat shifted from a fairly distant slow-to-develop prospective event to a much more imminent possibility of attack.  As indicated, by early 1999, intelligence estimates began to move up the likely deployment date of several potentially hostile states. The changed estimates still projected threats five years to a decade out at the earliest, leaving time for NMD deployment.

Further inflaming the situation was the public acknowledgment of Chinese espionage efforts aimed at acquiring access to high-tech especially nuclear, weapon designs.   The Cox Report alleged a systematic effort aimed at threatening the United States.[14]  As a result, political passions were engaged over the question of the nature and seriousness of the precise threat China posed for the United States.  From this evidence, the world became a more dangerous place, especially if one tied Chinese missile developments to purloined U.S. nuclear secrets.  The Cold War was not back, yet.  But, the threat, albeit in the future tense, was growing and more rapidly than anticipated even a year earlier. Despite the bipartisan composition of the Cox Commission, the wrangles over the report further hardened the positions of the respective antagonists.

Regardless, by the spring of 1999, the political logjam was broken, driven by a combination of presidential politics (a subterranean but potent influence) and with some apparent missile technology improvement by the rogue states. Congress now pushed hard for establishing a firm date for a presidential deployment decision.  The initial reaction by the administration was to threaten to veto the proposal, but, after a series of accommodating amendments, agreed to set a firm date for a deployment decision.  In the summer of 2000 the president planned thoroughly review the situation both in terms of threat probability and technology development before deciding whether to deploy an initial NMD architecture.   If agreed to by the president, NMD deployment would occur in the 2002–2005 time frame.

Technically speaking, what was to occur in the summer of 2000 was a Deployment Readiness Review (DRR) at the DoD level.  This review assessed whether sufficient technological progress had occurred to support a deployment decision.   The actual decision would be made by the national command authority (the president and his advisors) after assessing four factors: the nature of the threat, the status of the technology, the affordability of the system, and an assessment of NMD's impact upon the overall strategic environment and U.S. arms control objectives.[15]

Both sides were aware that the spring 1999 compromise represented merely a presidential commitment to fully review the question and make a preliminary decision. From one perspective, the 2000 decision point tracks the earlier ABM deployment choice in 1967–1968 in that any first choice must be reaffirmed by President Clinton's successor. Republicans still perceived the president as unlikely to assent enthusiastically to deployment but knew that presidential politics might influence the choice in their favor—that is, in the summer of 2000, the presidential campaigns would be well underway. A negative presidential decision would be useful, as graphically illuminating what Republicans clearly perceived as disastrous administration defense policies. For this reason, the pressures upon the president were to agree initially with the real decision to be revisited in 2001 by the new presidential administration regardless of which candidate won. The Democrats, if victorious, might further stretch out NMD development while Republicans conversely might expand and accelerate deployment although there were real questions whether political choices could appreciably impact the actual construction process. The weather and physical terrain in Alaska, (a projected radar site) limited available construction options. The real question arises in 2001 although the summer of 2000 deadline solidified the general attitude that NMD was moving toward another crescendo in its lengthening history. The sense of the proponents was that a major policy window was opening—one that, however, might be abruptly shut. Their gut feeling was that external players, the rogue states or states of concern, would engage in behaviors sufficiently disruptive to keep up the political momentum for deployment. The question would become not deployment per se but the scope and size of the relevant NMD architecture implemented. Democrats, it was expected, would most likely opt for a treaty-compliant minimum system while Republicans would implement a more open-ended NMD architecture.

The technology side came more fully into play later in 1999 when several events occurred that added greater political momentum to the possibility of NMD deployment. First, in the fall, the THAAD finally achieved two successes in a row as test vehicles closed on incoming targets. Those successes added further political fuel to the fire. In response, the administration cancelled the last two preliminary flight tests, pushing THAAD along to the next developmental phase.[16] Whether the technology was sufficiently advanced to allow such a gesture was unclear but the political realities were such that the administration felt the necessity to do so. As usual, the politics of the situation overrode the technical side. Ironically, greater THAAD success potentially endangered the NTW program budget-wise. On the other hand, it drew additional support from Japan's agreement in September 1999 to participate in accelerated development of a joint TMD system to protect Japan. Also, during the period between the two successful THAAD tests, the PAC-3 and Israel Arrow TMD systems were tested successfully. Israel in fact deployed the latter system in early 2000.[17]  Arrow represented the first deployment of a system designed explicitly to fill the TMD role.

Their importance in all three instances was in physically demonstrating the basic interception concept that missiles could in fact be successfully struck by hit-to-kill vehicles.  Even though the systems were all theater level, this demonstration of success was fundamental for shoring up sagging confidence, especially given the persistent earlier THAAD mishaps.  However, the large leap forward sought for THAAD development was essentially an act of faith that all problems had finally been resolved.  Supporters seized upon this evidence (two successes) as vindication, rejecting the idea that so few successes after multiple failures should dictate caution in moving forward.

Further bolstering that confidence was the October 2, 1999, interception by an NMD HTK vehicle of an incoming target vehicle, a simulated missile attack.  That again suggested to NMD supporters that the time was now ripe for deployment with a high success probability expected.  NMD opponents, analyzing the test results, found what they perceived as too rosy an evaluation of what was actually accomplished.  During the kill vehicle's flight, target acquisition was not acquired—and would not have been except for the fact that a bright balloon decoy accompanying the target attracted its attention—leading to detection of the less visible target vehicle and the final kill.  Critics felt that the kill vehicle was too easily deceived, undermining their confidence in its probability of success.  BMDO rejected that view, seeing the kill as evidence of resolving problems with a robust detector system overcoming initial adversity.  Both sides acknowledged the strike; but the implications drawn were very different.[18]  Subsequently, on January 19, 2000, the kill vehicle failed to strike the target, losing target acquisition just six seconds before final contact.[19]  The result was, temporarily, at least to derail further progress because one standard of evaluation was achievement of two successful interceptions in a row.  Opponents argued the concept remained undoable while the proponents proclaimed these events as just more examples of the difficulties inherent in successfully developing any high-tech weaponry.  The specific NMD deployment architecture options will be more closely considered in chapter 6.  The debate was further complicated by the March 2000 announcement that the next round of testing would be delayed into the summer from spring due to issues posed by the January test failure.[20]  That delay undermined the argument that testing to that point had been successfully completed.  Instead, the secretary of defense would have to recommend a course of action without all the facts but the decision could not be delayed for reasons clearly related more to the necessities of presidential politics than NMD policy.

With the impending decision on NMD deployment growing closer, the opponents ratcheted up the counterpressures.  An analysis by the Union of Concerned Scientists argued that the HTK vehicle could be easily deceived by decoys and shielded warheads—options they felt were easily achievable by the rogue states, a view rejected by the BMDO.  The BMDO through its director responded that the "report's conclusions are based on assumptions that tilt in favor of the offense and against the defensive system we are developing.

Indeed, the report's conclusions are based on assumptions that would indicate more 'knowledge' than anyone—even I—have regarding the capabilities of the more far-term 'C3' NMD system, a system for which we have not finalized plans."[21]    In addition, a concurrent analysis of the testing program by Theodore A Postol at MIT suggested that the BMDO had dumbed down the specific tasks to be accomplished by the interceptor.  Essentially, the tests had been made easier, allowing the HTK vehicle to distinguish the target from the decoys accompanying it.  Otherwise, it was argued, the missile was not capable of reliably intercepting the target.[22]    Such an argument, if successfully made, undermines the system's credibility as an effective defense.  Persistent criticisms had been made that the NMD testing program was excessively truncated with the deployment decision coming after the fifth test in a projected series of 19 or so attempts.  The argument by BMDO has been that any failures to this point have not been showstoppers and further delays would push deployment out to the 2010 and beyond time frame.  The security threat is growing so time is of the essence became their counterargument.[23]

The growing realization that the president was moving toward some decision on NMD deployment increased the pressures on both sides.  The external factors impacting any decision were presidential politics and the physical terrain and weather in Alaska, the location selected for the first X-Band radar site.  Presidential politics revolved around Republican efforts to paint the administration as weak on defense while the Democrats sought to defuse the issue.  Republicans in Congress pushed ever harder for a decision while George W. Bush, the soon-to-be Republican presidential nominee on May 23 2000, criticized the proposed Clinton deployment as inadequate.  However, the governor's speech was light on specifics as to his actual alternative approach except that he would do more and better.[24]    Closeness to assuming office or the prospect of doing so tends to make presidents or presidential candidates more cautious about their promises especially expensive ones.  NMD was not a centerpiece issue to which irrevocable commitments need be made.

Because of the physical terrain and weather conditions on Shemya Island on the Aleutian Islands chain, a decision in the summer or early fall of 2000 was necessary to allow construction to commence in 2001 for a projected 2005 deployment date.  Any delay in decision pushed deployment back a year or more.  The latter fact added urgency to the Integrated Flight Test 5, already pushed back from April until July 2000.  Success there would provide the two successful interceptions thought necessary to authorize initial deployment.

By late spring and early summer, international reaction intensified in its negativism toward NMD deployment whether the ABM treaty was abandoned or simply amended.  Russia, in fact, rejected any immediate efforts at amendment while European countries generally were hostile.  Several European states, Denmark and the United Kingdom, were critical since X-Band radar would be positioned at already existing radar sites at Thule, Greenland, and Flyingdales in the United Kingdom.  The Chinese were particularly vocal in their hostility to possible U.S. NMD deployment.

The entire process was temporarily immobilized in July 2000 when the test ended when the booster failed at separation of the interceptor, negating any attempt at interception. The booster employed was not the booster to be used in the final system configuration but a temporary expedient to allow warhead and detector testing, especially verifying acquisition of the right target. As a result, there were not two successful intercepts in a row, a standard continually referred to by the DoD. Subsequently, the next test was rolled deeper into the fall and ultimately rescheduled for early 2001.[25]

In response and following his earlier skeptical views regarding NMD, President Clinton on September 1, 2000, pushed the decision point forward into early 2001 for his successor to decide whether to deploy by declining to approve start of construction.[26] The president's decision was based upon his desire not "to pay the big front-end costs if he was not sure this thing would work."[27] Among the costs considered were both fiscal and political ones with the latter appearing to outweigh the former. All of this was buttressed by a sense that the technology was not sufficiently advanced to ensure operational success. This sense of futility was reinforced by the July 7th test failure. The interceptor had not engaged during that test but that excuse did not negate the failure.

The president's speech analyzed the world situation saying it as contained significant threats to the United States, especially in the future. Therefore, prudence dictates that NMD be pursued as one security avenue along with diplomacy and deterrence to protect American security. However, in the president's judgment, "though the technology for NMD is promising, the system as a whole is not yet proven. Therefore, I have decided not to authorize deployment of a national missile defense at this time. Instead, I have asked Secretary Cohen to continue a robust program of development and testing. My decision will not have a significant impact on the date the overall system could be deployed in the next administration, if the next president decides to go forward."[28] Further comments by the president highlighted the possible international repercussions if deployment occurred at that time. President Clinton's decision was consistent with his long-established and publicly known views so surprise at the choice was muted. Public disinterest in NMD as a critical national priority was further mirrored in Washington after the Clinton decision to delay construction. According to one count, of eighty-three speeches reported in the *Congressional Record* six days after the decision to defer, only one dealt with NMD. A survey focusing explicitly upon NMD as an issue found a majority supported the president's choice.[29] Survey results are driven by the question and how it is phrased, but the reality was that NMD was not a visible issue during the election—its invisibility tracked that of defense and foreign policy issues generally. Strong NMD supporters were generally Republicans so that the issue got rolled into their larger objection to the Clinton administration and by extension the Democratic candidate.

In fact, immediate reaction was more muted than one might expect, given the earlier rhetoric, but that quiet reflected the political reality that NMD remained a specialized issue. Vice President Gore supported the president's decision, especially the testing and development aspect. His approach remained one of possibly amending the ABM treaty as a step to keeping any arms race under control. Governor Bush's view was simply that the administration had missed an important opportunity to push forward on a critical military initiative. The Republican campaign organization's initial response was comparatively mild while it assessed its relevance to the electorate in November. Overall, the 2000 presidential election was clearly not a contest in which NMD loomed large as an issue driving voters, either as a surrogate for large defense questions or on its own. During the three presidential debates and the single vice-presidential one, no mention of NMD occurred—with, in fact, only minimal emphasis put upon international affairs despite the continuing clash in the Middle East between Israel and the Palestinians. The election was fought over purely domestic questions including the economy and moral rectitude. The result was a narrowly divided electorate with neither candidate able to claim a mandate although George W. Bush claimed victory in the electoral college while Al Gore won the popular vote. NMD for the public never penetrated the surface of American politics, rather the question continued as an elite-centered issue, generally remote from public concerns. When prodded, the public expressed general support for the concept but that support evaporated during the heat of the campaign. The major candidates did not raise the question in any serious way while Patrick Buchanan, the battered Reform party candidate, never got on track during the election process. After a raucous convention splitting the Reform part and some personal medical issues, Patrick Buchanan faded to less than 1 percent of the vote.

The intensity of the general NMD debate had been re-ignited across the decade of the 1990s at least at elite levels. The justifications for NMD have not changed fundamentally but have varied in their specifics and the aggressiveness with which each proposal is put forward at any particular point in time. As was indicated, four purposes appear to summarize the general arguments consistently made for implementing NMD. There do exist other parallel reasons since proponents have been fertile producers of justifications upholding BMD. Likewise, opponents have assertively denied their validity. In both instances, the parties have dealt in hypothetical situations, flavored with a light sprinkling of test data and conjectures concerning what might be true given certain assumptions and models.

## PROTECTING THE SOCIETY

The first and most obvious public purpose for BMD becomes protecting American society from the ravages of missile-delivered weapons of mass destruction. A fundamental and historical purpose of American security policy is protection against all external enemies by whatever means they threaten the United States. This goal, for example, justified maintaining a large navy at the turn of the nineteenth century through the twentieth century. The fleet's mission was to prevent, if possible, any invasion by hostile powers whether coming from Europe or Asia. Such a perspective explains the naval war plans drawn up after

World War I in which both Japan and Great Britain were projected as potential naval threats against the United States. By that time, the latter was thought to be a highly improbable enemy but caution dictated advance preparation. Prior to the end of the nineteenth century, U.S. security had relied, despite its bellicose rhetoric, upon British naval dominance and the protection afforded by the vast distances from likely enemies. Since World War II, the United States has embarked upon a steady succession of efforts aimed at solidifying American immunity from outside threat. The pain inflicted in retaliation would become so enormous as to deter aggression but, failing that, punishment would automatically follow if the United States were being attacked. Earlier efforts at aircraft defense using missiles and jet interceptors were implemented in the 1940s and 1950s with BMD being merely a logical extension of that approach. That search for national security eventually evolved into the deterrent relationship inherent in the cold peace existing across the 1950s until the early 1990s, that phase ending with the death of the Soviet Union.

Such a strategy, however, was in the end a reactive one, essentially striking back once attacked although with devastating power. For many, that basic relationship was unacceptable, given the damage likely inflicted first upon American society. This reaction regarding the ballistic missile threat was most clearly displayed in President Reagan's personal conception of Strategic Defense Initiative (SDI) in its original form. As the president apparently conceptualized the program, SDI would provide a complete shield of protection against nuclear threats from the Soviet Union; he particularly emphasized initially the shield aspect. World War III would not find the United States a radioactive ruin—though victorious in the aggregate nuclear exchange—because no significant national military effort had been expended to defend the population. SDI was classically American in the sense that the population defense provided was to be independent of any civil defense program with its implications of a more intrusive state. A total civil defense program to be successful required a degree of societal regimentation that was not acceptable to many Americans, plus it demanded great expense. That effort had effectively died by the early mid-1960s. In practice, SDI substituted technology for imposing excessive social discipline and fiscal costs on the citizenry. Costs would be high but much less than providing shelters for the entire society or at least the urban areas. The SDI technology effectively operated independently of the people, as did the strategic nuclear forces. The irony was that the original ABM system proposed in 1967–1969 with its nuclear warheads to ensure interception demanded the sheltering of the civilian population if they were to be protected effectively. That gap or failure to provide sufficient shelter meant the simple act of defense itself might prove harmful to those being protected due to radiation and fallout.

This perspective also rejects the deterrence logic embedded in mutually assured destruction (MAD) with its assumptions that the shared risks of mass destruction between states will prevent the outbreak of nuclear war. From a MAD perspective, national populations become explicitly hostages to the other side. Each side, being capable of effectively annihilating the other's society, is deterred from acting so irrationally because of the horrors of the inevitable outcome.  By definition, nuclear attack becomes irrational.  This view was reenforced in popular culture with earlier movies depicting the end of human civilization including *On the Beach* and *Planet of the Apes* (the original movie). President Reagan was reportedly personally shocked at discovering the full import of that MAD logic and American society's vulnerability to such a terrible outcome.  The 1984 television movie, *The Day After*, purportedly also greatly affected Reagan personally and added to his fervor regarding SDI, despite often intense criticism.  This movie described the world after a nuclear exchange with its devastation and societal dislocation.  Proceeding from such a posture, rejection of the amoral logic embedded in MAD becomes a natural outcome. The search then becomes one of seeking an acceptable alternative solution other than surrender.  BMD is an obvious candidate, especially if the seeker is particularly attracted to futuristic technological solutions as Ronald Reagan was personally.  Lou Cannon in his unofficial biography of Ronald Reagan refers to his abiding personal interest in science fiction with its descriptions of space weaponry capable of destroying missiles in flight.[30]

The earlier 1960s debate over ABM, which culminated in the fall of 1967 limited deployment decision, found similar expressions regarding the moral necessity to protect American society from possible nuclear devastation.  Those expressions, while reflecting a more pessimistic evaluation regarding achieving successful missile interception, tend to focus upon overall civilian casualty reduction rather than achieving total defensive success.  (Remember the comment by Senator Richard Russell regarding the last two survivors, that they be Americans, which was merely a statement of the obvious.)  The expectations were still that civilian casualties would remain high but significantly less than otherwise expected under a pure MAD war scenario.  Public descriptions of SDI quickly moved from a scenario of providing total protection to a situation assuming some leakage, reflecting greater technical realism as the program moved away from the Oval Office to the military technologists responsible for actual development.  Their evaluations, while generally positive as to ultimate technological feasibility, became extremely sensitive to the enormous problems that must be conquered in order to establish successful missile defense.  This realism especially reflected the extraordinary success achieved in developing new missile penetration aids, all of which further complicated the defensive effort.   MIRV alone with its volleys of warheads simply overwhelmed most defensive arrangements.  There were too many targets, and they were moving too quickly for an effective defense to be mounted.

The current posture, as articulated by proponents, often returns to the moralistic overtones of the Reagan initiative in arguing for achieving the maximum protection possible for the national population.  Both during SDI and currently, the arguments are based upon very positive projections of technical success in achieving interception.   The redundant, layered defense being suggested maximizes overall interception potential.   The earlier 1967 deployment, being basically a terminal or point-defense configuration, was assumed less capable of achieving total defensive success, a fact clearly recognized in their casualty projections. Casualties were reduced, but losses would still be high. The critical weaknesses are obviously the predictions of successful interception; a failure to intercept constitutes a breach in the moral trust so publicly assumed by proponents. False hope may be more damning than no hope since humans are often quite resilient during crises otherwise perceived as hopeless when they begin from a position of realism.

Advocates of missile defense from this perspective raise the ante because rejection of their arguments for whatever reason becomes a moral question not simply a political judgment. Emotionalism often becomes a central theme in their presentation with the moral integrity of the opposition directly challenged. Caveats are brushed aside as mere political temporizing in the face of evil. Such moral certainty rarely permeates most political questions. At one level, proponents in some cases have cast the argument on an emotional and moral level equivalent to the abortion debate. Opponents have generally been more guarded, relying heavily upon more pragmatic factors such as level of technology development and world political stability. This situation patterns in some ways the emotional debates in the 1950s and 1960s over nuclear weapons and their use, but with the sides switched in many cases.

## PROTECTING STRATEGIC ASSETS

The second reason most consistently publicly advanced has been that of protecting U.S. strategic weapons, meaning primarily its ICBM fields and bomber bases. The submarine-based missiles are presumed protected by their dispersal across the wide and deep oceans. This position implicitly assumes that the national population will be partially shielded through civil defense programs (which do not actually exist), but the central focus concentrates upon maintenance of the U.S. capacity to respond overwhelmingly in the event of a Soviet nuclear attack. By ensuring the survival of at least a minimum level of strategic forces, the United States during the Cold War guaranteed the effective devastation of the Soviet Union. Such a finite deterrent approach predated the 1967 deployment since, by the late 1950s, the United States had embarked upon establishing its triad of ICBMs, bombers, and SLBMs. Ensuring retaliation through redundancy became the central theme. That weapon redundancy has now been severely reduced (see chapter 3) but continues as the primary operational principle.

Ballistic missile defense becomes critical because, if successfully implemented, that program ensures the launching of a massive counterattack even if the enemy totally surprises the United States. The recurring nightmare undergirding American security policy since at least December 1941 has been that of avoiding a nuclear Pearl Harbor—whether by bomber earlier or missile attack presently. Such attacks now are immeasurably more devastating than the actual aerial attack on Pearl Harbor in December 1941, which used using conventional weapons. Significant assets survived or were repairable. Nuclear weapons cause massive destruction, even if the warhead delivery is somewhat inaccurate, and collateral damage alone can render a society prostrate in the face of its enemies. That defensive posture has expanded in recent years to incorporate other forms of interstate aggression, but here our focus concentrates on BMD. However, spoofing the defensive system may be the most efficient way to achieve total tactical surprise especially if one's missile arsenal is significantly smaller than that of the United States. In fact, the dependency of successful BMD upon electronics constitutes a potential vulnerability of massive proportions. Recognition of this vulnerability was driven home by Serbian hackers' attacks against DoD computer sites during the 1999 air campaign. The U.S. Space Command has been assigned responsibility for offensive and defensive warfare activities. This protection rationale for BMD highlights that vulnerability on several dimensions, given the critical nature attached to protecting the nation's strategic assets.

The clearest expression of this protective logic was embedded in the earlier 1972 ABM treaty when the ICBM fields and the nation's capital were the only assets explicitly designated as needing protection. The former site supplied the military component for ensuring deterrence while the latter location embodied the national command authority. The latter was critical for waging war within the nuclear holocaust—as an act of political will, not a spasm of mindless violence. Nuclear exchanges were not to be haphazard affairs triggered by some event and running to completion. Within the horrors of such a conflict, the national leadership was presumed to be controlling the application of nuclear weapons. How realistic such assumptions were is fortunately unknown since no nuclear exchange took place during the Cold War period. Regardless, protecting the national capacity to wage such war remains an important justification for NMD.

## ENSURING CRISIS STABILITY

Here, the justification or rationale for deployment shifts, becoming psychological in nature as much as physical power. This differs from the previous purposes in that the focus falls upon the actual crisis as it unfolds rather than simply riding out the nuclear holocaust. Ballistic missiles have proven to be extraordinarily horrifying mass terror weapons, disrupting normal life. Warheads fall without sound (being hypersonic) out of the sky with often little or no effective warning. From the target population's limited perspective, these attacks become almost random events in their strikes, the military equivalent of a lightning strike on a mountaintop. As a result, civilian populations have become terrified by that reality—the capriciousness of such armed attacks with no defense available. Beginning with the V-2 terror bombings of London during World War II, ballistic missiles on several occasions have been systematically employed to disrupt and cower societies. For example, in the 1980s, Iran and Iraq engaged in the "war of the cities," the firing of missiles at the other's capital for psychological coercion purposes. During the Gulf War, Iraq attempted to draw Israel into the conflict by attacking its civilian population. At the same time, Scud attacks terrified the Saudi Arabian population and disturbed coalition troops in the area.  In 1996, China bombarded the sea lanes around Taiwan, disrupting ship traffic and panicking the population.  Migration from Taiwan reportedly escalated during and after this incident, reflecting the uncertainty created by such terrorist attacks.  The North Korean missile passing over Japan in August 1998 caused widespread distress as the population discovered its vulnerability to such actions.  In all cases, the psychological comfort most citizens feel in the general expectation that their government will protect them is permanently shattered.  In not one case was any effective military counteraction taken although in all instances, the governments were able to maintain social control and persevere through the crisis.  Such an attack even if only a singular one using WMD, could likely totally disturb a society for a time while it waited for the other shoe to drop.  Reactive retribution would likely be insufficiently swift or accurate to recover that sense of national well-being existing prior to the assault.

Thus, BMD at both the national and theater levels becomes critical for calming or reducing popular fear.  Given that situation, the actual success or failure of the BMD system may be unclear at the time of engagement.  However, simply making the effort calms many individuals, at least, temporarily as occurred in Israel where Patriot anti-missile batteries fired away unsuccessfully into the night.  This picture of some counterresponse deflects the pressures upon the political leadership in deciding what actions to take.  For example, the coercive potential of simply owning missile technologies has become so highly sensitized that in some cases merely pursuing the technology promotes the rogue state's agenda.  For example, North Korea in the fall of 1999 was effectively bribed not to test its Taepo Dong-2 missile.  These weapons posed a direct threat to Japan, and possibly with modifications even to the western United States.  One argument concerning North Korea strongly suggests that their threatened missile tests and launches are simply bargaining tools through which economic and other concessions are coerced.  Without such weaponry, the society would be ignored and allowed to decline into chaos.  North Korea's economic and political isolation is such that a decline of such proportions would in fact draw little world response except for its missiles.  North Korean economic problems have existed for years with little effective action by outsiders until the missiles became an issue and eventually a bargaining chip.

In fact, the Central Intelligence Agency (CIA) has altered its threat assessment methodology to explicitly focus upon a state's initial development of ballistic missiles rather than awaiting their often long delayed deployment.

Because countries could threaten to use ballistic missiles following limited flight-testing and before a missile is deployed in the traditional sense, we use the first successful flight test to indicate an "initial threat availability." Emerging long-range missile powers do not appear to rely on robust test programs to ensure a missile's accuracy and reliability or to intend to deploy a large number of long-range missiles to dedicate, long-term sites. A nation may decide that the ability to threaten with one or two missiles is sufficient. With shorter flight test programs—perhaps only one test—and potentially simple deployment schemes, the time between the initial flight test and the availability of a missile for military use is likely to be shortened. Using the date of the first projected flight test as the initial indicator of the threat recognizes that an adversary armed with even a single missile capable of delivering a weapon of mass destruction may consider it threatening. Using the first flight test also results in threat projections a few years earlier than those based on traditional definitions of deployment.

Their argument now focuses on the psychological coercion that comes from mere possession; regardless of the actual numbers at hand or whether significant deployment ultimately occurs.[31]    States such as the United States traditionally consider actual deployment as the time when coercion becomes possible.    This definition of the situation was based upon an expectation that active military engagement was likely at some point.    The political needs and agendas of many rogue states instead emphasize the symbolic aspects.    One now possesses the physical means by which to threaten the hegemon in its lair.    The fact that a successful attack would lead to the annihilation of their society becomes immaterial to the domestic and regional political point being made.    For one thing, most believe that the United States will not retaliate—a fallacy indulged in by Iraq in 1990.

Given these apparent irrationalities (from a U.S. perspective), NMD becomes essential for sustaining national capacity to make rational policy choices during a confrontation with another state.    Calming and stabilizing public fears remain an essential part of this foreign policy equation.    Given the sharp divisions within the United States over its role in the world, policies leading to apparent (whether real or not) national vulnerabilities become very unstable.    The U.S. role in world affairs demands in theory that its decisions be coherent and thought out, not knee jerk or panicky reactions to threats and pseudo-threats.    Those advocating a more activist U.S. international presence of necessity must consider this issue and how to address it.    Whether that consideration leads them to support NMD is not clear, given differing assessments concerning future world trends and technology.    From this point of view, NMD does not provide political wisdom, just (if successful) time to think through consequences and options.

When nuclear threats arise, NMD, it is argued, reduces the pressures upon the national leadership.    It does not eliminate those pressures, just lessens their intensity, especially if NMD is successfully implemented.    This aspect draws support from both internationalists and isolationists.    The former perceive NMD as allowing greater power projection overseas while isolationists see NMD as protection from outside threats, allowing the United States to ignore the world unless it wishes to become engaged.    Whether any technology is in fact that robust is an unanswered question.    BMD in all its facets becomes critical for restraining public anxieties regarding the uncertainties inherent in world affairs.

## POLITICAL AND MILITARY POWER PROJECTION

Protecting U.S. military assets when deployed overseas becomes critical for a society highly sensitive to the possibility of its casualties. Therefore, TMD becomes the logical concept to pursue when ballistic missile technologies proliferate across the globe. In addition, successful BMD, at both national and theater levels, in principle discourages other states from aggressively pursuing their objectives beyond a certain point. U.S. forces and population will be safe from coercion at least in the form of ballistic missiles.

Projecting one's political power on occasion demands the direct employment of military means. Normally that translates into the threatened use of force and placement of U.S. military forces into potentially awkward and dangerous situations—awkward because those forces while projecting U.S. intentions are clearly subject to armed attack by the other side, creating a danger of defeat. Historically, one of the great fallacies of military leaders has been the tendency to plan their operations as if the enemy will do nothing, remaining frozen in place like lambs led to the slaughter. In fact, enemy actions often disrupt and defeat the best-laid plans. Their decisions add great uncertainty and danger to the situation. Now, by contrast, American politicians are often obsessed with any actions by the other side and their potential for inflicting casualties. Military interventions, whether large or small scale, by definition mean those American personnel committed are placed in harm's way.

Two situations arise as a result. First, successful missile attacks by the enemy can physically disrupt or defeat American forces. Therefore, protection of American forces in the theater of operations becomes absolutely essential for mounting an effective military effort. In previous wars, during interventions, appropriate defensive measures were taken; appropriate that is to the time and existing technology. Air defense is the most obvious analogy, and it is now being extended to cover missiles. Counterbattery fire by artillery represents another form, as do anti-submarine operations protecting an invasion convoy. The goal in all cases is preventing the defeat of U.S. forces while minimizing possible casualties.

Second and more delicately stated, the politically well established American aversion to unnecessary casualties means that maximum effort must be expended to protect the lives of U.S. personnel. Failure to do so or, more accurately, the appearance of failure (or, even worse, of indifference) undermines political support. The degree of sensitivity to American casualties can be best illustrated by a speech by the chairman of the Joint Chiefs of Staff, General Henry H. Shelton. General Shelton proposed that any intervention has to be subjected to the "Dover Test." Dover Air Force Base, Delaware, is the entry or return point for all U.S. military dead. Forensics experts, for example, accurately identify if possible all unknown casualties. As a result of their efforts, the Unknown Soldier from the Vietnam War buried at Arlington was subsequently identified and moved to another cemetery. The Dover Test is simply this: "Is the American public prepared for the sight of our most precious resources coming home in flag draped caskets into Dover Air Force Base?"[32]

**Table 4.3**
**Theater Missile Defense**

| Lower Tier (Point) Defense | Warhead Type | Range (km) | Deployment Date |
|---|---|---|---|
| Patriot PAC-2 | Blast Fragment | 10–15 | 1991 |
| Patriot PAC-3 | Hit to Kill | 40–50 | 2001 |
| Navy Area Defense | Blast Fragment | 50–100 | 2003 |
| **Upper Tier (Area) Defense** | | | |
| THAAD | Hit to Kill | >100 | 2207 or later |
| Navy Theater Wide | Hit to Kill | >300 | 2007 or later |
| Arrow (Israel-U.S.) | Blast Fragment | >100 | 2000 |
| **Boost-Phase Defense** | | | |
| Airborne    Laser (ABL) | Directed Energy | >300 | 2006 |

This view is much different than simply protecting American society. Here, the expectation is that the deployed forces will in fact be placed in a potentially or actually dangerous situation. The government is responsible for providing as complete protection as is humanly possible. Joint Vision 2010's full-spectrum protection summarizes this priority. The DoD in JV 2010 laid out an expectation that, in effect, a bubble of protection would be put in place covering all possible threats from afar whether air, sea, or space. The imagery is reminiscent of the space shield implications embodied in SDI, but is scaled down to a theater of operations as opposed to national coverage. At one level, TMD represents a trial run for NMD—multi-layered defense against ballistic missiles.

As a consequence, theater missile defense (TMD) has become a political given within the larger BMD debate. Clearly, the TMD effort picked up critical political momentum during the 1991 Gulf War—a situation solidified by the Clinton administration's desire to defuse growing pressures for NMD.[33]

Also, pursuit of TMD becomes central for any overseas deployment of U.S. forces in the not too distant future. As missile technologies proliferate, U.S. forces will encounter more situations where such weapons will pose a very real threat. No administration could deploy troops without some semblance of TMD protection, that is, if it wished to survive politically.

Table 4.3 lays out in tabular form the relevant TMD systems either under development or deployable at this time.[34] Lower tier involves systems capable of a point defense, usually endoatmospheric, meaning defense of specific locations (less than 100 kilo-meters) rather than broad vistas. Upper tier refers to area-wide defensive capabilities extending out beyond 100 kilometers and possessing exo-atmospheric capabilities. All of this is incorporated into what the BMDO characterizes as a family of systems concept. This family concept envisions different weapons systems being developed to operate in a diversity of environments. Land-and-sea based systems are to be incorporated in both tiers, upper and lower. This allows for defense of the littoral regions where U.S. troops may be committed while land-based mobile systems follow troops deeper into the interior.

According to the ABM treaty, the critical difference distinguishing NMD and TMD systems is their range and speed of the interceptor. NMD interceptors close at speeds in excess of 6 km/sec while TMD interceptors operate at 5 km/sec and slower. However, upper-tier interceptors, notably the THAAD, operate exo-atmospherically so that interception occurs at higher speeds. As a result, that system and the Navy Theater Wide (NTW) violate the 1997 understanding. This has led to suggestions that those systems may be potential low-grade NMD components especially operating as sea-based systems.[35]

According to the ABM treaty, the critical difference distinguishing NMD and TMD systems is their range and speed of the interceptor. NMD interceptors close at speeds in excess of 6 km/sec while TMD interceptors operate at 5 km/sec and slower. However, upper-tier interceptors, notably the THAAD, operate exo-atmospherically so that interception occurs at higher speeds. As a result, that system and the Navy Theater Wide (NTW) violate the 1997 understanding. This has led to suggestions that those systems may be potential low-grade NMD components especially operating as sea-based systems.[36]

An entirely different TMD option is the Airborne Laser (ABL), which allows for the possibility of boost phase interception. This approach has the virtue of knocking down the missile before it reaches full flight power, meaning lower speed and altitude for interception. The laser reflects a major technological advance if successful since it has obvious implications for the even more long-range Space-Based Laser (SBL). In a sense, the ABL is a continuation of the research avenues pursued by the SDIO in the 1980s. Boost phase interception, as will be discussed, is an option being strongly pushed as an alternative to the problems encountered by the present NMD ground-based interceptor configuration. The questions of laser power, focus, and range are still not completely answered. The ABL destroys the missile by heating its sides, igniting fuel, and dropping the missile and its payload back onto the enemy.

The Arrow represents in an interesting manner an extension of the earlier Gulf War controversy over the success of the Patriot's. Israeli officials were very skeptical of the originally reported successes of the Patriot PAC-2. Those successes proved ephemeral, vanishing upon closer and more dispassionate analyses. But, that experience clearly demonstrated the necessity for a TMD to protect Israel from its neighbors. A joint Israel-U.S. program has developed the Arrow, which was first deployed in the late summer of 2000 in Israel. The system is interoperable with the PAC-3, the U.S. Army's now standard lower-tier system. In addition, the United States is cooperating with Germany and Italy to produce the Medium Extended Air Defense System (MEADS). The latter system is a modified PAC-3 configured for army corps–level defense. The difficulty has been that the army for a time did not perceive MEADS as a priority. That posture has changed although European defense reorganization in the aftermath of Kosovo has put all expensive programs up for grabs until Europe decides how it wishes to handle different issues, a lengthy process. In addition, Germany has objected to U.S. requirements that certain PAC-3 technologies be "black boxed," meaning not accessible to German scrutiny. Resolution of that issue will require the United States to reconsider its willingness to share critical technologies—a an item of concern given the controversy over Chinese acquisition of such militarily sensitive technologies. Depriving one's putative allies on the other hand just perpetuates the technology gap between the United States and its allies, Kosovo revisited. Solutions to this vexing issue lay outside the parameters of this analysis, but do impact TMD policy if the United States is to lead future coalitions to redress international problems.

## CONCLUSION

Missile defense has been supported by a number of rationales over the years. The prominence of each has reflected the particular moment's political needs. Protection of the society and of American forces committed in harm's way has dominated any discussions. NMD covers the former while TMD is concerned with the latter, but the overlap between the two is becoming more substantial than most are aware. The distance of the United States from its likely foes leads to an underestimation of that overlap. For example, for Japan, TMD, especially sea-based system, could have substantial NMD characteristics with regard to North Korea and China. If the technology exists or is thought possible, fertile minds will expand the possibilities for use. Even more long term but totally destructive of current distinctions between TMD and NMD interceptors is the deployment of space-based antimissile systems. Their reach will be global, erasing the distinctions between theater and national level defenses. All missile threats will be handled by the same defensive system. In principle, a seamless web will be put in place, ensnaring all air and missile attacks. Total global defense will be become a physical reality, ushering in a completely different strategic environment for all the parties, both the major powers and the lesser ones.

## NOTES

1. James Glanz, "Antimissile Test Viewed to Be Flawed by Its Opponents," *New York Times* January 14, 1999, A1, A20.

2. Alexander A. Pikayev, Leonard S. Spector, Elina V. Kirichenko, and Ryan Gibson, *Russia, the US and the Missile Technology Control Regime*, Adelphi Paper 317 (New York: Oxford University Press, 1998).

3. The United States several times was confronted with the issue of initiating a preemptive strike against a rising rival. That option was rejected in the late 1940s when the United States had a nuclear monopoly but the question was revisited during the

Kennedy administration with regard to China and its budding nuclear arsenal. The Johnson administration rejected that choice, preferring to employ political means to accomplish its goals. William Burr and Jeffrey T. Richelson, "Whether to 'Strangle the Baby in the Cradle': The United States and the Chinese Nuclear Program, 1960-1964," *International Security* 25 (Winter 2000-2001): 54–99.

4. Philip Butterworth-Hayes, "Joint Strike Fighter Divides Europe," *Aerospace America* (April 2000): 4–7. The size of the JSF program, possibly up to $400 billion, has distorted the marketplace because this program is the only large-scale military aircraft purchase planned for the next several decades.

5. "Proposal on ABM: 'Ready to Work with Russia,'" *New York Times on the Web* April 28, 2000, accessed June 9, 2000.

6. Anthony L. Velocci, Jr., "LockMart Gets Daring With COO Selection," *Aviation Week & Space Technology* (April 16, 2000): 23–24.

7. Standing Consultative Commission, *First Agreed Statement Relating to the Treaty between the United States of America and the Union of Soviet Socialist Republics on the Limitations of Anti-Ballistic Missile Systems of May 26, 1972* (September 26, 1997).

8. Donald H. Rumsfeld, Chairman, *Report of the Commission on the Ballistic Missile Threat to the United States* (Washington, DC: U.S. Congress, Government Printing Office, July 1998).

9. Dinshaw Mistry, "Explaining and Predicting the Operation of International Security Regimes: Ballistic Missile Proliferation and the MTCR" (Paper presented at the Annual meeting of the American Political Science Association, Washington, DC: September 2000).

10. David A. Flughum, "U.S. Doubts Korean Space Launch Claim," *Aviation Week & Space Technology* (September 14, 1998): 58–59. The satellite that was launched was in space so briefly that no good fix could be taken of the vehicle, indicating that the effort failed although the political point of North Korean missile capability was not lost on Japan or the United States.

11. Roger Handberg, "Changing Parameters of Japanese Security Policy: The Advent of Military Space in the Post Cold War Environment" (Paper presented at the Annual Meeting of the Southern Political Science Association, Savannah November 1999).

12. Cf. Rex R. Kiziah, *US-Led Cooperative Theater Missile Defense in Northeast Asia: Challenges and Issues* (Maxwell Paper No. 21 Maxwell Air Force Base, AL: Air War College, July 2000).

13. John Wilson Lewis and Xue Litai, "China's Search for a Modern Air Force," *International Security* 24 (Summer 1999): 64–94.

14. House of Representatives, *Final Report of the United States House of Representatives Select Committee on U.S. National Security and Military/Commercial Concerns with the People's Republic of China* (Washington, DC: U.S. House of Representatives, Government Printing Office, January 1999).

15. Ballistic Missile Defense Organization, *Statement of Lieutenant General Ronald T. Kadish before the Senate Armed Services Committee, Strategic Forces Subcommittee, February 28, 2000.*

16. Robert Wall, "Pentagon Considers Thaad for Fast-Track Development," *Aviation Week & Space Technology* (April 24, 2000): 80.

17. David A. Fulghum and John D. Morrocco, "First Arrow Battery Deployed near Tel Aviv," *Aviation Week & Space Technology* (April 10, 2000): 66–67. The Arrow battery will be linked to existing Patriot batteries already in the country with expansion to other U.S. TMD systems expected.

18. James Glanz, "Antimissile Test Viewed as Flawed by Its Opponents," *New York Times*, January 14, 2000, A1, A20.

19. For the technical description, see Ballistic Missile Defense Organization, *National Missile Defense Integrated Flight Test Four (IFT-4)* Fact Sheet 124-00-11 (Washington, DC: Ballistic Missile Defense Organization, 2000).

20. The announcement of the delay in the testing schedule came on March 21, 2000. The delay was the result of an intensive technical reexamination of all components. Their view was that an obstruction occurred in the cooling system for the infrared detectors, which caused it to fail just prior to closure with the target. *DoD News Briefing* (Washington, DC: Office of the Assistant Secretary of Defense [Public Affairs], March 21, 2000).

21. Union of Concerned Scientists, *Countermeasures: A Technical Evaluation of the Operational Effectiveness of the Planned US National Missile Defense System* (Cambridge: Union of Concerned Scientists and MIT Security Studies Program, April 2000). The counter-critique of that critique came in a statement before Congress by Lieutenant General Kadish, Director of the Ballistic Missile Defense Organization, *Statement before the House Subcommittee on National Security, Veterans Affairs, and International Relations, Committee on Government Reform*, September 8, 2000.

22. William J. Broad, "Pentagon Has Been Rigging Antimissile Tests, Critics Maintain," *New York Times on the Web*, June 7, 2000.

23. Lieutenant General Ronald Kadish, "U.S. National Missile Defense: Looking Past the Headlines" (Address to the Year 2000 Multinational BMD Conference, Philadelphia, June 5, 2000).

24. That earlier Bush speech was more specific than his later statements during the fall campaign when details proved hard to discern. Roberto Suro, "Bush on Defense: Details to Come," *Washington Post* September 21, 2000, A01. Early statements in office were firm in indicating that NMD is a priority but specifics lay in the future. Mike Allen, "Bush Affirms Defense Plans," *Washington Post*, January 27, 2001, A1.

25. Eric Schmitt, "Pentagon Likely to Delay New Test for Missile Shield," *New York Times*, September 1, 2000, A1, A3.

26. Robert Suro, "Clinton Defers Missile Defense," *Washington Post*, September 2, 2000, A1, A14; Eric Schmitt, "President Decides to Put Off Work on Missile Shield," *New York Times*, September 2, 2000, A1, A6.

27. Robert Suro, "Woes Undermined Missile Defense Cause," *Washington Post*, September 3, 2000, A4, A5.

28. "A Call for Realism and Prudence: Excerpts from President Clinton's Speech," *New York Times*, September 2, 2000, A8.

29. The question asked was: "President Clinton recently decided not to deploy a national missile defense system right now and to leave the decision about whether to deploy a national missile defense system to the next president. Do you agree or disagree with the President's decision not to deploy a national missile system right now? Do you feel that way strongly or not so strongly?" The question was asked to 1,000 adults, 18 years of age or older by telephone. The overall results were: "37%—strongly agree, 21%—not strongly agree, 10%—not strongly disagree, 20%—strongly disagree and 12%—Don't know." "Council for a Livable World, 58% of Public Support President's Missile Defense Decision: Politicians Ignore the Issue," http://www.clw.org/ef/nmddecision.html.

30.  Lou Cannon, *President Reagan: The Role of a Lifetime* (New York:  Simon & Schuster, 1991), 292–295.

31.  Robert D. Walpole, *Statement for the Record to the Senate Foreign Relations Committee on Foreign Missile Developments and the Ballistic Missile Threat to the United States through 2015* (Washington, DC:  Central Intelligence Agency, September, 16 1999).

32.  Kevin F. Gilmartin, "Shelton Outlines Role of Military in 21st Century," *American Forces Information Service News Article*, January 21, 2000, accessed January 26, 2000.

33.  Michael O'Hanlon, "Star Wars Strikes Back," *Foreign Affairs* (November 1999): 69–70.

34.  Table 4.2 is a derivative of the table reported in O'Hanlon, Ibid., 72–73.

35.  Robert Wall, "NMD Flight Testing Slows: Boost-Phase Intercept Bolstered," *Aviation Week & Space Technology* (August 28, 2000): 50–51; and James Glanz, "Other Systems Might Provide a U.S. Missile Shield," *New York Times on the Web* September 4, 2000.

36.  Robert Wall, "NMD Flight Testing Slows: Boost-Phase Intercept Bolstered," *Aviation Week & Space Technology* (August 28, 2000): 50–51; and James Glanz, "Other Systems Might Provide a U.S. Missile Shield," *New York Times on the Web* September 4, 2000.

# 5

# Agreeing on NMD or Not?

## INTRODUCTION

As is clear, national missile defense (NMD) remains the biggest political bone
of contention in the ballistic missile defense (BMD) field while theater missile
defense (TMD) is, practically speaking, considered to be a politically done deal.
At a very generalized level, the latter remains true, but the pesky technical
questions regarding TMD have not necessarily been fully addressed. The
dominant assumption seems to be that whatever technical problems presently
exist will be successfully resolved when the several theater-level missile systems
progress further toward deployment, another example of technological optimism
at its finest. Quite obviously, the technological imperative permeates the entire
field, with its adherents seizing upon any and all apparent testing successes in
order to advance the likelihood of deployment. In fact, opponents counter with
some evidence to support their assertions that test results have on occasion been
so distorted as to virtually constitute fraud. The most obvious case occurred in
1984 when fudged results were used to convince the Soviets of U.S. success in
overcoming the major obstacles to interception success. Retrospectively, it was
suggested that the deception was successful in forcing the Soviets to build up
their strategic forces, effectively bankrupting themselves in that process. The
validity of this latter assertion has been questioned but is immaterial for the
present debate. The larger policy issue is the suspicion regarding unreliability of
critical evidence for making decisions concerning NMD. Once such deceptions
are disclosed, all subsequent test results become subject to challenge and real
doubt, an under current impacting the present debate. Ambiguity becomes

interpreted as deception because the credibility bar has been lowered artificially. Essentially, both sides talk past each other.

Regardless, success is now believed by many though not all to be merely a matter of time and money, especially the latter. In fact, the assumption is that once theater-level deployment physically occurs, that overall process will become irreversible unlike the first situation in the 1970s. Then, NMD stood effectively alone, a technologically beleaguered and isolated system. The much commented upon incremental nature of defense policy making comes into play—each decision being merely a marginal adjustment from the status quo. The Theater High Altitude Area Defense (THAAD) program, the leading theater-level program, clearly benefits from that expectation, jumping from two-test successes after multiple failures to an accelerated development schedule in the fall of 1999. Whether the THAAD can in fact operate successfully in a combat setting remains unclear. That decision to accelerate forward, however, reflects strongly held worldviews against which facts do not often resonate.

As detailed earlier, the political imperatives driving TMD deployment have become so apparently overwhelming that their derailment would signal the possibility of a massive U.S. withdrawal from world affairs, at least in a military sense. Such a dramatic event could conceivably happen, but TMD would be only a peripheral item within the context of a tremendous upheaval in American domestic politics. The ripple effects for globalization would be profound, given the central position of the United States in the world economic order including protecting that fragile system from disruption. That capacity would be lost because U.S. forces would no longer be readily available for use unless there arose a presently nonexistent political willingness to accept major military casualties. Most societies likely would not miss the hegemonic role of the United States except when they invoke its protection or leadership in the absence of the will to proceed on their own. Domestically speaking, protecting American forces overseas from casualties as much as possible has moved from an expectation to an absolute political necessity. Once a theater-level option becomes available, failure to implement it would be extremely politically damaging for any administration, undermining the ability to convince Congress (in its present mood) of the necessity for any deployment. There is some evidence that the public is more realistic about the possibility of casualties occurring than politicians, but that realism is always qualified by the expectation that the mission has a purpose that is understandable to the public.[1] Politicians are usually searching for a hammer with which to beat their opponents—emotional appeals in terms of casualties are effective, at least in the short term.

Conversely, NMD, even more so than TMD, fits the category of an issue being driven by worldviews or ideologies often fairly disconnected from the operational realities of the relevant technologies. As Robert Jervis has observed of earlier nuclear weapons debates, the ideological intensity becomes high because the facts or experiences are thin on the ground.[2] Ballistic missile defense mirrors that situation of often certainty expressed in the absence of any real data except that generated through computer simulations. Such simulations are at best guesses about likely outcomes given certain assumptions. Spinning out elaborate scenarios is an important cottage industry among defense intellectuals. Such scenarios are predicated on the basis of worst case analysis, combined with heroic assumptions of technological optimism, a heady brew often intoxicating for its authors. NMD allows articulation of some of the boldest visions, both pro and con. After World War II, there was much discussion of nuclear weapons as the final absolute weapon—nullifying previous understandings of warfare. NMD as the absolute defense against the most unstoppable of military weapons holds similar attractiveness for grossly simplifying the world. Boldness in action would no longer be an invitation to attack because the other side would realize the futility of their efforts. Mistakes might occur but the United States behind its missile shield would possess absolute power to decimate the other societies. That other threats might nullify NMD's relevance is not considered germane.

In this chapter, the discussion focuses upon the various ideological groupings that drive the larger debate over NMD deployment. Whether NMD deployment occurs quickly or not at all will ultimately reflect the relative political power wielded by these participants at the moment of choice. World events will likely remain unsettled enough to provide ammunition supporting both sides. Plus, barring unforeseen events, the technology will also remain sufficiently marginal in terms of reliability to fuel concern about its ultimate effectiveness. The dialogue remains one between the deaf, whose worlds only intersect of necessity when the situation demands a collective decision. However, regardless of the specific deployment decision rendered—positive or negative—the debate will continue. Historical precedent—when the much sought after original deployment was subsequently cancelled in light of experience and shifting national priorities — clearly establishes the instability of such choices.

## THINKING ABOUT THE WORLD

As has been eluded to earlier but not discussed in detail, three major ideological clusters have become extremely visible over the course of the drawn-out debate over ballistic missile defense (BMD) and, more straightforwardly, specifically regarding deployment at the national level. Theater missile defense tends to be debated more in terms of effectiveness issues since the potential adversaries can be anywhere and anyone. The ideological nature of the national level debate is not a new idea. Robert A. Bernstein and William W. Anthony found that the 1968–1970 Senate votes on the ABM deployment were heavily driven by ideology to the exclusion, at least originally, of constituency interests or political party affiliation.[3] This finding was extremely interesting since constituency-based concerns so often drive congressional choices. In fact, ideology had even greater impact as the lines over ABM deployment were drawn and hardened over the subsequent three-year period leading up to cancellation.

The ideological clusters examined here correlate loosely to the distinctions made between arms controllers and national advantage adherents, at least at the extremes.    The binary nature of that distinction, however, washes out the importance of the larger middle group whose policy choices actually determine the specific directions pursued by the United States.  Arms controllers provide a direct counterweight to those only advocating pursuit of national advantage although if even there, their argument is one usually premised upon the deeper understanding that arms control properly implemented gives advantages to the United States by leveling the field and reducing the possibility of dramatic change, especially that contrary to U.S. interests.  That logic has been played out in the often-baroque debates between the United States and the former Soviet Union over highly technical issues thought to have enormous potential impact in the future.   Given the uncertainties inherent in any discussions concerning nuclear warfare, such caution was thought necessary but the overall goal remained arms reductions in order to help sustain the peace or, at least, reduce the probability of war and the damage that would ensue.   The realistic underpinnings of the arms controllers' views of desirable outcomes to be achieved were often ignored in the hurly-burly of political exchange.  The public debate occurred in terms of slogans and oversimplifications:  appeasers versus warmongers.

By contrast, national advantage proponents assume that the United States, given its current technological superiority, will of course dominate all possible unbridled weapons competitions.  That assumption is also driven by an expectation that the United States has and will expend whatever resources are necessary to remain ahead.  Such a nationalistic view, however, builds heavily upon the experience during the Cold War, a premise declining in vigor.  That frailty can be most clearly seen in congressional rhetoric opposing any military interventions overseas.    Regardless, the fragility of the present U.S. technological advantage is either denied or minimized in their minds.  From this policy perspective, technological leads, once seized, are never lost, a denial of history obviously but a common mistake when one extrapolates into the future based on present trends.  One does not have to assume the decline of the West or some such analogy to be aware that national advantages, despite their permanent appearance, often vanish quickly.    That possibility, it is often argued, is particularly germane when dealing with technological change where dramatic breakthroughs remain a distinct possibility.   A more subtle but similar perspective arises in considering the collapse of empires.    Technological advantages prove temporary while the empire becomes overcommitted in areas outside its sphere of vital interests.

The more central flaw in this national advantage perspective arises from proponent's blindness regarding the dual-use nature of the most relevant technologies.  The United States dominates military applications currently but that large lead is very fragile, given that other states are concurrently developing equivalent civilian technologies, readily transferable to military uses, albeit with modifications.  Much of the present American military advantage is premised upon continued U.S. willingness to invest heavily in weapons research and development (R&D) while likely competitors pursue other options.  That is reflected in the great disparity in comparative military spending (including secret and infrastructure expenditures). For example, the civilian Ikonos remote-sensing satellite provided startlingly clear images of the secretive North Korean launch facility, not quite military grade but fully capable of being upgraded.[4] In truth, the photos published in *Aviation Week & Space Technology* were sufficiently clear and detailed to classified definitely be as military quality for most states. Those states would otherwise lack access to such information. The satellite in this case was an American one but other states such as France, India, and Russia—through their widely available commercial endeavors— clearly possess similar military potentialities. In fact, India is reassessing its policies in light of images made of India by its own satellite that are commercially available to Pakistan.[5] That reality was evident even earlier in 1990–1991 when Spot Image (French) and Landsat (American) remote-sensing satellites provided vital imagery for Desert Storm operations. The images while militarily useful were routine imaging events commercially available, albeit much less detailed than current commercial ventures can provide.[6] Until 1996, civilian imagery was kept less accurate due to security restrictions—ones now dramatically relaxed with commercial considerations determining the acuity required.

The United States has long recognized that that relationship exists as typified by its leadership in the establishment in 1987 of the earlier discussed Missile Technology Control Regime (MTCR), part of which regulates (prohibits) dissemination of dual-use space technologies due to their military potential. Furthermore, during the Gulf War, U.S. dependence upon Japanese electronics in critical systems caused great unease due to possible Japanese restrictions upon supporting military combat operations. Therefore, the ultimate message is that the present U.S. lead regarding BMD technologies is more uncertain than acknowledged. The key inhibitor has been the other states' reluctance to unilaterally pursue such technologies or their budget priorities are focused upon fostering domestic economic growth. The historical competitor, the Soviet Union, died, and its successor, the Russian Federation, has other more pressing issues especially economic ones. Militarily, it is sustaining its conventional forces for internal security purposes and an adequate (by Russian standards) nuclear force for external defense ranks above NMD. All of those inhibitors are obviously subject to change if Russian concerns about the United States grow stronger. Many states are unlikely to pursue such technologies due to their present economic underdevelopment, but they have not posed the greatest military threat.

"Dual-use" in this context refers to technologies primarily developed for private sector usage but which contain significant military potential. Space applications clearly fit that situation in that civilian technologies can be readily rolled over into direct military uses. Space-based communications, remote sensing, and navigation systems clearly fit the dual-use model. More dangerous militarily in the long run are applications in sensors, computers, communications technologies, and materials sciences. All of these areas can shift readily from military to civilian use and back while employing the same basic technologies. Such applications are becoming a critical prerequisite for survival in the global economy.   Thus, sustaining national economic competitiveness aids military strength, especially in coping with change.   Innovation is accelerating in many fields with potentially major effects upon the aggregate military balance and U.S. position in the world.   In fact, there has evolved a concept referred to as "spin-on."[7]   Spin-offs are military or government technologies developed for specific military purposes that find usefulness in the civilian economy.   Spin-ons are the reverse pattern in which civilian technologies are transferred into the military sector as an improvement (often exponential) in capabilities.   The new military application was not the intention of the original developer but was recognized as potentially militarily useful.     Some technologies demand significant modification to be militarily useful, but many only need to be made more robust in order to survive combat operations.   For example, computer chips must be radiation hardened to survive nuclear exchanges (the electromagnetic pulse (EMP) effects can destroy a system) or redundancy built in to allow continued operations.

The national advantage perspective draws heavily upon one long-standing tradition in American politics.   Labeled the "Jacksonian Tradition" by one scholar, this perspective argues that the U.S. political culture contains a strain within it that advocates what might be termed "total war"—meaning that the war is fought "with all available force."[8]   There are effectively no rules limiting the imposition of the American will upon the enemy.   The argument is that American foreign policy makes no sense unless this cultural predisposition is factored into the situation.   One need not accept this explanation completely, but there is a strong historical record supporting the notion that, in time of war, the United States has not allowed any restraints to interfere with confronting its adversaries and that presidents who have acted in a restrained fashion have paid a political price for that behavior.   Jacksonian views are not necessarily more militant in terms of world affairs, but they provide an emotional base supporting the maximum utilization of available military technologies.   The purposes of that technology are to impose their will on the enemy and to minimize American casualties—two goals seen as compatible through the exercise of ever more proficient military technologies.

## SHAPING NMD POLICIES

One must note that individual viewpoints once clearly articulated by policy makers are rarely changed significantly.   By this, we are just referring to the fact that public officials once they clearly establish a defined public position on such issues are constrained by that public nature from major shifts in their positions. The obvious exception to this generalization is when, and if, a dramatic event occurs totally undermining the coherence and justification for the previous position. As has been described in chapters 2 and 4 in their historical overviews, NMD as a policy issue has not confronted such crescendos, except in the negative sense that the Soviet Union disintegrated, removing the urgency underlying deployment.   Even then, the sense of threat, while perceived as real by advocates, was fairly abstract in nature, involving throw weights and warhead dispersal patterns. The Soviet Union's demise removed an important justification for the original demands for NMD deployment. U.S. strategic forces and its peoples were obviously vulnerable to the Soviet nuclear juggernaut. The Russian Federation ostensibly entered into a period of détente with the United States—a condition reinforced by its economic and political travails. Efforts in 1991 at expanding the NMD rationale to incorporate rogue states and accidental launches were not as persuasive. The sense of urgency was lower and proved resistant to efforts to heighten that anxiety. NMD dropped off the public's radar.

For decision makers, arriving at a position, therefore, regarding NMD has come in two ways. For a comparatively vocal few, NMD is part of an ideological package regarding the state of the world. This can be either supportive or not. Others come to the question with proclivities in various directions but have not drawn conclusions yet. On many issues, their views will remain unformed regarding specifics until forced to assume a position. On most issues, such an explicit position statement is not demanded in advance. For congressional members, their positions are usually leanings or attitudes pointing in a particular direction, but over time those become more settled because passing legislation requires votes and in effect forces a position to be identified through that act. For the executive, especially the president, public pronouncements become part of the nomination and election process. In appealing to groups within the party while seeking its nomination, presidential candidates are generally required to explicitly indicate their preferences. At this preliminary stage, the candidate's effort still has some flexibility because of changing circumstances if and when he or she assumes office.

Presidential candidates often do make unequivocal commitments on specific issues but those are either absolute requirements if one is to be nominated or else they represent peripheral issues for which commitment is costless during the general election. Abortion is one such issue in seeking the Democratic or Republican presidential nomination. Political parties are buffeted by the intensity with which certain groups in the party hold tight to often very specific issues. Their influence is usually disproportionately great in the nomination process because comparatively few voters participate in primaries but often precipitously declines later during the general election, which is aimed at the wider electorate. NMD for Republican candidates is an easy agreement since the larger electorate is basically indifferent, at best, regarding the issue. Democratic presidential candidates have found the issue less compelling unless some connection occurs within the electorate. There are few groups within the party pushing the issue; most are indifferent, if not vaguely opposed. For Democratic candidates, NMD is normally rolled into a general defense policy posture of prudent action in the face of threat while not exaggerating the threat. This produces a mixed bag of symbolic support but less budgetary pressures than Republicans face.

But, even absolute or unequivocal opposition or support regarding NMD deployment may waver under the pressure of later events especially changing economic realities. The single act that usually forces hard choices is the allocation of budgetary resources when concrete decisions are required. Ultimately, all policy choices in this arena converge on budget choices. Rhetoric may be supportive or hostile but funding decisions determine whether any real action results. The widening gap between rhetoric and action is often most clearly embodied in budgetary choices. Many members vote for symbolic reaffirmations of NMD but, when fiscal resources are being allocated, find other, clearly more-pressing, uses in their judgment for scarce funds. Presidents likewise budget for NMD, but most have chosen to support continued research and development, albeit at varying levels depending on current evaluations of external threat, technological pace, and political necessities. From a presidential perspective, those amounts are equivalent to deployment, symbolic re-affirmations while preserving flexibility amid uncertainty. This scenario is not unique to NMD; rather it is a fact of American political life. The annual fiscal cycle embedded in American politics makes such outcomes both possible and routine, further confusing public understanding. Everyone is publicly supportive—how could a politician argue for a weaker defense? But, clearly major differences exist regarding the level of support thought absolutely necessary for NMD as a specific program.

The symbolic aspects of politics are especially potent in the arena of national defense; gestures often effectively substitute for definitive action. Publicly supporting defense spending generally or even specific weapons programs does not translate into deploying or using such instruments. But it does inoculate one politically from appearing soft on this critical issue during elections. This reflects the desire of all decision makers concerned to preserve their flexibility and freedom of action. Bill Clinton as president opposed NMD, but under pressure accommodated those who were much more adamant and public in their support. NMD policy development reflected that presidential ambivalence but also his concomitant willingness to accommodate those more committed. Accommodation did not translate into complete acquiescence to opponents' views but rather a measured effort to defuse their political impact. Enough was done to blunt any political damage but not enough to directly repudiate earlier presidential positions regarding the importance of pursuing arms control. The president's approach is reflective of the struggle's essentially ideological nature, especially at the extremes of support or nonsupport for NMD as a concept.

Major changes in policy direction have tended to reflect the addition of new participants into the mix rather than changing existing players' opinions. In addition, as will be discussed, marginal adjustments in the policy views held by the middle group can also translate into dramatic effects upon policy outcomes. This population influx is graphically obvious when a new presidential administration enters office, even when the political party does not change, for example from Reagan to Bush in 1989. The first Bush administration was publicly committed to NMD but clearly less fervent than its predecessor in supporting the concept. The change reflected both different presidential priorities and a drastically changing world situation. The Clinton administration in 1993 moved even further away from the Reagan vision, aided and abetted by a Democratic Congress.  Congress dramatically reversed its stance in 1995 when a resurgent conservative Republican majority assumed office.  In the latter case, NMD was directly incorporated as part of the party platform, *The Contract with America,* although how critical NMD was in that mix is unclear but it likely was of minimal public impact.  Military issues generally have become marginal political questions after the Gulf War in 1991.  Attempts to push such issues have floundered upon public complacency and indifference.  In both the 1996 and 2000 presidential elections, other issues were much more critical to determining the outcome.  Several foreign policy events, notably the deaths of American soldiers in Somalia, triggered a sharp reaction but the political effects quickly dissipated.  Interventions in Bosnia and Yugoslavia (Kosovo) created uneasiness about long-term commitments but the effects upon the 2000 presidential election appeared minimal.

However, the fact that the extremes hold fairly well defined almost rigid perspectives upon NMD is not unique to this particular issue; much of contemporary public policy debate in the United States has been a dialogue of the deaf.  Core antagonists (the most informed and motivated) often hold very inflexible perspectives on the key questions.  Their approach, however, becomes a constant hammering on the same points—any new information being fed into the maw of preconception.  For them, the fundamentals are already clear and unequivocal, and subsequent facts are only confusing.  Because of their obsession, such issue partisans are unable to comprehend why the general public remains disinterested.  Code words and phrases inform the devout what the proper position is on any aspect of the question, new or old.  NMD suffers from a high degree of abstraction that further deflects public understanding or interest.  When the issue does attain some public visibility, the question usually is cloaked within some larger concern with the state of national security rather than being the critical factor itself.  Therefore, public support remains problematic because there exists no real intensity in their support.  This allows cost and technical questions to determine the nature of public attitudes to the degree that they exist.  With the death of the Soviet Union, public views became even more disengaged—rogue states lack the same immediacy in terms of their potential threat to the United States, despite the frequent alarms sounded.  Public weariness regarding global threats has been reenforced by recurring failed global crises such Y2K meltdowns and Ebola fever epidemics.  The public is not indifferent to possible threats, but their immediate credibility remains suspect.  Americans have historically been an insular people, self-obsessed and ignorant of other countries.  Even in a global age, that reality has not changed, and has possibly even grown worse with the continued references to U.S. primacy in the world.

Although the public may perceive certain segments of the world as very hostile to the United States, that threat is usually assumed to be long term and possibly not directly military in nature.  More debilitating to any general sense of alarm are the recurring attempts to cast various states as future adversaries, not necessarily military in nature.  These possibilities have included Japan and Europe with the Russian Federation and China more often seen as direct military threats. For the public, at least presently, none of these examples are terribly credible in the short term while the rest of the world is perceived as lagging far behind those states. As a consequence, no public official argues that public demand or outcry drives his or her position regarding NMD. That situation may change, possibly quickly, but the reality is that ideologically driven think tanks and policy groups interacting with sympathetic officials in both the legislative and executive drive the debate both pro and con. NMD remains elite politics in its rawest form—the decisions made reflect elite evaluations regarding the necessity for NMD. For example, much moral outrage was expressed by NMD partisans over the fact that the U.S. population remains exposed to the ballistic missile threat. They quote surveys done prior to the 1994 congressional and 1996 presidential elections describing public outrage (accessed through focus groups) at discovering the population's defenselessness before the missile threat.[9] The difficulty was that the outrage did not translate into changes in electoral choices. More critically, focus groups are readily manipulated into expressing reactions to questions otherwise not relevant to the individuals' lives and therefore unimportant. Much of the analysis tracks a pattern of self-fulfilling prophecy on both sides.

Policy change in this area comes through the addition of new participants and marginal shifts among the undecided or indifferent. These new participants may not have explicitly focused on the issue before the most recent eruption or else their views are essentially unformed due to their lack of knowledge. As indicated above, congressional members often have general leanings on issue categories but lack substantive knowledge or interest in a specific area. Their electoral survival is predicated upon their positions on other issues, among which NMD looms small. Republican candidates are more likely to espouse supportive postures but that is normally a minor aspect of their campaigns. Domestic questions affecting the economy are first, followed by social issues; NMD is normally not on their constituency's radar. But, the pressure to vote on specific legislation leads inexorably to the member taking a position, one that hardens over time. Generally, incumbents tend to focus linearly upon those issues most immediately germane to their constituency and institutional position within Congress rather than range widely across the possible issue spectrum. Therefore, changing one's position on NMD once a view is established can force consideration of other already settled questions. Congressional decision-making does not begin *de novo* each year but rather builds upon previous choices, assuming those did not lead to obvious disaster.

Making policy regarding NMD occurs between two principal institutions, the executive and Congress with outsiders willing to intervene. Congress reflects a combination of individual and institutional perspectives. Individual members of Congress stake out positions consistent with their political affiliation and ideology as influenced by their future ambitions. For example, Vice President Albert Gore became more supportive of NMD during the latter years of the Clinton administration than previously while serving in the Senate or House (prior to 1993) especially as the 2000 presidential election drew nigh. Republican presidential contenders and candidates support NMD, but their enthusiasm is more muted than the issue partisans' desire.[10]  In addition, the political parties in Congress have gradually staked out general policy views regarding such issues.  Adherence to any position remains tentative although over the past thirty years, the parties in Congress have become more ideologically homogeneous in their views, further solidifying the partisan lines.

In fact, NMD is generally submerged into the large issue catalog of both parties.  The Democratic party exhibited greater hostility to NMD when in the majority, but even during the Reagan years and SDI that opposition was always tempered by caution.  The old Cold War Democrats had literally died out by the early 1980s but the Cold War itself did not end until later.  After the 1994 election, the effects were interesting as the more moderate and conservative Democrats were defeated, which led to an initial opposition to Republican demands for NMD.  Opposition became muted as more moderate Democrats entered Congress, diluting liberal dominance of the party.  President Clinton and the New Democrats (in their self-description) dominated the public debate on the issue—straddling a position of domestic reform and defense preparedness (a less intense version of the earlier Cold War Democrats).

The Republicans on the other hand have reached a general party consensus on the necessity of NMD but do exhibit differences on when and how much should be deployed.  Responsibility in terms of control of Congress has not decreased verbal support.  However, the exact degree of support is unclear due to the fact that until 2001, the president (Clinton) was effectively predisposed to limit deployment if not delay it indefinitely.  Rhetoric therefore has substituted for action in terms of unrestrained choice regarding NMD deployment.  Confronted by the prospect of actual deployment, possibly open end deployment, the decisions will become more difficult if a balanced budget remains a political necessity.  The larger Republican agenda focuses upon tax reductions, improved defense capabilities generally, and Social Security–Medicare reform.  Those choices consume or reduce tax resources and make decisions more difficult.  The present closely divided Congress makes all these choices much more contentious and difficult to make.

For the executive branch, the president symbolizes the particular view adopted by his administration but within the executive itself the parochialism of department and service heads may obscure the clarity of the views being presented.  Agency heads lead and represent institutions with often firmly held views regarding particular policy issues as they pertain to the future.  Within the Department of Defense (DoD) each of the military services has different institutional views regarding NMD generally and special programs in particular, reflecting that service's perceived interests.  On paper, all parties within the DoD are onboard but in practice real differences do exist—a situation that can be activated by knowledgeable outsiders such as Congress.  Congressional ability to elicit supportive commentary for NMD keeps the issue alive, even when technical problems threaten to terminate specific BMD programs.  Wrapped in military expertise, such optimistic statements provide rebuttal to carping critics, usually civilian and outside official circles.  The military services are fully aware that NMD represents a competitor for finite resources—as NMD grows they will become more stressed financially by its demands.

For policy makers, remaining open minded regarding NMD becomes difficult and usually is driven by calculations of relative political cost-benefits, including individual, institutional, and national variables. The latter remain the most fluid because the passage of time can render dramatic changes in external threat perceptions, evaluations of NMD technology effectiveness, and the desire for certainty. The latter refers to judgments about whether a decision at this particular point in time can "solve" the problem, or do the unknowns still prevent that degree of foreknowledge. Predicting the future becomes risky, and the usual approach remains only probabilistic. As a result, only ranges of certainty can be established, usually with wide degrees of error inherent in the evaluation process. The partisans at both ends of the NMD debate essentially deny that uncertainty, arguing that accepting their position will solve all the problems.

## WHY NMD?—THREE PERSPECTIVES

The question posed by the section heading might more realistically be phrased, "When NMD?" If national missile defense works, the United States would deploy the relevant system with comparatively little hesitation and possibly minimal debate. Other states' views, including those of allies, are frankly not that compelling if NMD met that single criterion. The United States does not perceive itself as alone, but recognizes that the demise of the Soviet threat has freed states from former ties driven by that threat. Conversely, the United States is likewise freed of such constraints, but obviously within limits. NMD has been portrayed as an issue upon which only the United States can make the judgment, based upon its self-interests. For over fifty years, the United States has aggressively pursued acquiring the best military technologies available. Cost was not irrelevant but not necessarily determinative regarding its decisions. Predictions as to the probable cost of Strategic Defense Initiative (SDI) were astronomical in some projected configurations, but that did not deter believers. It did, however, effectively turn away those less committed to the concept. The result is that tides of opinion appear to run through the debate, moving toward deployment and then away. Presently, the tide appears to be sharply rising in support of some form of NMD deployment.

The divisions over BMD deployment on a national scale are driven by two factors: (1) the differing assessments made of the disruptive impact posed by NMD deployment in terms of the United States and its relationships in the world, especially with its allies; and (2) the technological prospects for successful NMD deployment, successful in the sense of operating with utmost efficiency and effectiveness under the most stressful and conceivable battle conditions. Sharp differences in answering both these questions have deeply split the politicians over how aggressively to pursue national missile defense. Those differences represent fundamental and long-standing perceptions structuring their views of both military technological change and world politics.

In essence, ideologically driven worldviews force the debate and determine the resulting decisions.

The analysis here is framed in terms of polar ideological opposites, but one must note that even these are not totally divorced from one another. In fact, the actual political arguments are often articulated in terms of technical details and judgments, based upon those specifics but grounded in fundamental values. The ideological component becomes clearer when both sides address the same facts but continually draw diametrically opposed conclusions. The reason for this general congruence is that all the parties, even the most ardent opponents, as was discussed earlier, are heavily imbued with the technological imperative that totally permeates modern American defense policy debates. This simply means that all parties are driven by their strongly held understandings that, given sufficient resources and time, technological fixes can be created for almost all BMD problems, whether at the national level or not. Such a view explains the apparent rush to implement the THAAD system following two flight successes after multitudinous failures.[11] Individuals can differ markedly in their degree of enthusiasm for pursuit of these advances but for the most part the choices represent simply a cost-benefit calculation. Crudely stated, until recently, the expected additional national security benefits have been deemed insufficient to justify the demanded expenditures. Doubts such as these are what in the end terminated the first NMD, deployment albeit in the context of a broader negotiated arms control solution. It was a choice that minimized the domestic political risks for the Nixon administration given strong Democratic preferences for pursuing arms control solutions. Technological optimism at that point could not override the obvious limitations of the existing ABM technologies.

The other bias, aside from the technological aspects running through the controversy, that aids the NMD advocates is that no public official or, at least, no significant number, would publicly advocate apparent national weakness in the face of external threat. Therefore, opposition to NMD is framed in terms of alternative methods by which to secure national security—arms control and reduction being the most obvious other pathway. That perspective leaves those opposed to NMD subject to the vagaries of the technology development process and interpretations thereof. Advances in technology translate into pressure to deploy now, a choice congruent with previous defense decisions to pursue the best technological solutions possible for meeting national security needs.

All the debate participants deal with an uncertain world in which hard choices are made based on often extremely fragmentary information. Thus, NMD views are often intensely held at the ideological poles with a fervor that masks the very large uncertainties inherent in the total decisional process. Figure 5.1 organizes the three general perspectives articulated regarding NMD along a continuum. Movement between the polar positions is unlikely in the absence of war (as will be discussed) so any policy change results from the fluctuating perceptions held by the middle group. Their shifts in evaluation, in effect, determine whether NMD deployment becomes more or less probable at any particular point in time. This provides whatever fluidity exists within the larger debate.   In effect, these individuals represent the decision point or minimum winning coalition (MWC).

**Figure 5.1**
**Conceptualizing BMD Debate Ideologies**

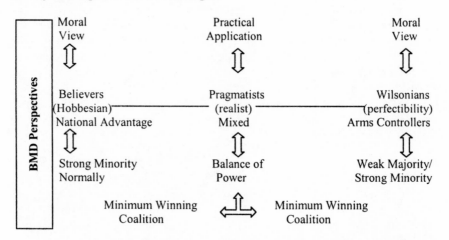

Given the fervor of the adherents at the issue's extremes, any decision to be implemented must acquire an extraordinary majority rather than a simple majority or the passage of time and the rise of new issues will undermine the original choice.  Erosion in support occurs in the middle group, whose views are more driven by specific events, especially those related to emerging technologies and changing budgets

Despite the sharp rhetoric exchanged, decisions regarding NMD are not simply up-and-down choices made only when new issues or choices repeatedly confront the participants.  The annual congressional budget process, as described earlier, forces a repeated revisiting of the question.  Thus no decision is ever completely final in the sense that the issue remains alive, assuming there continue to exist either sufficient opposition or support to challenge the previous choice.  That maximizes both sides' opportunities to finesse the issue until, at some unknown future point, when victory can be at least temporarily claimed. For example, President Nixon's 1969 Safeguard decision finessed the disruptive basing problems encountered by the earlier Sentinel deployments around urban areas.   But, the phased expansion of the ABM system to cover more intercontinental ballistic missile (ICBM) fields brought the issue back to Congress, allowing opponents to attack it anew.[12]  The result was a cycle of debilitating debates further undermining ABM support.   One should not underestimate the annual feature of congressional budgeting since NMD deployment would be a multiyear proposition.  That is especially true because the longer-range NMD deployment options involve space-based and other configurations that will demand a decade or more of development time, providing multiple chances for Congress to act.

As postulated, three distinct groups appear to exist: believers, pragmatics, and Wilsonians.  Quickly summarized, believers desire NMD deployment as soon as possible without equivocation in the largest configuration feasible, while Wilsonians reject NMD technology due to its capacity, in their judgment, to increase the possibility of war.  Pragmatists, as one might expect, repeatedly re-weigh their choices in light of changing international circumstances and technology issues.   These groupings represent particular approaches to considering the issues embedded in NMD rather than tightly organized political organizations.    Pragmatists are found in both political parties, but their distribution varies over time.  Equally clearly, there exist significant differences across each group regarding the intensity with which their particular views are held.   What issue fluidity exists within this policy realm grows out of these differences since, at the polar opposites, compromise is not thought possible. Each extreme wages an unrelenting marathon campaign to establish the views thought right by that group.

Delay, from the perspective of Figure 5.1, occurs because of the choices made by the middle group—the pragmatists.  Their tentative adherence to either side determines what is labeled the minimum winning coalition (MWC).  In fact, if the decision is made only through an MWC, that choice is unlikely to hold for long, given the multiple opportunities for reconsidering whatever congressional choice has been rendered.   Presidents may propose, but clearly Congress disposes.  Budget authority is the ultimate trump card.  NMD in some form has been on the national political agenda without resolution for so long that all sides assume the question remains open for perpetual reconsideration.  This behavior exists regardless of the particular administration in power.   Presidents can impact the NMD debate's intensity through their choices of whether to push forward a particular position hard or to defer to the current congressional majority.   Ronald Reagan pushed hard, but his leverage declined noticeably when the Senate reverted back to Democratic control in 1987.  That did not mean Congress did not respond to his demands, but the results were much more modest.    The program clearly encountered a stretch out—a very usual occurrence for expensive and contentious programs.   Likewise, President Clinton's obvious distaste for NMD influenced the debate, even after both houses became Republican controlled and in principle exceedingly favorable to the program.

**Wilsonians**

The three groups delineated are not evenly distributed so that each requires support from another faction in order to accomplish its goals.  As a result, the figure predicts two distinct minimum winning coalition possibilities—an alliance between Wilsonians and pragmatists or one between believers and pragmatists (the theoretical possibility of a Wilsonians-Believers coalition is not thought possible, given the intensity and opposition of their views). The Wilsonians are characterized by their moral abhorrence of NMD technology since it encourages nuclear weaponry proliferation and increases the possibility of its use.  The Wilsonians have consistently pursued international agreements aimed at controlling, even hopefully eliminating, NMD as an option within their larger effort aimed at arms control and, ultimately, total nuclear disarmament. Their drive is to continue the incremental spread of arms control agreements.

Their moral commitment is to a world characterized by adherence to the international rule of law with negotiated settlement of all disputes becoming the most strongly desired behavioral norm.  Force and its use, even defensively, comes as a last resort after all other possible avenues for peaceful resolution have been exhausted.  Self-defense is obviously not excluded but NMD itself is perceived as inherently provocative, capable of instigating conflict, including "first strike" scenarios by other states, notably Russia as successor to the Soviet Union.  Contrary to the believers' views, Wilsonians define NMD as at its root a passive yet aggressive posture for a state such as the United States.  The United States is already so disproportionately powerful that adding another increment to that power relationship frightens other states.  The states being disturbed include its putative allies and friends.  That disturbance could be seen in the Europeans' response to the Clinton moves in the early summer of 2000 to revise, even possibly discard, the ABM treaty.  Revision followed by subsequent NMD deployment was perceived as the first step toward igniting a new nuclear arms race a view not shared by the others but a question that will only be resolved in time.  Adversaries, current and potential, merely perceive NMD as making their task harder in the future event of conflict.  NMD from this perspective becomes strategically destabilizing and politically disruptive of the Wilsonians' larger efforts at maintaining world peace.  Deployment in their judgment negates any efforts at comprehensive nuclear weapons bans since other states will not leave themselves vulnerable to U.S. actions or those of others.  From this perspective, the Senate's rejection of the Comprehensive Test Ban Treaty was but a down payment for NMD and a future arms race.

This strand within the debate has been particularly refreshed by the Soviet Union's disintegration, removing the most imminent likelihood of nuclear war. That event has severely reduced in the Wilsonians' judgment the requirement for any version of NMD deployment, especially those provocative in nature. The argument being made currently by the national security apparatus that the collapse of the earlier Cold War duality has in fact increased possible missile threats is generally rejected as excessively alarmist. The rogue states or their states of concern equivalents have been present all along during the Cold War. Removing the big oak has allowed the saplings to become more visible to the eye, but they are not truly larger threats.  Their small missile forces remain potential threats, but other modes of weapon delivery are likely more dangerous and effective.  Their potential position, tactically speaking, emphasizes the technical obstacles inherent in successfully launching an ICBM accurately. Those technical obstacles will not immediately evaporate, and, even if they do, other leaderships are not irrational and suicidal.  Most leaders have struggled hard to reach power and desperately desire to sustain their position, not preside over a radioactive ruin.  The argument becomes that by its incessant ramblings on about NMD, the United States in effect feeds their interest (in many cases already existent) in acquiring ballistic missiles.

What would the United States do if such missiles really worked? Arms control efforts, therefore, are more productive endeavors than NMD. Such agreements should not just ratify the status quo, but leaders should pursue assertive efforts aimed at scaling back all the arms available to all parties. Thus, if armed conflict ensues, the damage and casualties inflicted will be less since war is in effect made less lethal. That view follows earlier efforts in the Middle Ages to make war less lethal, all of which failed. By completely banning NMD, no state including the United States is able to hide from the consequences of its actions. Choices will be made with the full realization that severe military consequences may result. That realization breeds caution. Their operative assumption also is that the United States would remain among the more heavily armed states up until the utopia of total disarmament is achieved. Most perceive that stage, if ever reached, to be very distant in time but a goal to strive for in the present. But, in the meanwhile, the potential scourge of war can be lessened, at least in theory. More pragmatically, treaties combined with prudent not confrontational behavior have been successful in putting off nuclear conflict for fifty years so that process should continue until demonstrated unsuccessful.

Historically, a concurrent strand of domestic policy has also run through their position, arguing that any resources not expended upon NMD could be more productively used for domestic needs. This argument becomes another variation in the "guns and butter" theme running through post–World War II American defense budgeting. The earlier Cold War Democrats, liberals domestically while realists internationally, grappled with this dilemma with mixed success. Military budgets represent discretionary spending, available for use elsewhere if not spent on the military. The argument becomes that the ultimate strength of the country is an equitable and just society, providing adequately for all its members. Otherwise, the United States becomes merely a shell—strong but brittle when the inevitable stresses come. One can argue political practicality as to whether funds diverted from NMD should go to the disadvantaged or be diverted into other social sectors already politically dominant.

Fundamentally, Wilsonians perceive the world not as always a benign one but rather as one much more amendable to nonmilitary solutions than is usually assumed. From this worldview, military force is not abolished (except at the extremes), but its influence and use is clearly kept limited in order to minimize the potential for igniting war. Military force becomes the last option not the first or at least it is not quickly invoked. Negotiated solutions are best because in open and free negotiations, both sides participate and agree, reducing future resentments and incentives to reverse matters. The Versailles treaty is often cited as the prototype for a war-producing instrument.

In fact, their argument becomes essentially that NMD contains certain unintended consequences, whose actual impact is to decrease the level of national security achieved. NMD in their judgment places the United States in a situation where others not possessing that defensive capability will come to perceive the United States as the ultimate "rogue state"—that is one capable of threatening other states with little chance of suffering proportionately as a consequence. In effect, the end of reciprocal deterrence occurs since the United States moves beyond retribution. The situation is one perceived as too internationally unstable, creating hostilities that ultimately undermine U.S. security interests. NMD from this perspective is primarily a source of instability and insecurity, feeding other states' paranoia. Total security becomes a chimera leading the United States to ignore the reality that its greatest sense of national security comes in a world of actively engaged peaceful states capable of resolving most problems through nonmilitary means. Therefore, the Wilsonians explicitly reject the believers' willingness to treat the ABM treaty as a mere scrap of paper no longer binding upon the United States due to the Soviet Union's death. These scraps of paper have meaning in that they guide different states in the quest for peaceful solutions.

### Believers

The "believers" also approach NMD, especially national deployment, as a moral commitment but from the perspective that the good government protects its citizenry against all conceivable external threats.    The effort must be expended even when success is problematic—to do otherwise is to deny the government's responsibility for protecting its people. Their worldview comes from the opposite direction than that of the Wilsonians. The world from this perspective is best described as a Hobbesian jungle, dangerous and conflict ridden with no international order possible except through individual states being strong enough to defend their particular interests. Simply put, strength has kept the United States secure, not pieces of paper. That strength is firmly grounded in economics but expressed militarily at least in the twentieth century and into the new era. President Dwight Eisenhower in the 1950s emphasized the economic competition inherent in the Cold War not in the sense of rhetoric but in terms of comparative economic capacity. That economic competition in his judgment would determine the outcome.[13]

For earlier generations, that economic strength represented the potential to mobilize immense human and industrial resources. More recently, forces in place have become the shield behind which the United States prospered and grew. From this perspective, treaties with potential enemies are made to be broken—their usefulness is limited if the other party is determined to cheat or otherwise evade the agreement. In their view, most states will cheat, especially those already adverse to the United States. Certain states such as Canada and the United Kingdom are clearly not perceived as threats because of their historic ties to the United States but even their interests are defined as different. For example, in the spring of 2000, the vice-commander of the U.S. Space Command, Vice Admiral Herbert Browne, stated that if Canada did not join the impending NMD effort, it would be left unprotected in the event of a rogue state attack. You either stand with the United States or against it; there can be little middle ground in the struggle between good and evil. This attitude was seen in earlier U.S. hostility toward neutralist and nonaligned states during the clash of the two superpowers. In this worldview, the United States unfortunately often stands alone in defending freedom, at least as the United States defines it. The lone pioneer myth is strong in American culture. Henry Kissinger, while national security advisor to President Nixon, described himself as the lone scout out ahead of the wagon train.

If there exists any remote possibility that American civilian casualties can be significantly reduced or effectively prevented in the most optimistic scenario, the moral imperative becomes pursuing and deploying that technology as rapidly as humanly possible. In contrast to the Wilsonians, legalistic restrictions such as the ABM treaty are not to interfere with this single-minded pursuit of the higher national good. Other states and their desires become only obstacles to be manipulated, not accommodated. As a consequence, this group remains exceptionally optimistic, almost giddy, concerning NMD technology development in both its current and future prospects. In fact, most implicitly assume that actual NMD deployment will unleash a multitude of future technological advances rendering the system even more effective than expected. Politically, their position becomes one of pushing its development as hard as possible with deployment occurring as soon as it can.

Testing and other technological failures are consistently explained away on the faith that expending even greater resources will conquer all problems. To outsiders and nonbelievers, technological optimism permeates this group to the point of unreality. In fact, this worldview believes that even a partial or possibly inadequate NMD system is a preferable deployment option to none at all. Given the uncertainties, potential enemies are deterred by the possibility that the NMD system might, in fact, work as claimed. All this leads the believers to be significantly less concerned about possible disruption of American foreign relations with either its allies or any possible adversaries. Those, being merely political problems, pale beside the overwhelming moral imperative of protecting American society from harm. This position also clearly rejects the implications of mutually assured destruction (MAD) as a national nuclear strategy, one leaving American society naked to nuclear attack with no defense possible or even attempted. That particular mutual suicide pact they see as incomprehensible for any national leadership.[14]

At the extreme, their view denies all the premises underlying nuclear deterrence, emphasizing the inevitability of nuclear holocaust as the consequence of human mistake and malice. That sense of inevitable doom in the absence of NMD fuels their passion, perceiving the other perspectives as Pollyannaish or treacherous or both. Only from a position of absolute military superiority, both defensive and offensive, can the United States be truly safe, or at least as safe as fallible humans can make things. This perspective implies a general enlarging and maintenance of American military capabilities at all levels. Whether such expenditures are politically sustainable over the longer term remains improbable. The United States, even during the Cold War, repeatedly pursued such strategies only to retreat from the fiscal implications.

In their more absolutist technological expressions, total defense was implied as the desired, even expected, outcome.    Ronald Reagan's early statements regarding SDI represent some of the clearest expressions of this vision of a world in which nuclear weapons are rendered powerless.    Technological reality has largely eliminated that view, at least publicly and now the usual goal is achieving significant reductions in risk.    Layered defenses imply a much higher capacity for destroying attacking missiles through redundancy.    One possible effect is that nuclear war becomes thinkable because the United States would survive any missile attack and be capable of retaliating overwhelmingly, devastating any enemy.    This understanding ironically also motivates the Wilsonians—both sides view NMD, if successful, as liberating the United States from fear of military reprisal.    Other forms of reprisal including economic reprisal may be more effective, especially in the energy area.    Each side draws different conclusions—Wilsonians perceive the potential for the United States to become overly aggressive while Believers see it simply as empowered— empowered in that the United States is able to project its power when necessary to influence events globally.    Since believers perceive the United States as a historically unique society, the expression of liberal values in an imperfect world, this empowerment will obviously be used for the greater good. Remember Ronald Reagan's invocation of the United States as the city on the hill, the beacon of liberty and freedom.

Others more simply argue that the government has a fundamental moral obligation to do whatever is technologically possible to protect its defenseless members.    Therefore, NMD becomes the logical extension of that moral imperative.    Their opponents, Wilsonians and Pragmatists, while acknowledging the imperative for maintaining an effective national defense, disagree strongly as to whether NMD will actually further that goal.    This disagreement is not resolvable because the initial value premises are so fundamentally disparate. Where one sees enhanced security, the other perceives heightened danger.

### Pragmatists

The pragmatists are not pacifists, a fact that becomes clear whenever they evaluate NMD's technological feasibility.    Like the believers and Wilsonians, they too have drunk deeply at the well of the technological imperative and its sibling, optimism.    Believers still hold strongly to the faith or expectation that NMD is, in fact, technologically possible, just not at this particular point in time. This expectation of the ultimate likelihood of technical success leaves pragmatists prisoners of events, especially technological ones.    But, it also explains their constant fluctuations in their support for NMD.    They perceive themselves as empiricists rather than ideologues as the other factions stake out their absolutist positions in attitude and rhetoric.

Their goal becomes not achieving perfection despite the jabs of the believers but rather demonstrating a clearly and unequivocally demonstrated capacity by NMD to work in real-time situations.    This capacity, they believe, does not presently exist.    The continual THAAD failures before testing success was achieved in the seventh attempt (in June 1999, with the first actual interception in August 1999) illustrates for these observers the inherent difficulties in assuring success in combat. Even though THAAD is a theater level system, the technical issues for NMD are thought to be similar, just more difficult. Plus, the Believers touted the 1991 Patriot "successes" as demonstrating the BMD concept. In a sense, those premature claims of operational success repeatedly come back to haunt the field. Striking a single target is one thing, stopping multiple, possibly evasive, warheads represents another entirely different level of difficulty.

Therefore, immediate NMD deployment in their judgment becomes disastrous at two levels. First, the United States expends enormous resources on a technology possibly doomed to operational failure or, more devastating, partial success. Pragmatists perceive economic costs as a very real world constraint—moneys are not unlimited and the value received must be maximized. Success is never assured when military technologies are stretched beyond their capabilities. More prudent use of funds could mean modernizing existing weapons systems or developing new ones, employing proven or doable technologies. For pragmatists, NMD is not a fetish but rather a program like all others that must meet the harsh test of practicality. NMD must be robust, accurate and reliable, issues clearly not totally resolved at present. Believers' rationalizations for each test failure ring hollow in their ears since the economic costs incurred are not trivial or apparently ending.

Second, NMD deployment in itself may produce a more politically unsettled world, significantly increasing the possibility of military conflict. Those conflicts will likely not rise to the level of actual missile attacks upon the United States but rather assume the form of lower-level events. Given the domestic divisiveness surrounding U.S. interventions overseas, the final outcome may be a reduced U.S. role in world affairs. In addition, other states have positioned their international postures, especially military ones, assuming no NMD regime operates outside the confines of the ABM treaty. Unraveling that agreement leads to a lessening of U.S. ability to negotiate new arms control measures or sustain those already in place. The Senate's rejection of the Comprehensive Test Ban Treaty in late 1999, for example, has already damaged U.S. capacity to influence other states' actions regarding such matters.

For pragmatists, arms control agreements have historically translated into cost efficient mechanisms for enhancing overall U.S. security. NMD becomes a disrupter of that cozy arrangement, without considering unresolved technical issues, and actually enhances national security. As a result, their political posture continues to be one of advocating further pursuit of NMD technology development while deferring any final deployment decision. Ongoing political events (domestic and international), combined with sporadic and erratic NMD technology demonstrations, drive their responses. The believers represent a constant goad for immediate deployment but the hard reality of testing reduces their political effectiveness. In part, the believers' frustration is that, in their opinion, since no weapons system can ever guarantee 100 percent efficiency, an unduly rigid and unfair standard is being imposed here. However, if an interceptor such as THAAD cannot work during six straight tests (successful only in the seventh), one's confidence is not dramatically increased regarding its likely reliability in the chaos of battle. Events do not become easier or simpler away from the controlled conditions of the test range, especially during the chaos of the battle at the rim of outer space. One must note, however, that the pragmatists are not fundamentally opposed to NMD as the Wilsonians are, both in principle and practice. From the Wilsonians' view, BMD encourages war and heightens the threat of violence while for Pragmatists NMD is but another arrow in the quiver.

A lesser factor but not an inconsequential one, is the thought that the large resources needed for NMD deployment could be better applied elsewhere. The application need not be military; the moneys could be used to address other national needs. This aspect of the pragmatists' worldview is not held equally strongly by all. But, unlike some Wilsonians, the possibility of alternative use is not ideologically driven, for example, programs for the disadvantaged. Pragmatists are more agnostic as to where any saved moneys might be used. Other organizational players within the DoD have already attempted to divert such funds for their purposes, arguing greater value received for the funds expended. Even Republican presidential administrations are not necessarily blank checks for military spending, especially in the absence of a direct threat to the United States.

## POLICY OUTCOMES

The situation has resulted in a policy process driven by the believers who continually force responses from the others. The Wilsonians reject entirely the very concept of NMD but the pragmatists hold the balance of decision. This produces the zigzag pattern so typical of the BMD policy process generally and NMD in particular. Threat definition first and then cost and technology effectiveness become the critical variables driving the policy process as perceived through the prism of foreign policy. All three are interrelated, but each has an independent effect upon policy deliberations and decisions at different points.

Figure 5.2 provides a perspective on the middle group, pragmatists, and illustrates how NMD policy is made. The three clusters are treated here as essentially equal in size—in fact, pragmatists constitute the largest groups followed by believers in more recent years, and finally by the Wilsonians. The intent of the figure is to make clear that the pragmatists lean in both directions. There exist adherents who lean toward the believer end but are troubled by the costs and practicality questions still extant.

**Figure 5.2**
**Conceptualizing the NMD Policy Process**

Wilsonians ⟵=======A=====➔ Pragmatists ⟵=====B===➔ Believers

Other pragmatists are attracted toward the arms control perspective but not with the same fervor as the Wilsonians. Their ambivalence comes with regard to the questions of compliance and verification of arms control agreements. Failures in either case can lead to adverse events endangering the United States. That possibility colors their response to the Wilsonians' advocacy of nonmilitary options.

Collectively, the pragmatists' support or nonsupport for NMD programmatically is very much time and event sensitive. The recent allegations of heightened rogue state or states of concern missile activity raises their willingness to consider the possibility of NMD deployment in a more favorable light. When pressed, their expectation or desire is to retain both aspects, the ABM treaty with its arms control aspect and NMD, running simultaneously if at all possible. If forced to choose, their decision will be heavily situational that is: driven by ongoing events both political and technological. Perfection in either NMD or arms control is not expected, rather the choice made reflects the immediate judgment of which approach would work best at that point in time.

For example, in Figure 5.2, the point "B" illustrates the pragmatists' general movement toward the believers' position over the past five years. The continual argument that the world is a threatening place has acquired more resonance in recent years with the demonstration of increasing missile capabilities by several states considered hostile. Prudence, both politically and militarily, moves the pragmatists to a posture more generally supportive of NMD. Wilsonians continue to argue the contrary but even their arguments become more technological in tone in order to elicit pragmatists' support. Pragmatists do not perceive the world as necessarily a benign one: therefore, one takes reasonable precautions. There is no rush to judgment but rather a continual hedging of one's bets as long as possible in an imperfect world. Believer attacks upon their commitment to national security are rejected as overly emotional and alarmist— the sky is not falling although the clouds may be darkening. For the Wilsonians, the question is, Does NMD make the clouds darker faster? The pragmatists hear both sides and respond based on their evaluation of the world and technological capabilities.

Point "A" reflects the periods after 1972 until 1983 and from 1989 until 1997 with regard to NMD. Pragmatists (or moderates) supported R&D efforts but resisted any rush to deploy. This reflected their evaluation that other approaches were more practical, including sustaining nuclear deterrence and initiating negotiations to reduce the threat of war. NMD as a program was perceived as both destabilizing and ineffectual, a deadly combination. However, prudence again dictated that NMD development be continued in the hope of future success. During those periods, Pragmatists and Wilsonians were effectively aligned although fundamentally divided on the long-term necessity for NMD.

Pragmatists' flexibility reflected the conceptual bases of their judgments: changing threat definitions, cost factors, and technology effectiveness. These specifics do change over time, meaning that their views on NMD change, albeit with a lag effect. The lag occurs because events may move faster than their attention to the issue. NMD remains an obsession for only one group, the Believers. So, the other factions have to be sensitized to the issue—an issue that already has a history to which new participants are quickly brought up to speed and enticed to join one side or the other. Continued stability in the international system negatively impacts the believers' ability to affect attitudes regarding NMD.

Such flexibility also means that policy can shift quickly from a more proactive NMD posture to one less so. The reality is that the institutional bias becomes one of sustaining NMD as a developmental program. One never knows what might happen in the unknowable future so one covers as many bets as possible. The consequence, however, is to maintain NMD development, always a strong policy possibility. The virtual disappearance of ABM issues in the later 1970s did not mean the program's demise as a developmental construct—those efforts continued to be resurrected in SDI.

A technology that exists, especially one as expensive as NMD has been to develop over the years is likely ultimately to be implemented. Otherwise, the money appears wasted. Even though present decision-makers did not pick out the original and subsequent allocations, inertia builds up over time, pushing the program forward. Final rejection of a program is extremely traumatic, as witness the B-70, the B-1 (cancelled by President Jimmy Carter and then brought back by President Ronald Reagan), the supersonic transport, and the Superconducting Super Collider. The more usual pattern is to finish a program once started—witness NASA and the International Space Station or the B-2 bomber (while reducing the number of planes actually built as costs escalated).

## CONCLUSION

National missile defense has become a political litmus test for certain political factions—one's support or nonsupport (and how fervent) automatically places one in a particular position on national security issues generally. Within the general NMD debate, those extreme views do not dominate but clearly influence the tenor and direction of the overall controversy at particular points in time. Wilsonians on this question are an embattled minority, but their more general advocacy of arms control approaches continues to draw support based upon demonstrated success at reducing military confrontation in the world at least at the nuclear level. Believers keep NMD alive as an issue, repeatedly drawing pragmatists to them because the world remains an uncertain place. Pragmatists, a shifting group in terms of membership, dominate the debate by their choices but cannot resolve it.

# NOTES

1. Peter D. Feaver and Richard H. Kohn, "The Gap," *The National Interest* 61 (Fall 2000): 29–37.

2. Robert Jervis, *The Illogic of American Nuclear Strategy* (Ithaca, NY: Cornell University Press, 1984) Chapter 1 provides some interesting examples of certainty amid ignorance.

3. Robert A. Bernstein and William W. Anthony, "The ABM Issue in the Senate, 1968–1970: The Importance of Ideology," *American Political Science Review* 68 (September 1974): 1198–1206.

4. Joseph C. Anselmo, "Commercial Space's Sharp New Image," *Aviation Week & Space Technology* (January 31, 2000): 52–54.

5. K.S. Jayaraman, "Imagery Deal Spurs Indian Policy Review," *Aviation Week & Space Technology* (January 17, 2000): 3, 20. Similar concerns arose over the possible use of satellite-based telephony by guerrillas in the border fight over Kashmir. K. S. Jayaraman, "India to Tighten Security on Mobile Communications," *Aviation Week & Space Technology* (July 3, 2000): 3, 20.

6. David N. Spires, *Beyond Horizons: A Half-Century of Air Force Space Leadership* (Peterson Air Force Base, CO: Air Force Command, 1997), 252–254.

7. Richard J. Samuels, *"Rich Nation, Strong Army": National Security and the Technological Transformation of Japan* (Ithaca, NY: Cornell University Press, 1994), 26–32.

8. Walter Russell Mead, "The Jacksonian Tradition and American Foreign Policy," *The National Interest* 58 (Winter 1999/2000): 23.

9. Ernest J. Yanarella, *The Missile Defense Controversy: Strategy, Technology, and Politics, 1955–1972* (Lexington: University Press of Kentucky, 1977), 146; "Poll Results Bolster Republican NMD Push," *BMD Monitor* 10 (27 January 1995): 22.

10. For example, in May 2000, the leading Republican presidential nominee, George W. Bush announced his support for a larger national missile defense program than what was termed the "flawed" Clinton system. The point was that his support while positive remained vague on specifics—the very issues that proponents often split over. Governor Bush signaled his support but maintained his flexibility to adjust to future conditions. Terry M. Neal, "Bush Backs Wider Missile Defenses," *Washington Post*, May 24, 2000, A01.

11. This rush to accelerate THAAD development drew opposition within the DoD itself from the department's director of testing and evaluation, but those internal objections were overridden in pursuit of the political necessity to demonstrate progress. Gopal Ratnam, "THAAD to Stay on Schedule Despite Call for More Tests," *Defense News* (December 20, 1999): 3, 50.

12. Yanarella, *Missile Defense Controversy*. 152; Bernstein and Anthony, "ABM Issue," 1198–1200.

13. David Callahan and Fred I. Greenstein, "The Reluctant Racer: Eisenhower and Space Policy," in Roger D. Launius and Howard E. McCurdy, eds., *Spaceflight and the Myth of Presidential Leadership* (Urbana: University of Illinois Press, 1997), 17–20.

14. Mark T. Clark and Brian T. Kennedy, *Why Nuclear War Is Possible: The Common-Sense Case for a National Missile Defense* (Claremont, CA: Claremont Institute, 2000), 2.

# 6

# Deployment Options or Guessing about the Shape of Things to Come

## INTRODUCTION

Decisions whether to deploy a national missile defense (NMD) are not simply yes or no choices but incorporate within their parameters related choices as to which specific deployment configurations to pursue. A building block or modular choice has been suggested—allowing speeding up or delaying deployment although, at a certain point, one is committed to a particular arrangement. The political realities over the past decade or so have temporarily converged upon one national missile defense profile as most likely to be deployed initially. However, this original choice has already expanded several times since its original delineation. In fact the immediate decision as to future direction will be determined after the completion of this volume by the George W. Bush administration. The exact arrangement chosen and the rapidity of deployment will reflect that particular administration's view of the situation. Blind acceptance of the Clinton design choice will not occur as testing continues.

The reality is that the ultimate placement of NMD interceptors remains unclear as even more elaborate options are proposed, reflecting shifting political and technical judgments. President Clinton provided one benchmark against which other deployment choices can be evaluated. That particular deployment attempted to fudge several issues by providing expanded national coverage while remaining at least partially treaty compliant. Thus, the Clinton plan envisioned first a limited deployment (a 100 land-based interceptors) as the foundation upon which later program increments could be built. For the believers, their goal remains establishing the maximum NMD deployment physically possible. The boundaries of their particular deployment proposals are presently unknown, pending future technology and political changes.

In this chapter, our approach will be to first present the logical possibilities for deployment, and then, using that framework, to discuss the proposed deployment approach that has been most recently pursued by the United States. Whether any actual deployment decided upon subsequently will match the Clinton proposal is less important than the reality that such a decision draws closer. In fact, by early 2000, some analysts were asserting that the proper question had become not if NMD deployment should occur but when it will happen.[1] Even though ideological proclivities may ultimately drive the decision of whether or not to deploy, fiscal realities and technology assessments will not disappear, given the pragmatists' continued centrality in the debate. Costs and mission success remain critical factors for which only guesstimates are available.

## DEPLOYMENT AS A PROBABILISTIC CHOICE

What infuriates many believers is their continued awareness that any deployment decision concerning NMD remains a probabilistic one rather than a straightforward up or down choice. President Clinton in September 2000 again demonstrated that reality. As has been discussed, NMD as a practical matter remains a hard question for policy makers, regardless of their personal commitment to the larger concept. This degree of difficulty arises from the political uncertainties created by often rapidly shifting threat perceptions, the always present cost factors, plus continued technological uncertainties. NMD still remains a program plagued with major unresolved cost issues—available projections as to probable costs vary dramatically depending upon the specific deployment configuration chosen and the estimator's perspective regarding the concept. These high cost figures are usually rejected by believers as deliberate efforts to delay or stop deployment. For example, initial official estimates in 1967 were for $5 billion while opponents aggressively argued budget numbers ten to twenty times higher. In many specifics, the believers were right in their estimates, but the consistent historical pattern in American defense policy has been that any high-tech weapons program comes in well over budget.[2] That brutal reality gives pause even to those generally supportive of the NMD concept. Reagan's pursuit of Strategic Defense Initiative (SDI) was dogged by continual questions regarding likely costs if his grander schemas were put in place. Fortunately, for Reagan, the real costs were never truly known nor was he in office to make those follow-up decisions.

The low cost at program initiation in 1967 reflected efforts to "buy into the system" and then come clean on costs later (by dribbling out the escalating increases over time). This "camel under the tent" approach has an unfortunate side effect that traumatically impacts future program development. Simply put, weapon cost estimates are usually defined as unrealistic for one of two reasons: (1) the cost estimate is so overinflated that it can be severely reduced with no program impairment; or (2) the estimate is so fungible that changes can be readily made with no harm to the program since budget growth will occur in the future anyway. Along the way, the expectation is that the NMD budget can be raided for other more pressing purposes that arise along the way. Reprogramming budget items is a long-standing and important part of Pentagon budget rituals—a process only marginally controlled by Congress. Congressional efforts during the Nixon administration to control subsequent executive manipulation of congressional appropriations were prolific in terms of forcing reports acknowledging the executive's actions but led to only marginal control over executive discretion. Congressional choices must come long before the actual program expenditures occur so that the simple passage of time alone erodes congressional efforts at control. Furthermore, congressional leaders are well aware that the response to executive actions comes after the fact normally, often a substantial gap in time. That fact increases congressional skepticism regarding likely projected budget outcomes for any one program since the executive manipulates apparent outcomes so frequently. Remember Congress' final decision to terminate the original Grand Forks anti-ballistic missile (ABM) deployment in 1975 came only after discovering that the Department of Defense (DoD) was going to terminate the program anyway. Legislative action only speeded up an executive decision already made but concealed from Congress. Constant alarms are sounded in the media (based on DoD leaks) concerning how any such cuts are leaving America naked before its enemies. Such alarmist and erroneous rhetoric reenforces congressional skepticism.

Back when the federal fiscal year began each July 1, an annual Washington springtime ritual along with the cherry blossoms was the announcement that the Soviets were coming—ten feet tall and carrying new superweapons. The weapons were always the ones the United States either did not have or possessed too few of. So, the obvious lesson to be drawn was for Congress to increase appropriations to redress these now obvious deficiencies. Cynics point out the convenient nature of such intelligence estimates and their timing. Now, the fiscal year begins October 1, but the same scenario plays out in the early summer months. The rogue states are coming, more powerful and crazier than ever. The point is that congressional skepticism is fed by these recycled budget-related crises, making apparently arbitrary reductions easy to justify since no one is believed.

More troubling for any quasi-rational budgeting process, high-cost growth may merely reflect the inherent difficulties in accurately estimating total costs for truly innovative military technologies. NMD clearly fits the image of being both an innovative and extremely difficult technology to successfully implement—a situation pregnant with significant potential for cost inflation and partial programmatic success. For example, the actual interceptor vehicle had not been used in NMD tests up through the end of the year 2000. Given its centrality for the final product's success, the difficulties encountered in developing the interceptor clearly signal higher costs and possible delays.[3]

Thus, even generally supportive presidents and Congresses may find the final cost numbers for NMD difficult to swallow, especially in the light of possibly rapidly changing threat perceptions. Such cost uncertainties provide opponents the leverage through which to attack weapons programs that are opposed on other grounds. As has been discussed, annual budgeting, practically speaking, repeatedly reopens all previously settled issues for another round of debate and decision. Over the years, congressional attention shifts and intensity wanes—meaning that opponents may mobilize sufficient strength to crimp program growth. In addition, threat perceptions being inherently ambiguous are not always the same for all parties, further reducing potential support. Unfortunately for NMD advocates, the world does not stand still, preserving the status quo. When the missile threat declines (at least perceptually), the pressures will tend toward reducing or eliminating unnecessary expenditures—or, more subtly, allow the stretching out of previous commitments so funds can be currently employed elsewhere. Short-term needs are often more pressing, overriding those distant issues. When threats are measured in decades, the tendency is to focus upon more immediate needs.

Even more thoroughly disruptive are competing defense needs. For example, continued troop deployments overseas demand resources now, and these are demands not deferrable or often programmable, given the suddenness with which certain crises arise. The crisis may not be new in the sense that the particular situation has dragged on for several years, but U.S. involvement may increase comparatively quickly. U.S. troop commitments in Somalia and Bosnia came after years of internal turmoil, but the commitment decisions were made comparatively quickly. Long-term technology development programs as a result are routinely levied to support the more immediate deployment. That possibility of diversion is further enhanced when severe political conflict exists over the program. In fiscal years 1999 and 2000, funds were added to support BMD development along with backlogged deployment and modernization needs. As indicated earlier, BMD generally and NMD in particular directly compete with other military service priorities. For example, the Space-Based Infrared System, SBIRS-Low, satellite constellation in the fall of 2000 was a candidate for cancellation despite its critical role for NMD. With the latter's deployment delayed, the air force attempted to shed that burden—one inherited from Ballistic Missile Defense Organization (BMDO) when its budget grew too large. The BMDO budget share was kept low profile in order to reduce its political visibility. SBIRS-Low now competes with other air force needs, new fighters, for example. The air force will probably not win but the message is clear, NMD in this case impinges on their critical interests.[4]

Once the 2000 presidential election occurred, almost regardless of whom was elected, the budget question returns to the table and will do so repeatedly. Republicans demand tax cuts and Democrats want new programs while both must act to preserve and reform Social Security and Medicare; the budget pressures will remain intense. NMD may rank as a priority ahead of many other

DoD programs, but it will have to kick into the "kitty" especially if the perceived missile threat remains distant.   NMD remains in concept future oriented since no one in authority has yet seriously suggested recreating SDI in all its grandeur with its capacity to adversely impact Russian capabilities to strike the United States.   The other likely missile threats are diverse but not equivalent to Russia even in its present state of comparative military decline.

## THE EVOLVING MISSILE THREAT ASSESSMENT

Missile threat assessments involve consideration of (1) capabilities, including present and projected; (2) intentions both current and future; and (3) predictions regarding future technology development.   All three factors contain substantial unknowns that can totally change the answers derived from first premises.   Capabilities as a concept simply refer to the other state's ability to successfully launch its ballistic missiles over known distances.   In practice, the range of their missiles is presumed to change—always to the disadvantage of the United States as more states acquire the ability to throw farther and more accurately their warheads.   These enhanced capabilities can come from internal development on purchase from other states.   This makes North Korea a critical player since its demonstrated desire is to sell its comparatively primitive missile technologies for hard currency to all comers.   Although primitive by U.S. and Russian standards, the weaponry marks a distinct improvement in accuracy and range for many potential customers.   That availability means that unequipped states may quickly acquire the military means otherwise denied them.   The Missile Technology Central Regime (MTCR) plus determined diplomacy can hinder proliferation but not totally stop it.   Those projected capabilities therefore become subject to widely divergent threat scenarios, based upon assumptions of expanded access to ballistic missile technologies.

Intentions represent the explicitly political component of the threat assessment process.   How does a particular national leadership assess its relationship with and toward other states.   More specifically, which national leaderships are so negatively motivated that their actions will be hostile toward the United States and its allies.   Is their current hostility situational in nature, based upon specific and addressable grievances or constant and generalized?   More critically, how intense are those attitudes—will hostile actions follow these attitudes?   Many states are ambivalent toward other states, especially their neighbors, but those feelings do not readily translate into hostile actions.   It is this fundamental disconnect between attitudes and actions that makes the threat assessment process so difficult; and prudence is not necessarily absent among national elites just because weapons are physically in hand.

The even more difficult aspect becomes determining whether the hostile intentions expressed or exhibited today will endure indefinitely.   State interests are permanent, but their active animosities may not linger.   Of necessity, intelligence estimates often project linearly into the future present political dispositions because the internal sources of change are outside U.S. control, possibly even its influence.   The United States often finds its best response is one of benign neglect while domestic groups within a society sort out their priorities. That distancing may produce anomalies in that changes in the other state's intentions may not be immediately recognized, leading to unnecessary provocations. The problem is that while capabilities can be thought to be reasonably clear (at least over time) because they represent identifiable physical phenomena, interpretation remains subject to the vicissitudes of human failings. The tendency therefore is to extrapolate the present into the future indefinitely until unequivocal counterevidence arises. Any such evidence, however, must overcome existing predispositions.

For example, Robert D. Walpole, CIA national intelligence officer for Strategic and Nuclear Programs, in evaluating Iran as a future threat, stated:

At the present time and for at least the next three years, we do not believe that the national debate is likely to produce any fundamental change in Iran's national security policies and programs. Recognizing the significant uncertainties surrounding projections fifteen years into the future and the potential for reformers' success in Iran, we have projected Iranian ballistic missile trends and capabilities into the future largely based on assessed technical capabilities, with a general premise that Iran's relations with the United States and related threat perceptions will not change significantly.[5]

The above presentation regarding Iran reflected all the ambivalence inherent in the intelligence estimation process, but its tone helps fuel pressure for NMD deployment.

Finally, assessment includes predictions regarding the direction and pace of future missile development. Technological development here does not refer to simply upgrading existing missile capabilities, which may involve merely incorporating standard technologies into otherwise deficient systems. For example, extending range and improving accuracy, while militarily significant, are not fundamental changes that move one's missile technologies to the next level. How fast and in what form will technological improvements occur? Do those advances change the strategic context by adding enormous complexity to each side's defensive and offensive calculations? For example, in building a NMD system, changes in penetration techniques can add measurable difficulties to the act of interception. In fact, major technological innovations may negate existing weaponry whether on the defensive or offensive side of the equation.

When one moves to directly consider the most likely ballistic missile threats against the United States and, by implication, its allies, several distinct scenarios arise. First, Russia and China by the size of their missile forces (especially in the former case) and relative sophistication represent one level of potential threat while a second group of states (North Korea, Iran, and Iraq) offer a more nuanced situation. Second, the threats in the latter group lay down the road time wise but substantial uncertainties exist as to how distant, in fact, the threat is:

**Table 6.1[6]**
**Selected Ballistic Missile Threats, Present and Immediate Future**

| Country | Status | Number | Approximate Range (km) | Approximate Payload (kg) |
|---|---|---|---|---|
| **China:** | | | | |
| CSS-N-3 | Operational | 12–24 | 1,700 | 600 |
| DF-31/JL-2 | 2003 | --- | 8,000 | 700 |
| DF-41 | 2010 | --- | 12,000 | 800 |
| **India:** | | | | |
| Agni 1 | development | --- | 1,500 | 1,000 |
| Agni 2 | development | --- | 2,000 | 1,000 |
| Surya | development | --- | 12,000 | --- |
| **Iran:** | | | | |
| Shahab-3 | 2000 | --- | 1,300 | 750 |
| Shahab-4 | development | --- | 2000 | 1,000 |
| Shahab-5 | development | --- | 5,500 | --- |
| **Iraq:** | | | | |
| Al-Tammuz | Development? | --- | 2,000 | --- |
| **North Korea:** | | | | |
| Taepo-dong 1 | 2000 | --- | 2,000 | 1,000 |
| Taepo-dong 2 | 2003 | --- | 4,000–6000 | 1,000 |
| Taepo-dong 2 ICBM | 2003 | --- | 12,000 | 200–300 |
| **Pakistan:** | | | | |
| Ghauri 1/ No/dong 1 | 1999 | 10 | 1,300 | 1,000 |
| Ghauri 2/ Taepo-dong 1 | development | --- | 2,000 | 1,000 |

Iran, Iraq, and North Korea are the usual suspects in the list of potentially threatening states. Third, India and Pakistan are even more distant concerns principally because of their nuclear weapons potential and their volatile regional context. The states most usually considered of interest in the NMD debate are described briefly in Table 6.1 in terms of their missile capabilities. Russia is excluded because its forces clearly overwhelm any presently projected NMD. Most of the evidence is accurate but deployment dates are estimates and are subject to dramatic shifts over short periods of time.

Russia and China are not officially considered objects of any projected NMD deployments although the latter state could be adversely impacted by U.S. deployment due to the comparatively small size of its missile forces. That uncertainty about U.S. intentions has triggered strong Chinese reactions despite repeated U.S. protestations of injured innocence. NMD deployment in principle would force an accelerated Chinese missile development effort in order to ensure their capability to penetrate possible U.S. defenses. U.S. strategists for thirty-plus years have taught the world the necessity of remaining technologically current with all potential foes. That message has been received and now blows back into the U.S. policy debate. Other states are not passive recipients of U.S. unilateral actions. Their domestic politics demand some response, how much is one of the unknowns in the equation.

Russia even under START I and II (Strategic Arms Reduction Talks) scenarios would possess sufficient missiles to saturate any early NMD arrangements. Whether that capability is sustainable in the event of a massive NMD deployment becomes less certain. For the Russians, their response might be influenced by evaluations of whether or not NMD will in fact work. According to Frances Fitzgerald, by the end of the Cold War, the Soviets had come to the conclusion that the SDI system could not be made to work effectively.[7] Thus, their concern declined, opening the door for the dramatic peace initiatives of the latter part of the 1980s. This view obviously stands on its head the notion that the Soviet Union collapsed due to fear of SDI.

Regardless, the present NMD debate is not conducted openly in terms of these two particular states. In the interest of world stability, Russia and China are defined as key stakeholders within the status quo, not to be disturbed excessively if possible. Competition tinged by cooperation characterizes U.S. policy toward both states. Verbal exchanges presently substitute for military ones but the potential exists for the latter, including employment of ballistic missiles in a nation-killing nuclear exchange.

The more relevant threat, at least in terms of the NMD debate, occurs among the less militarily advanced states. That situation has been characterized as follows:

The new missile threats confronting the United States are far different from the Cold War threat during the past three decades. During that period, the ballistic missile threat to the United States involved relatively accurate, survivable, and reliable missiles deployed in large numbers. Soviet—and to much lesser extent Chinese—strategic forces threatened, as they still do, the potential for catastrophic, nation-killing damage. By contrast, the new missile threats involve states with considerably fewer missiles with less accuracy, yield, survivability, reliability, and range-payload capability than the hostile strategic forces we have faced for thirty years.[8]

These states are assessed as actively working to acquire and expand their ability to engage the United States with ballistic missiles. Evidence to that point was their acquisition of newer missiles capable of longer ranges. North Korea was thought to be the state most immediately capable of developing an international ballistic missile (ICBM), the Taepo Dong-2/ICBM with two stages, which is physically capable of directly attacking some portions of the United States. The Taepo Dong-2 missile with a third stage could reach the entire United States. The limiting factor would be the small payload, meaning the most immediate weapons of mass destruction WMD would be biological or chemical. Warhead survival during atmospheric reentry would remain a technical issue to be solved unless outsiders such as Russia or China assisted.

Iran with its Shahab-3 with a 1,300-kilometer range has acquired the capability to reach Europe with further range extensions predicted. Russia has repeatedly been identified as involved in technology transfers to Iran, a fact that has been extrapolated to include a probable capacity to strike the United States by 2010. Such a capability was presumed to be very likely by 2015 as the domestic Iranian missile technology community matures through a combination of foreign assistance and growing experience. In fact, it is reported that Iran is already considering follow-on projects, the Shahab-4 and the Shahab-5 missiles, that clearly extend the range of its ballistic missiles to incorporate the United States. Iranian explanations that the boosters were potential space launch vehicles were not rejected, just extrapolated into a potential capacity for increased missile range.[9] Dual use of rockets has a long history, dating back to the V-2.

Iraq is currently hampered by the UN embargo on certain military technologies but not stymied in its pursuit of ballistic missile technologies. The obvious shortcut is purchase of a Taepo Dong-2 from North Korea, an option the United States is attempting to short-circuit through economic aid incentives to North Korea. Domestic development would take longer, reflecting start-up difficulties. Iraq's greatest impact would likely be within the Persian Gulf region in a manner similar to Iran, possibly disrupting states supported by the United States. Possession of ballistic missiles is most often a regional affair rather than a direct threat to the United States. Unfortunately, those regional neighbors are linked to the United States—a fact that draws the United States into the situation.

India and Pakistan are both developing medium-range missiles for use against their regional enemies (including each other) and possibly in India's case, China. The ongoing Kashmir border conflict provides a constant threat to escalate into a full-scale war. Pakistan has been assisted by North Korea and China according to some intelligence estimates. Neither state represents an immediate or projected threat against the United States, but both hold the potential to disrupt the peace because of their nuclear ambitions and ability to reach states such as China and eventually Russia and Japan.[10] It is against this background that the NMD deployment debate plays out.

## CONTINUING THE PROBABILISTIC COURSE OF DEPLOYMENT

A further complication becomes the unknowable fiscal realities affecting the federal government at the times when actual choices are made. NMD is not a single up-or-down choice but remains an issue destined to be revisited either annually as part of the general U.S. government budgetary cycle or at particular points when one developmental stage ends and the next begins. That occurred in September 2000 when President Clinton delayed deployment construction. The result will be, politically speaking, that the program will run the budget gauntlet again and again each year. Congress and the president will of necessity have to annually reaffirm their commitment or, at least, the intensity of their support as expressed in dollars. In principle, that is an easy choice in a rational actor paradigm—one makes the choice based upon the best available information at the time and then follows through on that decision. The problem is time and circumstances change. Information refers to the abstract level of military threat posed by others while circumstances describe the perceived likelihood of an attack by those states—two very different propositions.

When the rational actor paradigm works, decisions are made, based upon the best available intelligence. Unfortunately for decision finality, long-term programs encounter the situation where information changes quickly over time often even before the implementation phase is finalized. One can push forward,, based upon the original information regardless of its current fit to the new realities, or else further adjustments are made. Those adjustments open the issue up again. Given resource limitations, the latter most likely occurs, frustrating believers but considered responsible behavior by the pragmatists. What adds further confusion to this debate becomes the problem of whether those events occurring immediately prior to the decision are in fact truly changes or just foam on the ocean, to be swept away by later events more accurately reflecting reality. Even more disturbing for any implementation decision are events occurring subsequently—when new facts arise or different interpretations are attached to old facts. The 1967 deployment decision confronted that reality as its political and technological base eroded under the pressure of events. Later, public opposition became a major issue when ABM sites appeared in the neighborhood, changing domestic political dynamics. The public had been disengaged up to this point while NMD advocates assumed, possibly erroneously, that their support was assured once they become aware.

Intelligence estimates are not objective descriptions of events. Questions are approached from a particular frame of reference, often reflecting the new conventional wisdom and organizational imperatives. Threat levels may fluctuate for reasons unrelated to actual changes in the strategic environment. The CIA, for example, has been repeatedly criticized from both ends of the NMD debate for its estimates of likely missile threat. The agency struggles to remain objective while satisfying its political masters, who are split on the question. This situation arose in the late 1990s in assessing how quickly various states would acquire the capability to threaten the United States. After the Rumsfeld Report, there appeared greater convergence in the technology estimates but not in the intentions, the most nebulous aspect of the process. Whether the prediction convergence was real remains unclear but politically inescapable for an agency deeply immersed in the politics of national defense.

Drawing upon our earlier descriptions, the fungibility of the decision process, including the budget, can be seen in the meandering trail NMD traced across the 1980s and 1990s. President Reagan in 1983 proposed the Strategic Defense Initiative (SDI) as a major administration strategic and political priority. By 1984, the technology development and demonstration phase was underway albeit resisted by Congress in its more grandiose forms especially after the 1986 elections when the Republicans lost control of the Senate. That put SDI on a slower pathway, a situation not appreciably changed during the Bush administration. The slowdown reflected changing information; the Soviet

Union was clearly in decline while the missile threat posed by other states was not thought sufficiently pressing yet. In fact, the major Bush initiative was the Global Protection against Limited Strikes (GPALS), a downscaling of the larger SDI concept. This was the Bush administration's response to changes in the world, and it provided an underpinning for the new world order. The Clinton administration, upon entering office in 1993, effectively cancelled NMD. The new Republican Congress reversed that decision at least in principle in 1995. By 1996, the newest Clinton administration programmatic option was the "three plus three" program. In the spring of 1999, a fragile agreement was hammered out to render a decision on deployment in mid-2000 with deployment by 2005. Technical issues pushed that decision point later into 2001 as President Clinton deferred resolution to the new president. The point is simply that NMD decisions have proven more flexible than one might expect in the abstract. In sum, irrevocable choices have not existed, a distressing fact for believers but reality for most public policies such as NMD that are carried out over significant time periods. The opportunities for reconsideration are too plentiful for nothing to happen, given the lengthy time interval involved.

In addition, the blunt reality is that other national priorities exist, especially in the domestic sphere. In the absence of dire military threat or actual conflict, those domestic priorities will continue to dominate the agenda. For example, if the United States pursues and sustains its commitment to a balanced federal budget (or some reasonably close approximation), then the decisions regarding NMD expansion become even more problematic. A truly balanced budget demands that hard choices must be made between equally deserving national priorities. The Truman administration (and later even the Eisenhower administration in the 1950s) was much criticized for its cuts in defense spending during the interlude between World War II and the Korean War. These reductions, it was charged, left the United States badly weakened in the face of Soviet aggression. The criticism ignores the political reality that after the Great Depression and world war, tremendous political pressure mounted to sustain a balanced budget at almost all costs. The fear was that of spending the United States into economic oblivion, a view shared intensely by President Dwight Eisenhower.

Those pressures continued in at least an attenuated form until the Nixon administration (remember the Congressional Budget Act of 1974). After that point, the concept became largely rhetorical rather than action oriented. At present, the political momentum regarding deficit spending remains tentative—the rhetoric is mighty but economic times have been so good that the pinch has been nonexistent. If the economy falters, the national commitment to balanced budgets will be severely tested. If strong, then the budget choices may become truly divisive and politicized. In that environment, NMD is not particularly privileged unless there occurs a dramatic heightening in national threat perceptions. For example, China or Russia could again conceivably pose a dire threat although China is more distant, at least strategically. Even in decline, Russian strategic forces remain a significant military force. With refurbishing, that situation could continue for several decades even if strategic arms reductions continue.  In fact, it has been argued that a failure to refurbish their strategic forces may place the Russian government in a situation of use it or lose it regarding their nuclear forces, an interesting scenario since deterioration has occurred faster than any NMD deployment.  U.S. policy appears premised upon continued Russian debility, allowing attention to focus upon clearly less formidable military threats.

In the absence of such an overt threat to national survival, the pressure will center upon controlling the budget in several ways.  The most obvious coping mechanism becomes imposing across-the-board percentage budget cuts.  Here, effectively, the fiscal pain is evenly distributed across all programs although with possibly dramatically disparate impacts.[11]   For example, a particular program may be reaching its crescendo just as the reduction occurs, meaning the program ultimately fails.   Pleadings for special consideration are usually unsuccessful because protecting one program opens up the door for all others to seek special consideration.  Congress often employs such budgetary devices in lieu of making those hard programmatic choices.  As one recent example of the fiscal approach, the Republican Congress imposed a less than 1 percent across-the-board percentage reduction in the fall of 1999 in an effort to carve out some budgetary relief so as to continue pursuit of other pressing political goals, including tax cuts.[12]   Attempts to segregate defense budgeting from such unilateral reductions are likely only temporarily successful at best and are not politically sustainable over multiple years.  The political risks are thought to be too high unless the threat to national security is significant and self-evident such as armed confrontations or actual fighting.  Bold scenarios regarding future potential threats are difficult to sustain in times of apparent peace with no overt hostile actions by others.  Ugly words by others do not constitute acts of aggression although they may hurt one's feelings and create anxiety.  Given public apathy regarding international affairs, the threat will have to be fairly explicit and supportable by evidence not hyperbole.

Again, whether assuming a balanced federal budget or not, the political realities historically have been for Congress to stretch out many weapons programs, reducing the procurement amounts provided (buying fewer copies at ultimately a higher per-copy cost), or reducing the capabilities of those systems actually procured.  The practical and immediate effect sought is to reduce expenditures during the present fiscal year, pushing those to the out years when the hope is that the budget will be larger or the other critical budgetary demands will be smaller (an unlikely scenario).  The resulting ripple effects from these decisions can be totally disruptive, even counterproductive, programmatically. The program ends up costing much more than originally anticipated, accelerating the pressures to later impose even greater reductions. Program advocates can rage against the decisionmakers' faulty logic but the reality is that, from their broader perspective, the choice was both necessary and unavoidable.  Short-term needs override long-term commitments because, from the decisionmakers' perspective, the commitment is in fact being met.  Better half a loaf than nothing at all is their judgment.  Given patience, the program gets most of what it needs—unfortunately, late, possibly short, and at greater cost.

All of the above budget stratagems were employed when deficit spending was the rule, and the political pressures or incentives will become even more chilling in a balanced budget environment. Thus, fudging the issue remains one very possible option because the external threats NMD confronts represent only estimates of the future rather than concrete events. These predictions are predicated upon accurate information concerning capabilities and even more reliable knowledge concerning other states' intentions. Intentions are the most fungible question of all since a simple change in leadership may move a state in a dramatically different threat direction. States do have permanent interests, but there exists great play in how those are exactly protected and pursued in practice. In fact, this is a lesson the United States has been learning over the past decade or so. U.S. intentions with regard to many states formerly its adversaries are in a state of flux as are theirs with regard to the United States. Given the inherent uncertainties in the intelligence-driven threat estimate process, there will exist sufficient fluidity to permit the other choices desired by political incumbents. For those Congress, they mostly include protecting their personal political position by bringing benefits directly to their constituents. NMD supplies such benefits to some officeholders, but likely too few to stave off all budget threats. Given these sordid political realities, the cost of NMD will be a critical question. As one can see in the Table 6.2 those costs are not insignificant. Anti-ballistic defense expenditures are estimated to have totaled at least $123.5 billion over the history of the effort through 1999. Table 6.2 lays out the distribution over time across program components or at least major categories. The figures are in terms of constant 2000 dollars. The point is that NMD and the other forms of BMD have proven expensive to develop, test, and yet not deploy.

**Table 6.2[13]**
**BMD Costs From the Beginning**

| Program | Period | Estimated cost (2000 constant dollars) |
|---|---|---|
| No explicit program | Pre 1962 | $1.6b |
| Nike Zeus | 1962–1965 | 3.5b |
| Nike X | 1962–1969 | 10.0b |
| Safeguard | 1968–1978 | 23.1b |
| Other BMD programs | 1962–1996 | 16.6b |
| SDI/NMD/TMD | 1983–1999 | 68.7b |
| Total | | 123.5b |

Since 1998, the deployment question has picked up greater intensity with escalating cost figures part of that package if expanded area coverage is required. Opponents such as the Council for a Livable World and the Coalition to Reduce Nuclear Dangers have used the constantly shifting official cost estimates to push hard the idea that the total costs are effectively unlimited. Their estimate in April 2000 totaled $120 billion through 2015. Such calculations included the possibility for deployed space-based lasers and interceptors, both options seriously suggested by proponents although down the road.[14]

The exact specifics of the cost estimates were not as important as the reality that the uncertainties as to which deployment option to pursue made all such predictions somewhat suspect. Believers want essentially a blank check in order to ensure the maximum coverage possible—that vagueness however plays to opposition appeals to the pragmatists. Pragmatists are not cost indifferent, rather their view is that one balances off conflicting claims for scarce resources, as budgets are not unlimited. Cost factors had been important back during the early 1970s debate over ABM deployment, especially when compounded by persistent effectiveness and reliability issues.

The point of this brief discussion is only to reemphasize the fragile nature of any NMD deployment decision. Once, the decision is reached by the president and Congress to pursue deployment, the program is clearly not assured of a smooth automatic implementation process. Instead, independent judgments based on continually updated information will continue to appear, regarding the scope, pace, and costs of the agreed-upon program. Richard Nixon was not opposed to NMD on principle, but his decision to pursue what became the ABM treaty in 1972 effectively signaled the end of the original NMD deployment. That presidential judgment reflected a mixture of domestic politics, budget needs, and political strategy commingled with military policy. To reemphasize the obvious, in the American political process, especially regarding its budgetary manifestations, no decision is ever truly final. The incrementalist nature of that process has the effect of undermining any such finality. Programs are continually being reengineered or tweaked. NMD is especially vulnerable to such incursions because of its long-term nature and the strong budgetary requirement for continued technology development. The latter means continued high levels of investment if and when the race between offensive and defensive weapons systems accelerates again. To assume a stagnant security situation is to ignore history.

One of the underlying issues not clearly addressed in much of the present discussion regarding NMD is the dynamic relationship existing between offense and defense. This question nourished Secretary of Defense Robert McNamara's reluctance to field a thick ABM field. The Soviets could overpower it through offensive innovations just as the United States could do to the Soviet Galosh ABM system. Many now automatically assume that NMD will be effective against presently envisioned primitive ICBMs for long periods because those states supposedly lack the technological capacity to upgrade quickly. That may prove a wish rather than a fact since the political incentives to upgrade for those states so motivated would be extremely high. To not do so is to accept political subordination to the United States, an unacceptable situation domestically for those leaders. This dimension has become muted recently because of the declining state of Russian missile forces where no upgrades are imminent. However, this ignores the dynamics created if approval of NMD deployment occurs. Russian leaders may feel compelled to speed up improvement of their offensive missile capabilities. Otherwise, they fear becoming dominated by the United States. Russian expertise and experience still exists although they are a depreciating asset the state merely lacks capital investment. NMD, even if approved in 2001, therefore will not have a free ride as others react.

There appears a feeling more than a factual assertion that the defense has caught up with the missiles most likely to be employed against the United States. The greater question is whether the technology, superior or not, will in fact work when required. A revealing quote regarding this issue came from Lieutenant General Ronald Kadish, BMDO Director, in May 2000: "One of the things I worry about a lot is that it's one wire that shakes loose in the system that prevents the test from being successful, or it's that plug or the water molecule in the plumbing system that gets you. It doesn't have to do with fundamental design as much as the complexity of the stuff we're building."[15] The general was referring to the testing situation, but his comments obviously extend to operational situations. Ironically, on July 7, 2000, General Kadish's worry occurred when the hit-to-kill (HTK) vehicle failed to separate from the booster, aborting the test. His comments subsequently were that the failed sequence was not even on his list of possible problems.[16]

Technologically speaking, NMD represents a dramatic example of modern warfare—automated, highly precise with unforgiving minor flaws. It is against this background that NMD deployment options are considered, both those thought possible and the ones being pursued in the short term. The question of what should be deployed remains open, even if the Clinton options (to be discussed) are pursued in the short term or immediately abandoned.

## DEPLOYMENT AS A CONTINUUM CHOICE[17]

Over the course of 1998–1999, the political tide dramatically shifted regarding the question of BMD generally and NMD in particular. The change occurred at several levels: the most obvious being an upgrading of the missile threats existing across the globe and, more subtly in the U.S. government's unacknowledged (at least publicly) view, the idea that NMD may become essential if the United States is to continue as an effective global power. These two levels are clearly interrelated although both were heavily marinated in partisan politics as the 2000 presidential election approached and passed. The critical contextual changes had come earlier in the political sphere, both domestically and internationally. Domestically, the shift in partisan control of Congress from Democratic to Republican replenished the reservoir of believers committed to some form of NMD deployment. More critically, this change also shifted the nature of the debate by creating a strong current of strongly held views always favorable to the concept.    Thus, technology failures were no longer politically devastating events but readily explained away as simply evidence of the Clinton administration's failure to aggressively pursue BMD technology development generally.    That can be readily seen in the tepid political response to the failed NMD tests in January and July 2000.    Those results were not considered devastating to the argument since worldviews now drive the debate.    The failures became bumps in the road rather than showstoppers.

Essentially, the argument becomes one that several "rogue states" or "states of concern" are moving toward establishment of effective ICBM capabilities faster than earlier intelligence projections had suggested.    For example, the Chinese are now testing an ICBM, the Dong Feng-31, with a 5,000-mile range, capable of reaching the United States with a 1,500-pound payload.[18]    As a consequence, according to NMD supporters, the missile threat to the United States grows steadily more serious, forcing NMD deployment as the most prudent and immediate measure.    Whether NMD deployment might generate a stronger and more immediate Chinese response is not thought germane to any American decision.    Their actions are presumed to be hostile to U.S. interests generally.

The latter part of the syllogism is not necessarily self-evident to all because the extent of deployment that is deemed absolutely necessary becomes the issue. The two are interconnected but not so compellingly that a decision regarding the first leads automatically to the second—that is: deciding what level of threat exists presently or will at some future point does not necessarily foreshadow NMD deployment as the obvious choice.    The latter continues to be heavily affected by cost and technology development factors.    That disconnect is what has made NMD policy development appear so erratic at least for Believers.[19] One must also remember the United States endured a long-term often-threatening confrontation with the Soviet Union without NMD—an adversary clearly much more dangerous in regard to its missile capabilities than any of the rogue states individually or collectively.    Thus, the most relevant historical precedent supports no NMD deployment, instead relying upon deterrence broadly defined along with disarmament and proliferation initiatives. Figure 6.1 lays out aggregate U.S. national-level NMD options in a very simplified form. Theater defense in principle represents the one point of agreement or departure and for that reason is excluded from the figure.

**Figure 6.1**
**NMD Deployment Coverage Continuum**

| Threat: | **Low** | Single | Multiple | Multiple-diverse | Multiple-unknown | **High** |
|---|---|---|---|---|---|---|
| | | +----------+---------------+-----------------------+ | | | |
| Coverage: | **Minimal** | Single Site (point/minimal area defense) | Multiple Land (area) | Sea Based (national) | Space Based (global) | **Maximum** |

Low ⟵===============Cost========================⟶High

TMD is limited in scope (by definition) and is treaty compliant at least generally in its current developmental configuration. Over the longer haul, that latter limiting characteristic may disappear, but presently TMD fits within the treaty parameters governing BMD although the THAAD and Navy Theater Wide (NTW) systems are on the margins. The latter lags behind the other developmentally although both still confront major technological issues. There have obviously been controversies over TMD because the boundary remains definitional rather than strictly physical. A highly capable TMD system can have national level consequences, especially for states such as Japan and Taiwan. Space-based applications still lie over the horizon, dependent upon future policy choices and technological success. The larger questions for TMD remain feasibility and effectiveness, given that the time pressures for achieving interception grow even more compressed with little opportunity for recovery if the incoming warhead is missed on the first pass. However, for Japan, TMD effectively constitutes its NMD profile since the most immediate (in terms of time) threat North Korea, is located so close.[20] Its capabilities with reference to China are more problematic, especially as Chinese ICBM capabilities improve.

Arrayed along a single continuum, two variables are being conceptualized, compared, and linked for analytic purposes with costs displayed as generally escalating from left to right as the NMD system becomes more complex and inclusive (or moves from thin to thick). On the topside of the continuum, the threat potential is ranked from low to high in terms of the number and diversity of possible ballistic missile threats. As depicted, the threat environment escalates from a single state or several states possessing minimal missile resources. Multiple states may possess limited ICBM capabilities but only one or two may in fact constitute a near-term security threat. Diplomacy and economic linkages likely will reduce the number of potentially hostile states especially since the United States is a status quo power with no territorial aspirations. The United States is not necessarily disinterested its interests may just differ. Weapons are more likely aimed at one's immediate neighbors with whom such territorial and other disputes are particularly relevant and active.

Obviously, this scenario excludes the Russian Federation, even in its present reduced condition as a result of the START I–driven weapons reductions and any additional reductions achieved through START II, if implemented. Russian missile capabilities are significantly reduced but not insignificant, which moves them clearly beyond the category of a minor missile power. Continued deterioration of their missiles and warheads may prove a more potent inhibitor on their actions than any NMD deployment. This situation historically was reflected in the earlier 1967 evaluation of China when domestic political considerations forced an obviously reluctant Johnson administration to proceed toward initial ABM deployment despite doubts about Chinese capabilities. The Soviets were not the immediate objective although that changed subsequently. As was pointed out earlier, the Johnson administration immediately hedged its bets in order to keep ABM deployment small by approaching the Soviets regarding strategic weapons negotiations at the fall 1967 Glassboro Summit.

Those efforts ultimately bore fruit in the ABM and SALT I treaties, finally leading to termination of the original ABM deployment by 1976.

The next point identifies multiple potential adversaries, each possessing a comparatively small but possibly growing missile capability. Their collective capabilities might be significant but that depends upon coordinated action by all parties. Individually, such states are not peer military competitors. The question here becomes the reliability of their missiles, combined with their estimated effective range. Developing and building ballistic missiles still remains difficult although purchase of such weapons is possible, but the more likely avenue is hiring international technical assistance. The latter occurs because international sanctions still inhibit, although do not totally prevent, the direct export of relevant missile technologies. States engaging in such exchange activities have found outside scrutiny difficult to deflect while economic incentives have been used to reduce their willingness. The United States has essentially bribed North Korea to slow its export traffic in ballistic missile technologies and nuclear weapons development. Other states may not be susceptible to such incentives, but one does not know until the opportunity arises. North Korea was once thought resistant to such economic incentives.

Regardless, there are now likely an increasing number of states capable of reaching the United States with ballistic missiles of various types and capabilities. Their collective capacity to inflict serious harm, however, could be great in the future, but these states presently remain too politically fragmented to implement any coordinated attack. This threat scenario, however, has become the focal point for the current debate over who possesses what weapons with which malign intentions. Answering these questions unequivocally is difficult because, for the intelligence evaluation process, one is commingling dimly understood military capabilities (present and future) with rapidly changing intentions.

By using the phrase "dimly understood," we are referring to the surprises that regularly occur when states demonstrate missile capabilities greater than expected. For example, the North Korean 1998 launch over Japan employed a third stage, an unanticipated occurrence expanding the missile's range. The Iranian missile test also, in 1998, demonstrated a longer range than originally expected. Other states work very aggressively to limit American intelligence access prior to events. A similar occurrence happened regarding the Indian nuclear tests in 1999—U.S. surveillance satellites were essentially spoofed prior to the explosions. This latter event was particularly disturbing since U.S. policy makers have heavily relied upon such national technical means to monitor different types of treaty compliance since 1972. These surprises are what keep the intelligence collection and analysis process so unstable; widely differing reports may be produced over very brief time spans.

Intentions are the most difficult to accurately access and interpret. Separating rhetoric from likely behavior becomes difficult because the involved parties do not act alone, even within their own body politic. Shifting domestic political coalitions and leaders can drastically change what finally translates into policy, especially during situations of international conflict. History is replete with national elites stepping back from a potential military confrontation while others plunge forward into the fray, often in a manner inimical to their ultimate political survival.    Fortunately, most elites are concerned with societal and personal self-preservation.  The problem for the United States becomes knowing when the situation has deteriorated to the point of anticipating probable military conflict.  Events in the Persian Gulf region and the Balkans have reenforced the reality that intentions are often obscure until the other party finally acts.

Thus, when combined with continuing intelligence assessment problems regarding capabilities, the situation becomes extraordinarily complicated.  In response, believers project the worst possible scenarios while pragmatists assume that any possible political divisions among and within those states will undermine their unity of purpose in striking against the United States.  Mere possession of equivalent weapons does not automatically lead to alliances, de facto or otherwise, especially for states widely scattered across the globe.  Their concerns and goals are likely too diverse plus over time these several states will develop greatly differing economic and political relationships with the United States, increasing or decreasing the potential threat.

Possession of BMD capabilities does not automatically mean the demise of diplomacy.    Regimes may be hostile but leaderships change, as do circumstances.    Analysts such as Samuel P. Huntington have argued that civilizational factors will meld such actors together in an overarching alliance of hostility to the West, especially the United States.[21]    These civilization differences are based upon fundamentally opposed religious and cultural characteristics that predispose certain groups of states to oppose the United States and the western civilizations it leads within the larger world context. Those states are held together as a power bloc by shared religious and cultural perspectives.  That scenario remains possible but assumes that the United States will not systematically act to disrupt economically if not diplomatically such collective efforts.  The United States no longer assumes an isolationist view of itself but rather acts assertively to protect its interests.  Unless another peer military power emerges to provide leadership, their diverse interests will make such counteralliances difficult to sustain.  Also, even within such groupings, major differences exist over social and economic policy, reflecting differences in their national circumstances.  Despite their Islamic character, for example, the oil states have different priorities than those states not possessing vast oil reserves.    In fact, the antagonisms among Islamic states can at times be as intense as any of their conflicts with industrial states.[22]

The third point along the continuum identifies a situation when a coordinated or larger-scale attack could be mounted.    This situation encompasses both the possibilities for multiple states cooperating in an attack and the existing situation of a large-scale attack by the Russian Federation.  In principle, China would be rolled into this scenario since the threat projection here becomes both large, diverse, and diffuse, with attackers possibly striking from several directions.  For example, the threat might come from land-based ICBMs located in different states or submarines stationed closer to the United States.  In response to such a hypothetical situation, U.S. policy after the demise of the Soviet Union aggressively pursued eliminating as many non-Russian ICBM forces as possible, the effect being to simplify the strategic environment. If the Ukraine or Belarus had fired missiles, U.S. retaliatory strikes would have ignited a Russian response since the missiles would have tracked along paths coming from the direction of Russia. Presently, Russia and China (the latter mostly in the future) constitute the two largest potential missile threats. China's capabilities (less than fifty missiles presently) are expected to increase although the future growth curve remains unknown. The other unknown factor is whether these two states could coordinate their efforts—a situation unclear presently and dependent upon future events. Each, China and Russia, has security concerns regarding the other since their adjoining border areas remain volatile and relatively porous, given their geographic isolation and distance from each state's metropolitan areas—especially for Russia. This question is even more pressing for Russia, given great disparities in population along the respective border areas. Illegal Chinese migration into the Russian Far East remains a flash point.

Within this context, the missile threat's scale and diversity are perceived as being at least a magnitude more threatening. The weapons employed are more robust and effective than those possibly launched in the second scenario. One underestimated aspect of ballistic missile technology is that the farther the missiles are sent, the more brutal the physical forces encountered by the vehicle and its warhead. Included in that calculation must be very critical issues of accuracy at impact, especially over such extremely long distances. Accuracy-at-impact problems plagued early ICBM research, an issue partially resolved by lighter but more powerful nuclear warheads, which allowed for some inaccuracy. The Circular Error Probable (CEP) remained large—several kilometers for years. The original V-2s had a CEP of seventeen kilometers but that still resulted in over 20,000 casualties in London during the missile bombardment. The greater the accuracy, the more efficient the weapon becomes in achieving its military goals, meaning individual missiles can be diverted to strike more targets rather than requiring redundant strikes upon the same target in order to ensure its destruction. Nuclear weapons allow some inaccuracy, especially against soft targets but conventional warheads have a more limited margin for error. A nuclear weapon with a CEP of one kilometer would still devastate a city. Thus, an attack upon the United States will most likely involve weapons of mass destruction although not nuclear ones.

Finally, the latter point on the continuum refers to large-scale capabilities wielded by unknown parties. This attack could come from a multitude of sources. "Unknown" simply refers to the fact that the future by definition remains unknown—new adversaries may arise or missile technological capabilities may dramatically change, empowering a state presently perceived as disadvantaged in ballistic technology. For example, China could significantly accelerate its missile program growth and development. In the first case, an adversary may acquire such assets through actual purchase or other means including disintegration of an existing state. This, in fact, occurred when the collapse of the Soviet Union temporarily posed a major proliferation issue. Second, technology change, since it is always ongoing, may provide an unexpected breakthrough, advantaging those earlier perceived as weak in terms of missile technology. This is a specific manifestation of the ongoing revolution in military affairs, an event totally reshaping the military environment. Such a radical change, while unlikely, remains possible. The result leads to temporary strategic instability during which NMD is defined as a bridging device for sustaining national security.    The usual pattern, however, remains steady improvement in known technologies by those not in possession of such capabilities earlier.    In truth, the most likely immediate participant would be a reinvigorated Russian missile force.    Time continues to erode that technology base, but in the short term (the next decade), its revitalization could occur with the most immediate impact being the refurbishing of existing weapons on an accelerated basis while new ones are developed.

## DEPLOYMENT OPTIONS

The bottom half of the above continuum identifies the various deployment options. Single-site terminal or minimal area defense is an option that is likely not politically viable currently because of its intrinsic geographic limitations. The operative term here is minimal defense since a single-site area defense remains the most likely national deployment option, but the coverage will be maximized by utilizing several site locations to expand coverage. Whatever coverage limitations exist is a direct function resulting from a terminal or minimal-area defense configuration.    Deciding what exactly to protect has become politically controversial in several ways. First, who is to be protected would become more difficult than in late 1960s when then-current strategic doctrine clearly identified sustaining assured retaliation capabilities along with the national command authority as the critical nodes.    Therefore, Grand Forks and Washington became the logical choices.    One protected an ICBM field while the other sheltered the national command authority.

Such a choice is no longer politically viable since the believers have made total national defense a moral necessity; therefore, it is not to be compromised. This places greater pressure to deploy an NMD configuration that is maximally structured to cover the contiguous states along with Alaska and Hawaii. Technologically speaking, that stresses the system since outlying areas will be more susceptible to attack especially by submarine-launched missiles.    The answer becomes the believers' view that the goal is expanding the system as quickly as possible to ensure maximum coverage.

Second, believers reject this initial option because, politically speaking, due to its geographically limited nature, this particular deployment remains too easy to kill off politically, as happened earlier.    Termination of such an NMD deployment would have minimal political effects because so little actual geographic area was covered.    More realistically, a truly single point or minimal-area terminal defense arrangement becomes simply an enhanced TMD capability against submarine-launched missiles.    Therefore, a more realistic political proposition would be deploying such a partial system which is clearly conceptualized as the initial building block within a larger area defensive arrangement.    Such an understanding, however, would mimic the 1960s deployment when the believers perceived that decision as the entering wedge for further ABM expansion, only to be disappointed when the ABM treaty, assisted by rapidly developing offensive missile technologies, negated the original decision.

In fact, this precedent bolstered the believers' profound distrust of the Clinton administration despite its earlier 1999 public acknowledgment that NMD's time had come.    The imprecision of that understanding was not in the words per se but rather their awareness that the Clinton administration had not come on board NMD wholeheartedly.    Instead, the agreement merely provided the administration and Vice President Al Gore political cover against allegations of neglect of national defense during the 2000 presidential election.    The subtlety came in their abrupt realization that the administration was not attempting to placate the believers, who are beyond hope in the administration's judgment, but the public at large, who ultimately decides elections.    By agreeing, in principle, the political edge was excised from the issue.    In form, a possible repeat of the 1967 ABM deployment, choice was created.    Lyndon Johnson defused any potential controversy regarding ABM during the 1968 presidential election year by acceding to a very limited initial deployment albeit one that could be expanded or easily cancelled.

The failure of the original ABM deployment to automatically roll forward has undermined any simple faith among believers as to the historical inevitability of their position.    The reality has been that political solutions rather than NMD deployment have been the dominant historical pattern.    However, this judgment must be strongly qualified in that research and development (R&D) has continued (albeit with varying emphases at particular points in time) as a hedge against future missile threats.    For the believers, vital momentum is continually being lost although never completely extinguished through this continual stop-and-start political process.    What this means is that the possibility of pushing forward with greater emphasis always remains a very plausible future policy option.    Rather than shutting down completely, the essentials are maintained in place, making fairly abrupt changes in policy emphasis entirely possible.    One saw that scenario played out in the continuing saga of NMD policy over the course of the Clinton administration (1993–2000).    This is especially true, given that most of the effort until 2000 focused on various stages in the R&D process so that one could always pick up the thread again.    In fact, the developmental emphasis was truly easier as long as the core team was kept intact.    As was discussed earlier, the THAAD program suffered when critical personnel moved on to other programs reflecting the slowness of the program's development.    Those individuals were desperately needed elsewhere by Lockheed Martin, a corporation in serious distress from management shortcomings.

The other points arrayed along the deployment continuum increase both NMD coverage and flexibility.    Multiple sites reflect a thicker NMD defense but one still oriented in particular directions, based upon threat analysis.    This is the option the believers have pursued for over a generation since the late 1950s and the inception of NMD as a concept.   SDI was a variant in that developmental process; as it was scaled back, the defensive configuration became even more conventional in approach.   The intention here is to provide maximum security against multiple strategic threats defined in advance.   By doing so, the NMD system can be oriented for maximum effectiveness at least total cost.   The difficulty is that now the possible threats are no longer as clearly delineated as during the Cold War era; therefore, an NMD deployment must retain some flexibility regarding the direction of likely threats.   As a result, what becomes unstated is how NMD will be exactly positioned although the limitations imposed by the ABM treaty would likely be superseded since most proposed deployments would ultimately exceed the restrictions of the two original locations (later limited to one in 1974 by a supplemental protocol).   Even if the deployments are restricted to two locations, they are unlikely to be the same sites chosen earlier due in part to changes in NMD technologies and strategic philosophy.   Russian willingness to allow treaty changes appears minimal under any circumstances.

This deployment approach essentially "solves" the ABM treaty problem of restrictions by ignoring or rejecting them.[23]   The view is that the United States must do whatever is necessary to make the NMD technology nominally effective, regardless of any international restrictions.   That political "nonpolitical" approach has been consistently rejected through 2000—Meaning that this thickened defensive alignment remains only an option, not a reality. Republicans in Congress since 1999 have perceived this approach as an achievable political goal regardless of the Clinton administration's obvious reluctance.   Their earlier optimism reflected their expectation that a Republican president would assume office in January 2001.   That eventuality has occurred but budgetary constraints could nullify even that commitment.   Remember earlier, a reluctant Democratic administration initiated the first ABM deployment, only to have that action terminated in a controversial political process crossing two successive Republican administrations.   In addition, President Reagan never fully confronted the economic price for full SDI deployment, only the early developmental costs, which were steadily escalating. The annualized budget process (as has been discussed) reenforces this concern for immediate costs because each year decisionmakers must readdress the question of how much is enough.   As other programmatic demands especially domestic ones press in on a new administration, even strongly supportive presidents may waver because of other priorities.   The year 2001 is clearly not 1969, the strategic imperatives are different.

Cost factors clearly enter here, however, because such an expansive approach contains no intrinsic limitation except total saturation coverage. Believers often vehemently argue that continued failure to protect American society from the threat posed by ballistic missiles is intrinsically immoral. Therefore, once the deployment process begins, who can be left out?   No one. In reality, costs may make such choices necessary, forcing believers to announce who are the chosen, a politically divisive move if the public's threat perception increases markedly.   If the threat is real and the NMD systems work, why should particular regions be left naked before the enemy? Or, the coverage provided remains tentative based on best projections of future threats. Changes in coverage would follow changes in threat assessment. Depending upon the original deployment option pursued, which could prove an expensive decision if a system has to be reoriented. In that sense, space-based and sea-based NMD become more cost effective (assuming development costs are affordable). Land-based systems at some point become fixed sites, expensive to reconfigure. Sea- and space-based systems according to projections, are much more expensive to develop but also are much more flexible in terms of deployment changes.

Earlier, that question never arose in any significant way because the initial deployment in 1967 was specifically tailored for a limited threat, China. In addition, there existed (as does presently) significant doubt as to the NMD system's actual effectiveness. Persistent doubts concerning technological effectiveness meant that no one really felt left out by not being covered by the ABM system. Indeed, once expanded, citizens in the Washington, D.C., and Chicago areas became generally hostile to ABM deployment occurring in their neighborhood. This not-in-my-backyard (NIMBY) attitude has not vanished from American politics, and has been reinforced by a vast arsenal of political and legal weapons aimed at hindering such decisions and their rapid implementation. During war, the rules loosen up but that is too late in the nuclear age. For example, the current deployment configuration slated for Alaska required an environmental impact statement—a demand unthinkable in an earlier generation for a defense project.[24]

Unless the global threat perceptions held by Americans worsen dramatically, public reluctance to have an NMD system built nearby could render deployment very politically volatile. Single-site deployment does not confront the same political resistance because the most likely sites are initially in Alaska, possibly later in Grand Forks, North Dakota. The latter was the original ABM site for the earlier system deployment while the former occurs in a more remote geographic area, comparatively speaking. Opposition would remain both more muted and regional in scope although NMD's more general opposition is unaffected by its specific location. Ship-based deployment options likewise provide greater political cover since deployment there would likely be over the horizon from shore, out of sight and out of mind. Space-based deployment is even more removed from public awareness.

Sea-based NMD options have become a seriously discussed possibility only comparatively recently.[25] This reflects both technology improvements (although still far short of deployability in an NMD modality) and the changes occurring in threat perception. Latent U.S. interest has been fanned by the explosive growth in official Japanese interest in missile defense. North Korea's erratic and secretive regime has inflamed Japanese fears, especially after a failed satellite launch in August 1998 during which the launch vehicle traveled over Japan, shedding several stages as it flew overhead. That event conclusively demonstrated Japanese vulnerability to missile attack—a situation for which there existed no defensive capability or completely effective early warning system. As a consequence, the United States and Japan are intensifying their

TMD cooperative projects. For Japan these TMD projects are the equivalent to NMD efforts by the United States.[26] The immediate threat perceived by Japan is so geographically close and the ballistic missile technologies are still so comparatively primitive that sea- based systems appear feasible.[27]

For the United States, sea-based systems hold the prospect of providing flexible coverage, allowing prompt reorientation of the system in response to rapid changes in threat evaluation.[28] Depending upon the specific NMD technologies developed, the number of units necessary to provide a particular level of coverage may vary from three to twenty-two ships or platforms according to various projections. Such systems are not totally futuristic in that TMD ship-borne systems are already under development with deployment considered fairly certain although the date keeps slipping.[29] Scaling up to NMD, however, represents a more difficult set of challenges; one that is not guaranteed immediate success.

In June 1999, the DoD released an unclassified summary of its earlier 1998 study of sea-based NMD.[30] The conclusions were generally favorable to the concept but acknowledged certain issues were only conjecture, not fact. The program would be based upon an Enhanced Theater Wide system—one carried on AEGIS-equipped ships (primarily cruisers and destroyers) employing the Navy Theater Wide (NTW) Standard Missile-3 interceptor. That missile is envisioned as having three distinct configurations: (1) the Enhanced NTW with a velocity of 4.5 kilometers per second; (2) the Improved 8-Pack with a velocity of 5.5 kilometers per second, and (3) the new 6-Pack with a velocity of 6.5 kilometers per second.[31] Clearly, in its more enhanced forms, this system would shatter ABM treaty restrictions on TMD systems and those on deployment at sea.

The HTK vehicle and radars would be those employed on the existing NMD architecture. The costs estimated for a stand-alone sea-based NMD architecture are $16 billion to $19 billion. Integrating a sea-based component into the overall NMD architecture would provide expanded defense for Alaska and Hawaii. One cost factor is that a sea-based architecture in fact requires more interceptors due to ship rotation. Issues of weather effects upon operations are assumed manageable although possibly of concern.

The term "platform" is used advisedly since there could, in fact, be two forms of ship-based NMD. More traditional ship-based systems would be housed on normal ship hulls, being part of the general defensive capability for the fleet. Such vessels would be highly mobile, normally attached to various carrier battle groups or expeditionary forces. Being militarily oriented toward TMD, these ships would protect naval and littoral ground forces in order to facilitate the projection of a U.S. presence overseas. These ships would also be equipped to handle more traditional fire support missions. One limitation could come in the tradeoffs necessary to sustain traditional naval fire support missions and missile defense. Ships can only carry a finite number of weapon types effectively unless one returns to the battleship era. That is not happening, so compromises will be necessary.

The platform concept would envision vessels similar to the already proposed arsenal ships, but they would be developed explicitly for NMD deployment. Their mobility could be much slower, needing more bulk to handle larger missile inventories and necessary radars plus providing greater stability during launch and heavy weather. Capable of being moved constantly to reorient the system, such vessels would allow placement closer to likely attackers, possibly permitting defensive measures during the missile ascent phase. In fact, movement of such vessels could become the equivalent to the present deployment of U.S. aircraft carriers to a region, a symbol of political seriousness and forward power projection. In this case, the power being projected is defensive rather than offensive, but the implications for potential adversaries are similar. Their power to do significant harm is being challenged.

Space-based systems represent the most comprehensive option, especially when combined, with land-based systems, providing global coverage against any missile attack from the launch point onward. That degree of protection presupposes a very threatening world situation likely coupled with multiple large-scale adversaries. From one perspective, this deployment implies a world even more threatening than the Cold War because of the latter—multiple, large-scale adversaries. During the Cold War proper, the Soviet Union, while a massive threat, was conceptualized as a single agent with China an afterthought, albeit a potentially dangerous one, but clearly secondary at least for the short term.

A space-based technology means deployment capabilities well beyond what presently exists. Missile warning and surveillance systems are already positioned in outer space.[32] In fact, all the systems described (whether theater or national) are premised upon the expectation that such space-based detection and warning capabilities will operate successfully. Given the brevity of missile flight times, early and accurate warning becomes critical for making TMD technologies effective. During Desert Storm, such warnings were provided to the Patriot batteries in the Middle East from satellites positioned away from the Gulf region. The jury-rigged notification system worked during Desert Storm, but the process was cumbersome and prone to failures, given its ad hoc nature.[33] Newer satellite configurations aim at more localized and immediate coverage and alert procedures. Messages during the Gulf War were routed through several way stations on their way to the Patriots, an unacceptable delay now.

What is referred to here in terms of space-based NMD incorporates the original SDI vision as articulated by the believers.[34] Weapons of varying types (lasers, particle beams, kinetic energy, and possibly nuclear) are positioned in space so as to allow global coverage with near real-time ballistic and cruise missile killing capabilities. Any missiles launched at the United States would run a gauntlet of weapons, ensuring through repeated intense attacks that the bulk of the warheads are destroyed. Such a system, if built and successfully implemented, allows prompt response to any potential missile threat. In principle, that protection could be extended to all U.S. allies; thereby, solidifying their support for various international interventions. This would occur because like the United States, those states would be protected against adverse actions by hostile states, at least with regard to ballistic missiles.

Such an NMD system remains purely theoretical at this point although the basics are being laid in place at the R&D and conceptual level.[35] For example, directed energy weapons (including lasers) have returned to some prominence with several successful interceptions of small tactical rockets.[36] The assumption is that scaling up such weapons is possible as evidenced by the Airborne Laser (ABL) project.    Such an approach directly challenges international understandings regarding the peaceful uses of outer space plus more specific prohibitions regarding deployment BMD systems in space.  As of the fall of 2000, the first experimental demonstration of a space-based laser, the Space-Based Laser Integrated Flight Experiment, is projected for 2013, not exactly right around the corner.[37]  There also exists great uncertainty regarding the actual costs for such a massive weapons deployment involving multiple battle stations in low earth orbit in order to provide maximum global coverage. Orbital times limit any single battle station's coverage area since the most optimal coverage occurs in low earth orbit close to any prospective targets. This uncertainty reflects the great unknowns inherent in any efforts aimed at launching such new and exotic technologies.  Earlier experience with SDI demonstrated the potential costliness of such technologies, regardless of their combat effectiveness.  These technology effectiveness issues, combined with such projected high costs, muted interest eventually and provided ammunition for the SDI opponents. Obviously, threat assessment becomes absolutely critical for justifying such large expenditures and the resulting disruptions of long-standing international understandings.

## CURRENT DEPLOYMENT SCENARIOS

Accurately describing the most likely initial NMD deployment when approval occurs is much like describing a Broadway play when it opens out of town.   The script is continually being rewritten, depending upon audience reaction, and may bear only a tangential relationship to the original concept. NMD has a similar character in that the proposed deployment scenarios have continually shifted as events move forward and others in government respond to those changing variables. The following description reflects that uncertainty but provides a snapshot in late December 2000 of an ongoing policy process.

Clearly, the younger Bush's administration will revisit and decide the issue, but even that choice will likely change over time.  For example, the actual interceptor is not scheduled to fly until 2004.   That date may drift forward or backward some, but the reality is that the proof of concept has not been demonstrated yet.  No administration has demonstrated the willingness to totally ignore the physical evidence provided through testing, they just vary in their willingness to accept ambiguity.   That variability reflects the worldview informing how the question is approached.  With these caveats in mind, the proposed first deployment scenario can be discussed.

In designing an NMD deployment scenario, the entering assumptions become critical for determining ultimate outcomes.    By varying the assumptions, one changes the likely results.  The three most relevant variables to this point are the likely threat, the state of the technology, and political decisions regarding maintaining treaty compliance.  As we have traced out briefly, the threat perception has expanded and worsened in recent years.  More states are evaluated as likely future possessors of ICBMs capable of reaching the United States and possibly predisposed to employ them.  Technology development continues, albeit not without controversy over the question of how fast and how well the NMD program objectives are being achieved.  Opponents drawing upon the earlier discussed Welch Report argue that a "rush to failure" is in progress while proponents see steady progress, based upon successful testing, even if failures do persist.  As indicated earlier, differences in evaluations concerning test results reflected ideological predispositions rather than actual outcomes.

Treaty compliance refers to whether the NMD deployment will conform to the strictures of the 1972 ABM treaty.  Translated loosely, that means the interceptor site should be located at North Forks, North Dakota, while armed only with ground-based interceptors.  Such an approach excludes sea- and space-based weaponry and deployment sites anywhere else other than where agreed upon earlier.  Other modifications or interpretations regarding the treaty may or may not be deemed binding, such as the 1997 distinction between TMD and NMD interceptors.  Republican members in Congress have in the past rejected that distinction with its restrictions upon TMD technologies.

The Clinton administration earlier operated on two tracks.  Politically, its consistent position was that the interceptors conform to the treaty by being only ground based.  At the same time, research continued, albeit at a lower intensity level, regarding a Space-Based Laser (SBL).  Basing wise, the administration's posture at first was to remain treaty compliant while at the same time exploring alternative basing options for the interceptors.  In the latter instance, the Russian government was approached regarding modifying the ABM treaty to allow a different American site to be opened. That request was flatly and consistently rejected.    The Russians might change their minds since there exists the possibility for a joint NMD system covering both societies.  There were other suggestions that the Russians might be willing to negotiate some changes, allowing American deployment but minimizing its effects upon their strategic posture.  Whether either result is likely remains unclear at this writing.

In response, the Clinton administration pursued the Alaska basing option, a process interrupted by the president's decision to defer the next choice to his successor.    The president, however, essentially conceded the case that if deployment occurred, it would be noncompliant unless the Russians explicitly agreed to amend the ABM treaty.  A new administration may find greater Russian flexibility simply because it will have at least four years in which to negotiate, unlike Clinton, who was obviously a political lame duck by 1999–2000.

All of these choices remain subject to future revision, depending upon the realities confronting the newly incumbent president at the time of choice.  This interplay between technical and political factors has characterized the field since its beginnings. The 1960s deployment decisions (by Lyndon Johnson in late 1967 and by Richard Nixon in early 1969) reflected that process as the ABM system grew in size and complexity. The original "light" deployment grew, at least potentially, although that process was terminated in 1970 by Congress when it rejected new ABM sites and finally by the 1972 ABM treaty, along with the subsequent congressional vote to end deployment.

The current (early 2001) NMD system architecture under development includes five major components. These components include the Ground-Based Interceptor (GBI), the Exo-atmospheric Kill Vehicle (EKV), Upgraded Early Warning Radars (UEWR), X-Band Radars (XBR), and the Battle Management/Command, Control, and Communications System (BM/C3).[38] Space-Based Infrared Systems-High and -Low (SBIRS) will be employed for initial target detection and tracking, eventually replacing the existing Defense Support Program (DSP) satellites presently in operation.

Missile launches potentially threatening to the United States are to be first identified through the Upgraded Early Warning Radars (large, fixed, phased array surveillance radars) in conjunction with DSP and SBIRS-High satellites.[39] Notification to the BM/C3 initiates the battle sequence, alerting X-Band Radars (ground based, multifunction phased array radars) of the threat along with SBIRS-Low satellites.[40] Those detectors in combination will track the missile as it closes on the United States. The BM/C3 provides the electronic guidance to make the system operate successfully. If a launch occurs, "the commander in chief of the North America Aerospace Defense Command (NORAD) will control and operate the NMD system through the BM/C3."[41] At the final stages, once interceptor launch occurs, the system runs automatically to interception. The time parameters shrink below the threshold of human responsiveness, given the distances and relative speeds involved.

The GBI is the shaft of the spear in attacking incoming targets.[42] The objective is to attack the missile during the midcourse exo-atmospheric phase of their flight. The interceptor is launched on the command issued by the BM/C3 element. As the missile closes on the target, the EKV (the point of the spear) activates on its board sensors to acquire the target, based on a continual data stream from the BM/C3.[43] Target destruction occurs through the force exerted by the collision between two objects moving at hypersonic speeds. Each component must operate successfully every time. As evidenced by the testing failures in January and July 2000, that can prove difficult to execute in practice.

Table 6.3 summarizes the pattern since 1987 as various administrations have adjusted their programs to reflect changing national priorities and current realities. Four of the six phases, as was discussed earlier, occurred within the Clinton administration (1993–2001) as the decision regarding NMD deployment grew near. The latter two reflected the rapidly changing perceptions of threat and the current state of the technology. As a result, the deployment options pursued within the Clinton administration exhibited a shifting shape across time.

**Table 6.3**
**Changing Parameters of National Missile Defense**

| NMD Program | Mission | Defense |
|---|---|---|
| 1. Phase I (1987-1989) | Enhance deterrence of a Soviet first strike | 1000s of interceptors, ground & space based |
| 2.Global-Protection Against Limited Strikes (GPALS) (1989-1992) | Protect against accidental or unauthorized launch | 100s of interceptors, ground & space based |
| 3. Technology Readiness (1993-1995) | Prepare technology to reduce deployment time | Ground based system, deployment not considered |
| 4. Deployment Readiness – "3+3" (1996-1999) | Integrate systems; prepare to deploy 3 years after a future decision | 10s of interceptors, ground based only |
| 5. NMD Acquisition (1999-2000) | Prepare for initial deployment in 2005 | 10s of interceptors, ground based only |
| 6. NMD Acquisition Enhanced (2000-2007) | Prepare for initial deployment in 2005-06, completed in 2007 | 100 interceptors, ground based only |

*Source: National Missile Defense Program Evolution, BMDO Fact Sheet JN-00-04* (January 2000). Line 6 is a modification of the original based upon policy changes subsequent to its posting.

The original deployment option, Capability 1 (C1 or line 5 in Table 6.3) was to be very limited, consisting of only twenty interceptors.[44] The infrastructure (described earlier) supporting that limited initial deployment was to be put in place in a manner allowing for scaling up to a significantly larger force if deemed necessary. That necessity arrived much more quickly than the administration envisioned in early 1999.

By February 2000, Lieutenant General Ronald T. Kadish, director of the BMDO, was testifying before the Strategic Forces Subcommittee of the Senate Armed Services Committee regarding the new situation and the evolving plans to deal with it.[45] Essentially, the upgraded threat assessments had led to the expanded deployment option identified by line 6 in Table 6.3. "The Expanded C1 architecture will be capable of defending all 50 states against expected near-term threats."[46] This translates into the original deployment of twenty interceptors by FY 2005 or now possibly 2006 with the balance (eighty) deployed by FY 2007. Obviously, such an approach allows for further expansion but this particular configuration remains partially treaty compliant since the interceptors are ground based. Barring a change in Russian views, they are noncompliant if positioned in Alaska. This deployment was delayed by President Clinton's September 2000 deferral of the construction start until a decision is made by the next administration.

Table 6.4 provides a snapshot of the NMD deployment options under development across the spring and summer of 2000. Changes occurred subsequently but remained tentative depending upon presidential choices. These options reflected a gradual process of incremental growth as political factors pushed the Clinton administration forward to a large-scale deployment posture.

Obviously, they are now largely historical but are of interest in clearly illustrating the modular approach taken by the administration.

**Table 6.4**
**Progressive Deployment Options As of Late 2000**

| Component | Threshold Deployment – Capability 1 | Expanded Capability 1 | Capability 2 | Capability 3 |
|---|---|---|---|---|
| 1. Interceptors | 20 | 100 | 100 | 250 |
| 2. Launch sites | 1 | 1 | 1 | 2 |
| 3.X-Band Radars | 1 | 1 | 4 | 9 |
| 4.Upgraded Early-Warning Radars | 5 | 5 | 5 | 6 |
| 5.Interceptor Communications Facilities | 3 | 3 | 4 | 5 |
| **Support Components** | | | | |
| 6.Early Warning Satellites (SBIRS-High) | 2 | 4 | 5 | 5 |
| 7.Warhead Tracking Satellites (SBIRS-Low) | 0 | 6 | 24 | 24 |

Source: *Congressional Budget Office, Budgetary and Technical Implications of the Administration's Plan for National Missile Defense* (Washington, D.C.: Congressional Budget Office, April 2000), Table 1.

NMD remains a work in progress; presidents set very general parameters that allow advocates to continually expand the box, and the result is a progressive growth in system size, capability, and cost. The initial deployment pursued, the Capability 1, was the starting point—one already superseded at least on paper by the Extended Capability 1 described above by General Kadish. The objective of this wider deployment is to provide greater coverage plus redundancy. When multiple missiles attack, more NMD interceptors are obviously required. More critically, multiple missiles are needed to ensure interception success. There is no notion of one bullet, one target, especially in these early stages. If the first EKV misses, others will make the kill. Expanded Capability 1 provides that extra margin of protection although certain physical parameters limit the system's effectiveness.

Capability 2 expands the NMD system's ability to handle more sophisticated countermeasures. A major criticism of the NMD testing effort has been the question of whether the interceptor could in fact distinguish between the warhead and its associated decoys.[47] This added capability grows out of the deployment, of SBIRS-Low system and more X-Band Radar sites. These allow more precise targeting of incoming warheads and target discrimination. The number of interceptors does not expand under this deployment just their purported effectiveness.

A more significant program expansion occurs when, and if, Capability 3 is pursued. The second site, Grand Forks, North Dakota, is added with 125 interceptors to provide stronger coverage for the East Coast. In addition, twenty-five more interceptors are to be added at the Alaska site for expanded coverage and more capacity to respond to multiple-wave attacks. This capability requires more radar sites; both X-Band and Early Warning, to support the more geographically dispersed defensive arrangement.

The Congressional Budget Office (CBO) cost projections in Table 6.5 were consistently higher than administration estimates.[48] In fact, the Clinton administration never provided cost estimates for Capabilities 2 and 3, indicating its reluctance to pursue those options. CBO estimates, however, did not incorporate the SBIRS-High and -Low satellite system costs since those programs were expected to be employed for broader defense purposes than just use by NMD. In fact, about their deployments were not dependent upon NMD although some question was raised by the air force whether SBIRS-Low would in fact be useful in the absence of NMD. Regardless, the CBO estimates were consistently higher than the administration's estimates (for Capability 1 at $20.2 billion, adjusted for inflation) because it included operating costs for a total of $25.6 billion. Expanded Capability 1 was estimated at $26 billion by the administration while CBO projected in at $29.5 billion. The point is that cost estimates like deployment dates remained fungible, depending upon the assumptions made in the analysis. These cost projections and deployment dates were clearly tentative and already being revised in light of the September 2000 deferral of the Alaska radar site construction. The numbers and dates are provided here as a perspective upon the deployment sequence at a particular point in time. Acceleration or delay may force adjustments in both, but the reality is that physical factors on the ground (construction seasons in Alaska) heavily impact any decision.

**Table 6.5**
**Projected Budget and Deployment Dates**

|  | Capability 1 | Expanded Capability 1 | Capability 2 | Capability 3 |
|---|---|---|---|---|
| Deployment Dates | 2005 | 2007 | 2010 | 2011 |
| CBO Cost Estimates | $25.6b | $29.5b | $35.6b | $48.8b |

*Source:* CBO, *Budgetary and Technical Implications of the Administration's Plan for National Missile Defense* (Washington, DC: Congressional Budget Office, April 2000), Tables 1 and 3.

The cost figures are clearly quite tentative, reflecting particular deployment configurations. Deployment follows, based upon the pace of technological advancement. Remember the interceptor to be employed is still under development with critical testing not to occur for several years (a 2003–2004 time frame is expected). In fact, as discussed earlier, significant developmental issues appear to exist regarding its progress, endangering actual deployment regardless of the political debates. Technological shortfalls can be overcome, but that may not happen on the same schedule as the politicians' desire. That is the reality of dealing with difficult technological problems in a rushed environment.

Despite the political capital being invested in the current struggle over deployment, other options have been suggested as alternatives, indicating the lack of consensus even among NMD supporters as to the best choices. One must note, however, that these options face significant technological challenges. Recapping briefly, one that is considered a distinct possibility is an NMD system based at sea. Severe questions exist regarding the technology in terms of effectiveness plus whether the radars can be effectively housed on the ships.[49] The other option, clearly more futuristic, involves space-based NMD. This means positioning battle stations in low earth orbit. As was indicated earlier, the DoD has evaluated the prospects of the first positively but acknowledges large unknowns.

Both of these approaches raise the issue of whether boost-phase interception is truly practical. Significant defense figures have suggested that such an interception strategy possesses several distinct virtues from the perspective of the United States. First, the missile is interdicted at the most vulnerable point in its flight when evasion is most difficult. One can accelerate launch velocities to evade interception, but that capacity requires better missile technologies than most states of concern presently possess. Second, a missile destroyed at this point would fall back upon the attacker, creating damage within that society.

Such an interception approach demands an extraordinarily accurate detection and tracking system, one able to discriminate peaceful from hostile launches almost instantaneously. That preemptive approach may be technically feasible but politically risky if mistakes occur. Boost-phase interception, however, has from the U.S. perspective the capacity to reduce the technical concerns about mounting a successful NMD if the interceptors can be placed physically close enough to be effective. Unfortunately for proponents, space-based technologies for NMD, which are the most indifferent in principle to weather and other factors, are the most distant in terms of development. Weather at sea can make ship-based operations extremely difficult to execute successfully. NMD remains a difficult proposition to execute under the most optimistic scenarios. Thus, the search for technological fixes remains a constant one.

## CONCLUSION

NMD will never be a completely done deal because the technology keeps moving. As can be seen in the above discussion, deployment may become imminent, but there still exist significant issues because the technology remains clearly a work in progress. The reality is that work will continue even if NMD deployment occurs immediately because other states will pursue solutions to defeat any existing NMD system. Capability 2 in its fashion is a recognition of that reality. The technological imperative runs deeply in modern military thinking so that pursuit of technological change is always an agenda item.

The larger question becomes whether Capability 3 (250 total interceptors) represents the down payment on a truly comprehensive NMD deployment. It is system set up to the handle the largest possible missile forces. The logic of the game drives the United States in that direction. Even the Clinton administration was forced to make gestures that despite its opposition to the larger concept. That opposition is now history, but the choices do not become easier by simply changing the officeholders.

## NOTES

1. James W. Canan, "Setting a Date for Missile Defense," *Aerospace America* (May 2000): 34–41.

2. Lauren Hall, *Weapons under Fire* (New York: Garland Publishing, 1997), 115–118.

3. Stephen Young, "Take Long Look at NMD," *Defense News* (September 11, 2000): 15. At that time, the booster was thought to be eight months to a year behind the original schedule. The BMDO after the July failure found quality control to be a continuing issue and one that had to be improved. Robert Wall, "U.S. Missile Defenses to Undergo Greater Scrutiny," *Aviation Week & Space Technology* (January 1, 2001): 56–57.

4. Gopal Ratnam and Jeremy Singer, "Support Falters for SBIRS Low," *Space News* (September 18, 2000): 1, 36.

5. Robert D. Walpole, *Statement for the Record to the International Security, Proliferation, and Federal Services Subcommittee of the Senate Government Affairs Committee*, September 21, 2000.

6. Table 6.1 is derived from information gleaned from Dean A. Wilkening, *Ballistic-Missile Defense and Strategic Stability*, Adephi Paper 334 (New York: Oxford University Press, International Institute for Strategic Studies, 2000), Appendix 1; Aaron Karp, *Ballistic Missile Proliferation: The Politics and Technics* (New York: Oxford University Press, Stockholm International Peace Research Institute, 1996), 149–150, Appendix 1; W. Seth Carus, *Ballistic Missiles in Modern Conflict* (Westport, CT: Praeger, 1991), 85–91.

7. Frances Fitzgerald, *Way Out There in the Blue: Reagan, Star Wars and the End of the Cold War* (New York: Simon & Schuster, 2000), 407–411.

8. Robert D. Walpole, *Statement for the Record to the Senate Foreign Relations Committee on the Foreign Missile Threat to the United States through 2015*, September 16, 1999.

9. John Lauder, Director, CDI Proliferation Center, *Statement to the Senate Committee on Foreign Relations on Russian Proliferation to Iran's Weapons of Mass Destruction and Missile Programs*, October 5, 2000.

10.  Nazir Kamal and Pravin Sawhney, *Missile Control in South Asia and the Role of Cooperative Monitoring Technology* Cooperative Monitoring Center Occasional Paper No. 4 (Albuquerque, NM:  Sandia National Laboratories, 1998), section 2.2.

11.  Analyses of congressional defense budgeting have discussed programmatic and fiscal approaches.  The former involves evaluating programs and making explicit choices as to which programs should be supported.  The fiscal approach avoids such difficult and contentious choices by making generally uniform across-the-board budget cuts.  The latter, while politically easier, can be exceptionally disruptive programmatically since strong and weak programs are lumped together indiscriminately.  Arnold Kanter, *Defense Politics:  A Budgetary Perspective* (Chicago:  University of Chicago Press, 1979); Roger Handberg and Robert L. Bledsoe, "Congress and the Defense Budget:  Possibilities of Change in the New World Order.".  (Paper presented at the Annual Meeting of the Midwest Political Science Association, Chicago, April 1992.)

12.  Randy Wynn, "A Year of Grudging Compromises and Unfinished Business," *Congressional Quarterly Weekly* (November 27, 1999): 2848.  The cut was 0.38 percent across the board.

13.  Stephen W. Young, *Pushing the Limits:  The Decision on National Missile Defense* (Washington, DC:  Coalition to Reduce Nuclear Dangers, Council for a Livable World Education Fund, July 2000), 28.  This is an updated analysis based upon an earlier report in John E. Pike, Bruce G. Blair, and Stephen I. Schwartz, "Defending Against the Bomb," in Stephen I. Schwartz ed., *Atomic Audit:  The Costs and Consequences of U.S. Nuclear Weapons since 1940* (Washington, DC:  Brookings Institution Press, 1998), 296.  The table reported here was updated into constant 2000 dollars from the earlier one that was in fiscal year 1996 dollars.

14.  Council for a Livable World Education Fund, *UP, UP and Away! Missile Defense Plan to Cost $60 Billion; Republicans Plan to Cost Twice as Much*, http:www.clw.org/ef/cbobmdreport.html.

15.  Associated Press, "Proposed Missile Defense System Could Take 4 Years to Test," LATimes.com (http://www.latimes.com/editions/orange/ocnews/20000510/t000044046.html.) dated May 10, 2000.  Ellipses were in the original article.

16.  "Q: General Kadish, of all the things that could have gone wrong with this flight, was this at the very bottom of your concern list?  Kadish: It wasn't even on my list. We had good confidence in the reliability of this. It's worked very well before. And to have the kill vehicle not separate was not something we worried about." *DoD News Briefing* (Washington, DC:  Office of the Assistant Secretary of Defense [Public Affairs], July 8, 2000).

17.  This section also draws upon an analysis presented earlier by Roger Handberg, Stewart French, and Jennifer Robinson, "Ballistic Missile Defense and the New Age: Star Wars without Reagan or Star Wars, the Sequel" (Paper presented at the Annual Meeting of the American Political Science Association, Atlanta, September 1999).

18.  Seth Faison, "In Unusual Announcement, China Tells of a Missile Test," *New York Times*, August 3, 1999, A6. This unexpected announcement was part of the psychological warfare being waged between the United States and China.  The Chinese were attempting to convince the U.S. that deployment was useless if directed against their weapons program.  Any future deployment would be overwhelmed by sophisticated and plentiful Chinese missiles.

19.  Joseph Cirincione, "Why the Right Lost the Missile Defense Debate," *Foreign Policy* 106 (1997): 38–55; and Eugene Fox and Stanley Orman, "The Vital Role of

Policy:  Or "*What Happened to Ballistic Missile Defense,'*" *Journal of Social, Political and Economic Studies* 21 (1996): 243–252.

20.    Robert Wall, "Asia Examines Missile Defense," *Aviation Week & Space Technology* (June 14, 1999): 203.

21.    Samuel P. Huntington, *The Clash of Civilizations and the Remaking of World Order* (New York: Simon & Schuster, 1996).

22.    For a counter critique of Huntington and also Francis Fukuyama's "end of history" argument, see Ahmet Davutoglu, "The Clash of Interests:  An Explanation of the World (Dis) Order," *Perceptions:  Journal of International Affairs* 2 (December 1997–February 1998).  This critique was posted to the Web page of the Republic of Turkey's Ministry of Foreign Affairs, http://www.mfa.gov.tr/grupa/percept/ii4/II4-7.html.

23.    Bruce M. DeBlois, "Space Sanctuary:  A Viable National Strategy," *Airpower Journal* (1998): 41–57, Pat Towell, "Can U.S. Build Missile Shield Without Shredding a Treaty?" *Congressional Quarterly Weekly* (December 4, 1999): 2914–2919.

24.    This environmental statement was posted to the Ballistic Missile Defense Organization's  Web  site  (http://www.acq.osd.mil/bmdo/bmdolink/html/eis.html) allowing maximum public involvement in the siting decision.

25.    Robert Holzer, "Sea-based National Missile Defense Proposed," *Space News* (March 22, 1999): 14,Gopal Ratnam and Amy Svitak, "Interest Grows in Sea-based Missile Defense," *Defense News* (August 21, 2000): 1, 20.

26.    Cf. the discussion in Department of Defense, *Report to Congress on Theater Missile Defense Architecture Options for the Asia-Pacific Region* (Washington, DC: Department of Defense, 1999), which elaborates the RBMD options usable by Japan, the Republic of Korea, and Taiwan.  The effects in terms of coverage are equivalent to NMD deployment for the United States.

27.    Wall, "Asia Examine Missile Defense."

28.    John Deutch, Harold Brown, and John P. White, "National Missile Defense:  Is There Another Way?" *Foreign Policy* 119 (2000): 91–100.  For a counterperspective, see Charles V. Pena and Barbara Conry, "National Missile Defense: Examining the Options," *Policy Analysis* 337 (1999); for implications of different deployment options Ivo H. Daalder, James M. Goldgeier, "Deploying NMD:  Not Whether, but How," *Survival* (2000).

29.    Robert Holzer, "Warhead Glitch Threatens NTW Schedule," *Defense News* (June 19, 2000): 1, 28.  The NTW system is the linchpin for any U.S. naval BMD deployment, in this case TMD, but with implications for NMD.  The problems continued to plague the program with direct impact upon NTW progress.  Robert Holzer, "Naval Antiair Missile Hits Snags," *Defense News* (December 11, 2000): 4.

30.    Ballistic Missile Defense Organization, *Summary of Report to Congress on Utility of Sea-based Assets to National Missile Defense* (Washington, DC:  Department of Defense, Ballistic Missile Defense Organization, June 1, 1999).

31.    Robert Holzer, "DoD Weighs Navy Interceptor Options," *Defense News* (July 24, 2000): 1, 60.

32.    Bruce M. DeBlois, "Space Sanctuary: A Viable National Strategy," *Airpower Journal* (Winter, 1998): 41–57.  In fact, DeBlois argues that weapons in space are counterproductive to long-term American interests—the sanctuary approach to space (no weapons deployed) plays to U.S. advantages in technology and operational experience.

33.    Roger Handberg, *New World Vistas: Militarization of Space* (Westport, CT: Praeger, 2000): 102-103.

34.    Kenneth B. Payne, *Strategic Defense: "Star Wars" in Perspective* (Lanham, MD: Hamilton, 1986).

35. US Space Command, *U.S. Space Command Long-Range Plan* (Peterson Air Force Base, CO: U.S. Space Command, 1998).

36. Robert Wall, "New Missile Defense Technologies Pushed," *Aviation Week & Space Technology* (September 4, 2000): 96–97.

37. Jeremy Singer, "U.S. Air Force Finalizes Details for Space-Based Laser Program," *Defense News* (November 27, 2000): 6. The total cost of the experiment is estimated at $3 billion.

38. BMDO, *National Missile Defense Architecture, BMDO Fact Sheet JN-00-06* (June 2000). The list provided here differs slightly since the Space-Based Infrared Systems High and Low are being developed regardless of NMD deployment.

39. BMDO, *Early Warning System, BMDO Fact Sheet JN-00-13* (February 2000).

40. BMDO, *X-Band Radars, BMDO Fact Sheet JN-00-19* (June 2000).

41. BMDO, *National Missile Defense Architecture*, 2.

42. BMDO, *Ground Based Interceptor, BMDO Fact Sheet JN-99-09* (March 1999).

43. BMDO, *NMD—Exo-atmospheric Kill Vehicle, BMDO Fact Sheet JN-00-01* (January 2000).

44. BMDO, *National Missile Defense Program Evolution, BMDO Fact Sheet JN-00-04* (January 2000).

45. Lieutenant General Ronald T. Kadish, *Statement before Senate Armed Services Committee, February 28, 2000*, http://www.acq.osd.mil/bmdo/bmdolink/html/kadish28feb00.html accessed April 4 2000.

46. Ibid. 3.

47. Union of Concerned Scientists and MIT Security Studies Program, *Countermeasures: A Technical Evaluation of the Operational Effectiveness of the Planned U.S. National Missile Defense System* (Cambridge, MA: Union of Concerned Scientists and MIT Security Studies Program, April 2000).

48. Those higher cost projections by the CBO generated some controversy, but were generally assumed not to be too far out of line with likely projections if the larger capabilities were eventually deployed. Gopal Ratnam, "Higher NMD Cost Estimate Further Polarizes Debate," *Defense News* (May 8, 2000): 4, 36.

49. The larger questions may be fiscal as resources for NMD are not unlimited so that up until now sea based missile defense even at the theater level has lagged behind its land-based competitors, especially the THAAD program. Robert Holzer, "Pentagon Narrows NTW's Horizon," *Defense News* (January 17, 2000): 3, 28.

# 7

# Pursuing Future Policy or Taking Counsel of One's Worst Fears

## INTRODUCTION

Historically, foreign policy and, by extension, national defense as one component have always proven difficult tasks for the United States to handle effectively. That result is not because of any lack of effort but rather reflects severe domestic disagreements over the U.S. role in world affairs. The National Missile Defense (NMD) debate exhibits all of those characteristics of conflict and indecision. This difficulty in part reflects U.S. isolationist historical experience as interpreted through the prism of its favorable geography. The United States is effectively an island state, removed from any immediate security threat. Earlier, across the nineteenth century, the world was thought to be very distant from American shores, so that foreign policy's relevance to America was often questioned or else interpreted primarily through economic lenses. The question became, How could the United States expand its trade relations with other states while remaining firmly detached from their squabbles? Several times that quest tracked a protectionism turn but, until the twentieth century, tariff collections were a major source of government revenue (along with land sales). American isolationism was aided by its rapidly expanding domestic economy, which absorbed its attention and energies.

Foreign threats to American national security were not considered truly credible ones despite the enormous disparity in armed forces existing between the United States and the larger European states. For example, the British during both the Revolutionary War and the War of 1812 clearly possessed the military capacity to severely punish the United States and did so at times almost with total impunity but were unable to conquer the country.[1] Placing and sustaining an occupation force ample enough to be controlling on such a distant hostile shore was beyond the British forces' logistical capability. Logistics, as they have been for centuries, severely limited other states' capacity to invade and hold territory in North America. Sheer distance made supplying everything a very long haul.[2] Living off the countryside was the traditional method of military supply but that source required continual movement by the troops in order to secure additional supplies as the immediate locality was exhausted. Stationary military forces as in a siege or occupation, for example, demanded resupply from secure and nearby sources, but those of necessity lay over the ocean or, at least, outside U.S. borders. As the United States grew in size, the capacity necessary to conquer it grew exponentially.

Conversely, the United States likewise lacked the requisite physical means both by deliberate political design (an aversion to large-standing armies) and by historical accident to invade others so distantly removed from its shores. American activities overseas normally assumed the form of pursuing various types of economic enterprises. Those could and did involve trade with other states, for example, using the clipper ships. The navy as a result built its few ships to advance and protect American trade with other states but not for purposes of conducting long-term overseas military adventures. American expeditions against pirates in Tripoli, for example, were of short duration and limited purpose. Most American military conquests involved its domestic foes, the nearly exterminated Native Americans and the rebellious Confederacy along with a weak neighbor to the south, Mexico. Despite its apparent military vulnerability, Canada remained free from successful U.S. invasion despite several abortive efforts. Logistical difficulties cut both ways, as did the British capacity to inflict significant pain, an early example of deterrents in action. The benefits did not sufficiently outweigh the costs.

Once the United States fully, though reluctantly, entered the larger world as a player; however, its role shifted gradually from that of onlooker to that of an active military participant with potentially major impact. At first this potential impact was often much greater in rhetoric than reality, but the United States clearly became a major player once its vast natural and industrial resources were mobilized to intervene internationally. The outcome has been that the United States psychologically has felt increasingly empowered to act unilaterally in pursuit of its view of its national interest. This proclivity to intervene was initially encouraged by some states that perceived the United States as a simple tool to manipulate in order to redress the European balance of power in their favor. The United States was to be exploited, but there was little respect for its views. Regardless, this psychological empowerment was reenforced by the cultural awareness that until the Vietnam War, the United States claimed to have never lost a war.[3] Most European states could not make such a nationalistic assertion, given their lengthy historical records of military defeats and victories. That experience, however, provided the Europeans a long-term framework within which to implement policy. Immediate gratification was deferred in the interest of long-term gain.

During World War II, there existed some early American fear of enemy attack but not one of actual military invasion—quite the contrast with most U.S. Allies during that war for whom that fear represented a very real if not an actual experience. Random balloon-borne bomb attacks and submarine shellings and offshore ship sinkings, while frightening to the public, did not constitute an actual military invasion threat. In fact, Japanese strategists never envisioned physically landing large forces on American shores except possibly in raids. Their strategic goal was to implement a defensive shell or defensive perimeter sufficiently strong to discourage any sustained American counterattack since the United States, in their opinion, lacked the patience and will to fight a long war. The international stereotype of the United States was one of a state lacking the requisite experience and nerve to successfully engage in protracted or confrontational foreign policy despite its obvious physical power. This particular interpretation or arose during the century-long period of U.S. political isolation and self-absorption—a negative stereotype only reinforced by its subsequent abrupt withdrawal from a leadership role in world affairs after World War I. A return to normalcy meant political not economic isolationism although the United States did engage in efforts at disarmament in the 1920s and 1930s.

After World War II, fears of nuclear attack grew when the Soviet Union acquired nuclear weapons, but with the passage of time even that concern faded somewhat, at least among the public. That threat while real, remained in essence an abstract one since nothing would likely happen until literally all hell broke loose. Sheer physical distance from any immediate military threat, even the Soviet Union, reinforced these national feelings of effective immunity and especially disengagement. That is why the Cuban Missile Crisis was so prominent, not just for the confrontation but also because of its nearness geographically to the United States. Everything is "over there," wherever over there is physically located. That same attitude permeates current public views of rogue state or states of concern missile threats against the United States. More recently, the U.S. public in subtle ways has clearly returned with some concrete justification to that earlier historical perception of remoteness, that any possible military security threats are extremely distant or unlikely at least in the near term. For example, the failure of the widely heralded Y2K threat to materialize after immense media hype further reinforces the feeling that there exist no significant present national security threats on the American horizon. It is against this historical background of American exceptionalism and the reality of geographic isolation that the NMD debate has ensued. In fact, the disjuncture between public and elite attitudes regarding possible national security threats remains enormous, making NMD peculiarly an exclusively elite-based issue. Here, in this chapter, possible future policy options are examined in the light of the continuing debate over Ballistic Missile Defense (BMD) particularly the NMD option. That elite-based orientation can be seen in the heavily domestic focus inherent in the specific debate and has been reinforced by the peculiar context of the Clinton presidency. Only by linking to domestic questions has NMD survived as an important political issue.

Until 2001, national missile defense despite its obvious and multitudinous international ramifications has been largely framed not as a debate over the future of American foreign and defense policy (which it obviously is) but as a largely domestic political dispute. By being driven by primarily domestic considerations, international ramifications often get comparatively short shrift. This perspective became true for both NMD advocates and opponents. For example, the Clinton administration (as with the earlier Johnson and Nixon administrations) was moved to accept a steadily expanding NMD program because of its calculations regarding the program's potential domestic political ramifications. The earlier administrations ultimately moved in opposite directions in response to those pressures: Johnson's to deploy ABM while Nixon's reversed direction. The Nixon choices were clothed in an international cloak, but domestic pressures forced its hand. Public opinion, once engaged proved hostile to having interceptors based in their backyards. Only minimal efforts were expended by the Clinton administration to articulate and act upon a clear counterresponse and so through the infamous triangulation approach, NMD advocates were effectively, albeit temporarily, neutered. The immediate justifications were the need for Clinton to get reelected in 1996 and more recently to defuse the issue during the 2000 presidential election. Both these efforts fully met their short-term political goals. That emphasis, however, meant that the debate became in effect a continual process of fudging the larger questions regarding foreign and defense policies. But, the ultimate price of such a piecemeal approach was that NMD deployment grew steadily more likely over the 1990s despite the administration's strong misgivings regarding NMD. Republican suspicions that President Clinton was not supportive of NMD were totally accurate; they just were helpless to force his choices since there existed no public pressure to do so. But, when sufficient political force was exerted, the president responded with minimal resistance but also minimal results. The policy window opened, but little could be done, given presidential resistance. In 2001, with presidential support rather than resistance, the policy window is again open but the results may not be as positive as some believers imagine.

Embracing this domestic focus, however, fed directly into the NMD proponents' principal arguments, which emphasize population protection as the single most critical moral and political criterion for deciding what should be done. No one is advocating major population losses, but there do exist multiple ways to achieve equivalent results since NMD is not presumed infallible in protecting the civilian population. The overall debate has moved well beyond the shield in space although space-based concepts remain firmly on the table, just not today's menu. However, by this heavy moral focus, the believers have driven the debate emotionally, disarming the earlier Clinton's administration's will to resist strongly. Their effective psychological insulation or isolation from external or international considerations fuels the believers' emotional fervor and willingness to disrupt if not destroy existing international agreements, including the ABM treaty and more. However, by operating from such a narrow yet nationalistic perspective, most international considerations and by implication the future role of the United States in the world become minor considerations, even effectively irrelevant ones.  That apparent disconnect from international reality is what feeds continued international anxieties about U.S. choices regarding NMD.  American national security is not solely an artifact of an impregnable fortress, but is based upon strong relationships with other states in implementing mutual understandings.  The United States may be the hegemon but its ultimate strength is economic—a factor heavily dependent upon other states and their willingness to cooperate.

In its most extreme manifestations, there almost appears to be no realization by Believers that the United States is truly not an island unto itself, totally removed from the flow of international currents.  The physical remove of the United States from close geographic neighbors who are militarily threatening is no longer as significant but has not disappeared, especially as a psychological construct.  The United States remains physically difficult for other states to reach due to the sheer distances involved.  But, unlike Imperial China, the United States economically and otherwise is not removed from the world, nor does it wish to be removed.  OPEC nations continually impact the United States with their oil cartel, even possibly adversely, without unleashing a single missile or terrorist attack.  The U.S. population will clearly not be completely protected from all forces of change and possible disruption by its NMD shield.  Hopes to the contrary will be severely disappointed.  Military force is often not truly effective in gaining what the United States desires most—instead the United States reaches out to other states in nonmilitary ways.  The United States shapes world events by its actions and inactions to an extent often not truly appreciated by Americans themselves.  That disconnected attitude to the rest of the world allows NMD to be debated as if only the United States and its views matter or will be affected by its decisions.  The ripple effects from U.S. choices are powerful forces in world affairs.

## CONTRADICTORY EFFECTS OF NMD DEPLOYMENT

The discussion here will consider domestic political realities first and then international aspects.  But, first, there exists an anomaly permeating the ongoing NMD controversy that merits some brief consideration.  This anomaly reflects both the effects of military technology and perceptions of the United States as historical and present international actor.  Technology at least in the military realm has long been classified into the broad categories of being either offensively or defensively dominant in its effects.  Obviously, most weaponry is multifaceted in that, depending upon the situation, the technology can be usefully employed in either capacity.  But, there exists a general understanding that during certain historical eras when offensive weaponry is considered to have become dominant over the defense, the international situation becomes more likely to be militarily conflictive.  Various states seize the apparent opportunity if they are more proficient in or equipped with the requisite offensive technology to strike, overwhelming their adversaries by force of arms or through the intimidation factor inherent in their possession of such dominant weaponry. This dominance was initially attributed to nuclear weaponry until the fuller implications of nuclear weapons employment were understood. Nuclear weapons deter but are not applicable to all circumstances.

Conversely, the expectation exists that when the defense is presumed ascendant, the probability for war declines markedly. Conflicts may occur but remain below the level of systemic war. This situation arises because the toll extracted from the attacker is exorbitant in terms of number of casualties and treasure expended, including the very real possibility of national military defeat or, even worse, stalemate. Military stalemate further drains national assets as the attacking forces confront a superior, possibly devastating, defensive arrangement. Tactical adroitness and organizational efficiency can temporarily overcome the advantages assumed inherent in either dominant military technology, but this general relationship is assumed to hold and impact national choices regarding war and peace. Offensive dominance, roughly speaking, means conflict while defensive superiority translates into a more peaceful time or at least no overt military conflicts. National rhetoric may be bellicose but actions are much more circumspect in nature. Leaders shrink from the brink of war rather than rushing blindly over the precipice.

Surprise occurs not just in the tactical or strategic sense but when new technologies first enter the military equation. The implications of those untested technologies are not apparently understood but once applied, their influence becomes self-evident. Thus, offensive or defensive breakthroughs repeatedly occur and are subsequently incorporated into traditional military doctrine. On occasion, the power of specific technologies may be already demonstrated but their full implications not perceived clearly. That situation occurred with regard to the American Civil War when the cumulative consequences of entrenchment, modern rifles, and artillery for defensive domination were conclusively demonstrated but not fully realized in Europe until World War I with its enormous casualties. Earlier Prussian successes against Austria and France only demonstrated part of the equation. Or, even more recently, the full ramifications or synergisms inherent in the application of air power employing modern sensors, precision-guided munitions, stealth, and space technologies were not self-evident prior to the Gulf War. Air power visionaries may have articulated such radical thoughts, but the actual commanders in the field only realized their full impact as the air war raged on over Iraq.[4] Absorbing the implications of that event has proven contentious since contradictory conclusions have been drawn as more experience has been accumulated. Offensive dominance may exist but a peer military power can still inflict significant losses.

Interestingly, this purported relationship between offensive and defensive weaponry along with its impact upon the larger international system has acquired a peculiar twist in the current discussions regarding possible American NMD deployment. This twist did not exist during the original anti-ballistic missile (ABM) deployment debate when the world was not more peaceful but most strategic calculations were more dominated by the Cold War and the two superpowers. Current evaluations reflect the ambiguities inherent in the world today when the strategic overlay is perceived as more diverse and fluid while the United States is also dominant militarily.

The twist referred to is that NMD deployment is perceived by some as empowering the United States to become an internationally disruptive even hyper-aggressive state—one that is commonly defined as beyond the effective control of other states due to its disproportionate and demonstrated military performance relative to others. The Europeans for example were alarmed by the growing gap between their militaries and U.S. forces during NATO air operations over Serbia. Despite their First World status and NATO partnership, the United States at times danced alone, a situation disturbing to European states fully conscious of their place in the world. The troubling scenario this implied is that the United States will truly be able to selectively intervene militarily with minimal or no concern about effective reprisals by the impacted states. In this scenario, geographic distance plus an effective NMD are presumed to afford the United States such wide freedom of action that normal international constraints will not apply to the ultimate hegemon.

This perspective on NMD's implications reflects the perceived hegemonic nature of U.S. military power presently. That apparent status as the sole hegemonic power, it is suggested, liberates the United States from considering the views of other states—a peculiar interpretation in light of the alternative interpretation often proffered of an ever more globalized and intertwined world economy. In the alternative view, that globalized economy enmeshes states ever more closely to other states. This includes the United States, according to those domestic parties who are particularly fearful of those ties that bind. The United States has become a central participant in that global economy, accepting repeated restrictions upon its freedom of action albeit often after protesting. For example, the World Trade Organization has forced significant changes in U.S. economic policy regarding protecting national industries. The United States presumes greater benefits flow from those voluntarily accepted limits upon its freedom of action. But all states ultimately judge their willingness to accept any such limits against the costs exacted by nonparticipation in the international trade regime.

What particularly inflames these international suspicions appears to be the strident tone associated with the more adamant NMD advocates.[5]    Their rhetorical excesses imply a United States capable of intervening almost at its whim when others render some insult or injury. What transpires from their perspective is an erratic isolationism in which the United States huddles behind its military shield, capriciously striking out when events do not go its way.

This caricature of a foreign policy builds upon two facts. First, believers and isolationists (two separate but often related groups) at times have soared in their rhetoric regarding the moral imperatives they perceived as embodied in NMD. Such flights of fancy imply that the United States only becomes truly secure when it operates totally independently in the world. Since the United States has never truly been in that situation, at least for a century, the analysis is flawed because even a hegemon operates in a world of constraints. The constraints may be fewer, but they are real in their impacts. Military power obviously is a very useful but not unlimited tool and, commonly, is not applicable to all situations, a brutal reality rediscovered by every administration and generation.

Second, the United States, because of its global hegemonic role, has been repeatedly called upon to facilitate the application of military force to resolve or, at least, calm particular crises.[6]    Such multilateral interventions including Bosnia, Somalia, Kosovo, and East Timor for example were not made quickly or easily. Great domestic acrimony and strife, at least among elites, accompanied each venture as with the ongoing air interdiction in Iraq.    Other states on occasion have either disagreed with the specific action taken or have been incapable of resolving the situation before invoking U.S. assistance.    As a consequence, U.S. actions are often crudely painted as the willful choices of a state whose judgment is not well respected.    Long-standing rather condescending attitudes toward the United States as a world leader have morphed into this area, reflecting other states' differing national interests and their frustrations with their present secondary status. The decision of whether or not to deploy NMD has multiple consequences both domestically and internationally, but that decision alone will not change the United States and its hegemonic status for the short term.    The long-range implications may be profound and disruptive but all remain purely conjecture at this point.  Rhetoric does not automatically translate into policy on either side.

## DOMESTIC POLITICAL REALITIES

NMD advocates have repeatedly struggled to make the question of NMD deployment the 1990s, now the 2000s, equivalent to the "missile gap" issue raised during the 1960 presidential election or the "ABM gap" in 1967–1968 (the one that ultimately failed to ignite politically due to Johnson administration preemption).  The latter model was pursued by the Clinton administration in the late 1990s.  The earlier missile gap debate, however, was subsumed within a larger critique of the Eisenhower administration's domestic and international policies.  The differences between the recent 2000 presidential election and the earlier events are clear; the situation was not a rerun of the past.  The major contextual differences at presently were the dramatically altered international environment (the end of the Cold War), combined with its attendant changed domestic priorities including sustained domestic economic prosperity, at least through the end of 2000.

For NMD proponents particularly, their political problem becomes one of fostering sufficient public outcry to generate political momentum for deployment and sustaining the program once approved.    Waiting for a Republican president could work, but presidents, regardless of their party affiliation, often perceive things somewhat differently once in office as they confront hard budget and foreign policy choices.  The earlier cancelled 1967–1969 deployments provide instructive precedents for what occurs when political support declines or shifts or the question becomes excessively controversial when the public becomes engaged on a personal level. Public support for NMD in the abstract faded when the question became personalized—when missile sites were housed in the suburbs. The not in my backyard (NIMBY) syndrome kicked in with full force to the point that the city deployment option faded into oblivion. Public opinion became a two-edged sword, a reality not always acknowledged in the debate over NMD. A president interested in mobilizing support for NMD may not wish to inflame public insecurities too much regarding the state of national defense since that ultimately reflects upon his administration. Blaming your predecessor, in this case Bill Clinton wears off quickly as a political protection, especially when there existed no readily apparent threat sufficient to motivate dramatic action prior to the incumbent president's tenure. Clinton's foot dragging was firmly grounded in his awareness that the public did not consider NMD a true national priority. Therefore, does this current furor become an admission of present incompetence in handling the deterrence process with regard to the states of concern or rogue states?

Believers truly fear that the policy window that they perceived opening wide in the 1998–2000 time frame may abruptly slam shut. Large-scale NMD deployment may not occur immediately regardless of administration. Domestic priorities (Social Security, Medicare, and tax cuts—especially the latter) and pressing defense modernization needs may drain away the dollars available for NMD particularly especially in its more enlarged versions. Policy windows are temporary openings or targets of political opportunity that may be closed off inadvertently even by otherwise supportive administrations because of their policy choices elsewhere. For example, President Bush's desire for a thorough review of the entire military budget, along with the assorted issues that with that process, has already annoyed some supporters who assumed his election signaled an open wallet for defense.[7] NMD is not the only item on the national political agenda, and clearly is not perceived as the most critical once the argument moves beyond the narrow BMD policy community.[8] President Bush's early statements regarding defense questions provide mixed signals. On the one hand, he proposed to raise the Department of Defense (DoD) budget, but clearly signaled his resistance to excessive spending. That caveat marked his recognition that fiscal resources would be tight if tax cut plans were successful.[9]

That policy community may expand during certain time periods but generally remains small and concentrated. Defense policy issues draw upon a wider constellation of interests whose focus, however, is aimed toward more traditional military functions, including deterrence—NMD may not actually help achieve that larger goal because of the persistent uncertainties concerning reliability. Therefore, NMD proponents often become marginal players because of their one-note symphony.

In addition, the problem for NMD advocates is that public opinion has remained firmly fixated upon domestic priorities, especially economic ones across a period of unprecedented domestic economic growth, from the mid-1990s onward. For example, a *Washington Post* poll found in September 2000 that the voters were generally satisfied with the state of national defense and the military.[10] This result came after at least six years of intense Republican attacks upon the Clinton defense policy. When another sample was asked explicitly whether the United States was either stronger or stayed the same after eight years of Clinton leadership, a majority (52 percent) agreed.[11]   These numbers further reinforce the point that domestic politics drive the overall situation, negating NMD proponents' attempts to force the debate, for only the already convinced are listening. For example, Republicans were approximately three times as likely as Democrats to see the U.S. military as weaker (72 percent to 28 percent).[12]

·In the absence of an ongoing military crisis directly threatening the United States, public mobilization remains tentative although latent concern about multiple military deployments overseas does exist.   But, that fact does not necessarily play into NMD being the solution; changing foreign policy direction is more reasonable. The volatile Middle East region, for example, illustrates the irrelevance of NMD, the weapons employed against the United States are likely conventional and low tech in nature or economic. The small craft attack upon the "USS *Cole*" by apparent suicide bombers illustrates the problem. Missile threats still lie in the future, at least from the public's perspective. U.S. allies in the Persian Gulf are presently more at risk than the United States itself.  In fact, the *Cole's* refueling in port rather than at sea reflected a shrunken naval support force including tankers so that use of such potentially hazardous locations became necessary. For the DoD, expansion and modernization of such assets remain a bigger priority than NMD.

Daily fluctuations in the Dow Jones average draw more public attention than any military crisis to this point, including Kosovo, an armed conflict. The air operations over Iraq remain effectively invisible to the public. The one exception regarding international affairs has been continued fears of globalization and its impact on jobs.[13] Any serious international military threats are thought to lie far in the future, not demanding immediate public attention. Military policy questions have arisen in the context of American foreign interventions abroad and whether or not those are justified in terms of potential casualties, but these specific actions are not motivated by fear of attacks upon the homeland.   In that sense, the present situation differs from earlier crises when the argument was that a military threat against the United States existed. That argument was stretched in some instances, but earlier the "Munich analogy" still had resonance among the public and elites.   That cultural-historical-generational understanding has now vanished after the Cold War and Vietnam.  What has replaced it?  There does not appear to be an agreed upon commonly shared historical analogy for use in coping with present international threats, a fact that impacts the ability to intervene in many situations even if the elites agreed that was necessary.

In a very fundamental sense, the NMD debate amply illustrates the extent to which the United States has entered into a new political era.  The recent presidential election contained minimal discussions of international policy including future threat scenarios and what the United States should do in response. There was none of the earlier sense of urgency or public engagement. This lack of urgency persisted despite the violence that erupted in Israel and the

Palestine Authority during the campaign. There exists no Korean War, Suez Crisis (with its implications of a Soviet nuclear threat against France and Great Britain), and confrontations with the Soviets over Berlin or Afghanistan, or Vietnam War. All the security threats currently suggested are both less visible and less capable of threatening the United States directly than the Soviet Union did in its prime. The public does not see Russia and China, despite often-harsh rhetoric by both sides, as immediate military threats. The reality could change but not in the short term unless a dramatic change in regime policies occur.

BMD, especially in its NMD manifestation, possesses the long-term potential to unsettle that profound sense of domestic tranquility. Partisans of an expanded NMD deployment have essentially operated as if the responses of other states are fundamentally irrelevant. That can be most graphically seen in their repeated suggestions that the United States does whatever it wishes, ignoring other states' reactions, with regard to the ABM treaty. In the short term, given Russian economic realities and Chinese comparative military weakness, that attitude can generate much animosity but little immediate threat. Over the longer term, the potential to rekindle the nuclear arms race may prove significant. Such an event would severely agitate the American public whose expectations regarding potential international danger are much different than those of previous generations who endured World War II and then the Cold War. Creating a heightened national anxiety regarding missile attack may prove debilitating if the threat occurs in other forms. Rogue states lack threat credibility in the short term while the Russian and Chinese nuclear threats still produce some resonance if sufficient alarm is sounded. Such a shift in emphasis completely changes the debate context especially questions of ultimate cost. Stopping a Russian missile attack represents a different level of effort than intercepting a few missiles from a lesser state.

Then, the question shifts to consider simple cost-benefit calculations—ones in which NMD has consistently had problems presenting reasonable cost projections. Believers acknowledge the fact that cost projections are highly fungible but frankly do not care. Costs as a concept appeals only to the pragmatists as an overriding consideration. Believers and Wilsonians perceive the NMD issue from such strong, though different, worldviews in which such mundane considerations do not matter. Costs only matter if cost-benefit calculations are actually made. If the issue is fundamentally a moral one then such calculations become both irrelevant and misplaced. In addition, the more extreme believers assert that further reductions in domestic discretionary spending could be imposed to pay for NMD. Their conservative social and economic views find that tradeoff totally acceptable. Others find such stark choices more difficult to impose. Domestic priorities do vary, even within the same political party.

The essential question remains the penetrability of any missile shield or defense program being proposed. Rhetoric may dazzle in the short term, but consistent demonstrated results are what matter ultimately. Failures in testing can only be explained away to a certain point, especially when significant moneys must be committed to deploy an inadequate system. The looseness of the budget projections put forth reinforces ambivalence about NMD since the costs always appear to escalate rather than decline. These rising costs are being projected against existing threats not the even more sophisticated missiles possible in the future. Those will demand an even more capable and resilient NMD system—meaning further cost escalation is almost guaranteed. But, does it work? Technological optimism permeates the entire BMD field and plays to long-standing American public attitudes regarding the inevitability of technological progress. But, that optimism is not totally unlimited or immune to real events.

Moreover, the technological imperative is most resistible by Congress in the absence of a demonstrated national military threat. Other states may be extremely hostile to the United States, especially rhetorically, but that fact alone is insufficient to force large expenditures in the absence of a demonstrated capacity to strike the United States in some significant manner. Current cost estimates have proven extremely fungible, ranging from $13 billion to $48 to $60 billion, depending upon the time line taken along with the proposed system's sophistication level. System complexity, sophistication, and costs escalate as one conjectures multiple missiles, penetration aids and other assorted devices for ensuring a successful attack. Defensive systems have to keep pace or be rendered militarily valueless. Deterrence, despite its visible failings still remains the most politically reliable posture, demonstrated through historical experience. After the fact devastation of the enemy may be emotionally unsatisfying for some, but despite their rhetoric, most national leaders are not normally suicidal or stupid. Their calculations may be completely erroneous (a hopefully correctable factual situation), but on the edge of actual nuclear war most individuals retreat from the prospect of such a confrontation, especially when responding from a position of massive strategic inferiority. The United States has not envisioned disarming. Nuclear proliferation rather than missiles by themselves remains the truly critical international security item since possession of those weapons makes the other state's power curve effectively unlimited. Such power however can be exercised in ways besides missiles.

The larger question domestically may not be one of NMD but of ensuring that an assured destruction capability exists. Both delivery systems and warheads are aging with no replacements in sight. Modernization can extend effective weapon life spans, but at some point the next generation weapon delivery systems must be envisioned and implemented in the absence of viable worldwide nuclear disarmament. The last Minuteman 3 was built in 1978 while the Peacemaker production line closed in 1988. The Minutemen are being modernized but in a decade or so, a new missile may be necessary. Otherwise, deterrence would rely singularly upon submarine-launched ballistic missiles (SLBMs). The nuclear genie is clearly out of the bottle. Arms control algorithms may effectively eliminate most missiles, but other weapons platforms remain more than adequate replacements. That situation probably requires a return at some point to earlier defense budgeting strategies in which strategic weapons are a focal point.

As a domestic political issue, NMD consistently ranks extremely low in terms of demonstrated and unsolicited public interest. Up to now, its political key to survival, as a major issue, has been its strong resonance among conservative groups—a resonance clearly disproportionate to its military value. In fact, one could fairly persuasively argue that one of NMD's greatest values has been as another political club with which conservatives beat the president they loathed, Bill Clinton. Also, NMD as an issue possesses both nostalgic and amnesiac qualities among Republicans. In the former context, NMD evokes memories of the Reagan presidency, a golden era of triumph, especially in retrospect, for right thinking. Those memories grow more golden with the passage of time—the very real policy differences that existed are forgotten or muted. Part of that forgetfulness encompasses the collective failure to remember the severe splits that existed, even among Republican circles, as to what exactly SDI would accomplish if deployed. President Reagan and Secretary of Defense Caspar Weinberger pushed for the maximum program (the latter despite his apparent original misgivings), the missile shield in space. It is in support of this concept that the greatest claims to omnipotence for NMD were made. Many other Republicans accepted SDI as a general concept but defined the effort mostly in terms of an ICBM protection plan—a throwback to traditional strategic doctrines. Expansion to population protection was to follow later (if ever) when the requisite technologies were stabilized and made more robust. That earlier skepticism has receded in memory because NMD has been under siege for a time and its grasp on the political agenda is tenuous.

Many Republicans assume that any president of their party as a matter of course will automatically authorize deployment and follow through on implementation. Based upon past history, one must assume that view ultimately remains very optimistic. Cost factors are not trivial, especially for a party that preaches and occasionally practices fiscal discipline. Social programs may be gutted in pursuit of NMD, but if the economy hiccups that euphoria may not survive contact with voter discontent and fear. The social safety net is only necessary when you need it, but when that time comes, the public demand will be intense and unforgiving of any failure to implement it. Voters still envision government as their protector of last resort, especially in economic hard times. More generally, the NMD worldview may not be sustainable in the absence of dramatic changes in the world situation. Dust-ups with and within minor powers do not evoke public emotions equivalent to the depths of the Cold War when Armageddon was once thought just around the corner. Within the memory of a single generation, one dug a bomb shelter in the backyard and debated one's moral obligations to unprepared neighbors and other strangers.

Democrats generally support the arms control perspective—a posture consonant with their views of the world and the domestic budget. Moneys are to be directed toward solving critical domestic social needs, not military programs thought unlikely to work ever. Improving U.S. military preparedness is not rejected by Democrats as a critical national priority, but their skepticism is high regarding the actual usefulness of NMD. Being more arms control oriented, the broader implications of NMD trouble them. From this perspective, weapons beget weapons so that NMD deployment, if actually carried out, will only foster larger and more serious conflicts where previously either none existed or the seriousness level was significantly lower. This "chicken and the egg" debate is what makes NMD so intractable as an issue to resolve.

The worldviews driving both sides of the debate have been reinforcing in that the Republicans have largely shifted to the believer-pragmatist side of the ledger with the Democrats mostly clustered toward the pragmatist-Wilsonian end. There still exist significant numbers of pragmatists in both parties, but their exact numbers and partisan distribution fluctuate over time. Often they seek rhetorical protection by voting in symbolic terms both ways, supporting NMD deployment but advocating ABM treaty revision and continued arms control measures.[14]    Much like the Dodo bird of American politics, the moderate Democrat or Republican, pragmatists have found their skepticism less acceptable within both parties. The schism between the parties makes NMD such a political football so that minor shifts in political power create disproportionate effects upon policy. In the 1968–1970 Senate debates over ABM deployment, the original ABM opposition was drawn from both parties, liberal Democrats and moderate Republicans, but over time the issue was transformed into a liberal-conservative split. In the late 1960s, conservative Southern Democrats still existed as a significant factor, but over time the ideological purification of the congressional parties has eliminated much of that source of intra-party division. Democrats collectively have tactically voted for NMD—votes, however, that are generally considered purely symbolic not substantive. Agreeing to consider the possibility of NMD deployment is not the functional equivalent to deploying or funding that deployment.

Worldviews giveth and taketh away NMD deployment. In a peculiar way, NMD is the elite (inside the Beltway) domestic political issue par excellence. That means ironically that international repercussions in the end could have greater impact here than one would expect from the rhetoric. As discussed earlier, elites of both parties are driven by their general vision of an active U.S. role in world affairs, a vision not necessarily shared by the public. There has arisen major opposition within the Republican party, especially in the House of Representatives, to any proactive U.S. world engagement, but the composition and duration of that perspective remains a question. Again, their attitudes, while indifferent to world affairs, were further hardened by their animosity toward the then president, Bill Clinton. His positions became an automatic negative reference point for Republican partisans who dominated Congress for the balance of the 1990s. There are fundamental differences in perspective regarding the future U.S. role in world politics, the present and future international threat environment, and NMD, but all were further amplified by partisanship and high levels of personal animosity.

The arrival of George W. Bush in the White House will test the partisan division over the issue. Republicans nominally at least control all three branches so that they are now accountable for any choices made. The younger Bush administration may prove particularly disappointing in that his major advisors come from his father's earlier tenure, an administration supportive but not overly enthusiastic about NMD. That earlier administration was grappling with the implications of the Cold War's end—seeking arms control solutions to military issues while reducing American military forces. George W. Bush as a candidate never expressed the kind of concrete views on foreign policy or defense that would commit him immediately to move aggressively on NMD. His early statements on NMD as president were supportive but still loose as to details and how big a deployment was to be implemented.[15] Appointing Colin Powell as secretary of state and Donald Rumsfeld as secretary of defense puts supporters of NMD in office, but the view is likely different from the inside. Stating your despised predecessor's policies were failures does not foretell your future choices. In fact, the larger defense theme was rebuilding military readiness—restocking the shelves—and procurement—new weapons and their replacements. Those objectives are expensive but fully compatible with military service aspirations. BMD is part of that larger process but does not dominate the discussions.

The bigger question within which NMD will be decided is, What role the United States should play in the larger world? A strong assertive role implies a United States willing to use all its instruments of power in pursuit of its policy objectives. A less assertive posture reduces exposure militarily speaking to others in the world. Certain officials, including Vice President Dick Cheney, Secretary of Defense Donald Rumsfeld, and Paul Wolfowitz (number two at the Pentagon), are identified with a more assertive posture.[16] Thus, NMD's international repercussions will be critical.

## INTERNATIONAL POLITICAL REALITIES

Internationally, NMD, as a general concept and as a specific program, becomes divisive along several dimensions. First, the original Clinton deployment, as presently conceptualized and especially in its more expanded forms, clearly negates existing ABM treaty restrictions. This occurs even before any choices by President Bush. Those restrictive parameters have guided other states' foreign and defense policies, structuring their military strategies and procurement decisions. States normally seek stability in their dealings with other states as in order to preserve their interests. Therefore, their normal response to unilateral changes in well-established policy foundations is overwhelmingly negative. Such a reaction is especially probable with regard to a state such as Russia, one that fears the consequences of its recent military and economic decline.[17] U.S. actions demand an effective response or Russia will be further pushed to the periphery of world leadership. In time, Russia will eventually regain its international stature as a military player, but political leaders normally perceive time in human terms not historical periods. Therefore, actions need to be pursued in the short term that preserve and extend their power and by implication that of the state they lead. By unsettling the situation regarding the treaty, the United States puts forces in motion that it does not control or even completely understand.[18]

NMD supporters repeatedly refer to the Russian Galosh deployment in the 1960s and the subsequent upgrades that have occurred over the years.[19] Their perspective is that the United States is simply catching up to Russia. This perspective, however, ignores the psychological fact that most other states perceive the Russian deployment as completely authorized under the ABM treaty. Its existence is part and parcel of the ongoing arms control process and does not represent a change or new initiative. Other states accept a future U.S. deployment but within the confines of the treaty—meaning Grand Forks only. The Moscow deployment represents part of the status quo; therefore, occasions no comment, especially since Russia is unlikely at this point to unilaterally expand it. More critically, even with upgrades, its effectiveness remains an empirical question.

Second, NMD deployment, especially its unilateral character, inflames divisions between the American hegemon and other states.[20] Hegemonic influence presently is very different than during earlier periods of empire in that nuclear weapons allow other states to severely damage the United States if confronted. In the more immediate sense, NMD deployment is perceived as another example of U.S. reckless isolationism.[21] This American isolationism is perceived as reckless because it is highly situational in character and very judgmental about other states. One example sure to inflame international passions was the reported comments by Vice Admiral Herbert Browne, the deputy commander of the U.S. Space Command,. Browne asserted that Canada would have to actively participate in the NMD program or else risk being excluded from its protection. This statement elicited Canadian outrage over a threat based on a NMD system not deployed yet—not the best way to convince others of U.S. reliability in time of crisis.[22] U.S. policy is also perceived as subject to drastic mood swings that make its international actions erratic and difficult to predict. This is a characterization further amplified by the heavy emphasis upon domestic issues in its policy debates, compared to international, including NMD.

The result from their perspective is a society that repeatedly engages in disproportionate responses to particular events or problems. More troubling is the U.S. inability to follow through once it initiates another state's response to some crisis. There exists a tendency to overexaggerate U.S. failings, but those mirror a larger distrust of the United States as a society. There is growing disquietude among other states regarding U.S. economic and social influences. NMD crystallizes some of those anxieties because the United States is fairly accurately thought of as basically an inward-looking society. When it does engage the outside world, its actions are often dramatic and profoundly unsettling and are often in pursuit of short-term domestic goals. From their perspective, President Clinton's incorporation of NMD into his domestic agenda only further inflames the situation because other states became powerless to affect the U.S. decision regardless of the consequences for those other states. U.S. resistance to outside interference with its domestic policies is a long-standing national trait.

Third, internationally speaking, deploying NMD is expected to ignite a new nuclear arms race even as the Cold War steadily recedes into memory.[23] Those states ambivalent or hostile to the United States will strive to maintain their comparative[24] military strength and political independence. They assume that the United States, if militarily powerful and unchallenged will act to dominate others. Thus, preserving their national freedom of action requires developing counterweights to U.S. military strength. China, for example, has made clear its hostility to a U.S. national missile defense deployment and has indicated its willingness to push ahead harder its ICBM forces in order to overcome any possible U.S. action.

Since most states cannot compete across the spectrum of weaponry, attention becomes focused upon a few sectors: electronic warfare, nuclear weapons, and missiles being one combination. A new nuclear arms race will not begin immediately, given the economic challenges presently existing in the most likely competitors. However, once national leaderships perceive a threat or unsatisfactory security situation to be arising, actions to redress those perceived military imbalances will be taken. Even states severely economically challenged can mobilize extraordinary resources under the goad of hyper-nationalism, fueled by fears of imminent military inferiority. Expanding or creating nuclear arsenals, along with different methods of delivery, would likely be the route taken. Given that nuclear disarmament is not an immediate reality in any case, pursuit of such weaponry becomes critical for achieving some degree of independence from the hegemon.

Fourth, given their general skepticism regarding NMD's effectiveness, the concern is that these states especially in Europe, will endure enormous disruptions in their security policies for no purpose.[25] NMD will fail in the crunch, leaving the United States and its allies vulnerable to weapons of mass destruction (WMD) missile attack. Interventions in crises may be organized on the assumption that such protection exists only for catastrophic failure. The societal costs of such a technology failure would be incalculable. This fear is also grounded in plain geographic reality; putative U.S. allies are closer and more susceptible to missile strikes.

American disparagement of these legitimate concerns adds an edge to the NMD deployment controversy internationally. Geographic realities fuel clear differences in perspective. For example, the United States only grudgingly acknowledges that there might be a political necessity to extend NMD's protection to other states. Russian initiatives in the summer of 2000 to establish a European wide defensive ballistic missile arrangement were challenged by the United States as vague, but the United States failed to perceive their political attractiveness to those closer to the firing line.[26] The Europeans especially view the United States as too self-centered to fully appreciate their dilemma, a perspective fed by their long historical experience incorporating both victory and defeat. The context is one where the United States demands that other states follow its lead without accepting the fact that perspectives differ as to the consequences of NMD deployment for the different parties.[27]

That centrality to world order, while of concern to other states, has helped defuse some hostility among European states.  NMD is perceived as a peculiarity of American domestic politics and the hope is that the technology will fail prior to any necessity for use, but in any case large-scale NMD deployment is a decade away.  The thought appears to be allowing the United States to proceed while striving to minimize its disruptive aspects internationally.[28]  At times, the Europeans appear more concerned about the larger international ramifications than the United States.

The difficulty for presidents and Congress when they contemplate NMD deployment in the twenty-first century is that the world, as of this writing (mid-February 2001), stands generally at a comparatively peaceful point in history, at least for the United States.  Armed conflicts, often extremely deadly ones, do rage across the various parts of the globe.  The United States has by virtue of its dominant political-military-economic position been called upon to intervene or to support logistically and politically the global community's interventions into those often brutal situations, for example, East Timor.

Regardless, the United States, at least the public, does not consider those episodic eruptions threatening to American well being.  That disconnection adds additional fervor to the often-emotional debate over whether the U.S. forces should be physically committed (the "Dover test" referred to earlier).  If we feel no real sense of national danger, why intervene?

Economic arguments are not overtly made, even if they obviously lurk in the background.  The Gulf War fit that model—the motivation rhetorically was a reinvigorated Munich analogy even though the primary geopolitical justification was securing the world oil supply.  Oil, despite its critical importance to the world economy, was a bit too raw to pass as the major justification.  One must remember that the early expectation was that U.S. casualties would be very high.  Losing American lives to secure the profits of the oil industry was not politically acceptable although that was part of the reality.  The acrimonious vote by Congress over supporting U.S. military actions against Iraq reflected that ambivalence.  Aggression must be punished for the right reasons.  That does not mean the public is philosophically opposed to U.S. interventions, rather their perspective remains heavily situational.

As was briefly highlighted in chapter 1, the role of the United States has become that of de facto sustainer of international order in pursuit of democracy, human rights, and economic freedom.  All those goals are endangered by the creation of unnecessary conflict, especially military conflict.  Such engagements, however will not normally involve NMD unless the opposing party possesses a significant missile capability.  Whether missile proliferation can be limited through the Missile Technology Control Regime (MTCR) or some equivalent agreement remains a very live question.  Also, consideration must be given to explicitly incorporating cruise missiles into the MTCR.[29]  Clearly, the MTCR has not been leak proof; the empirical question is whether it made a difference.  In one sense, the debate over NMD versus MTCR resembles the earlier debate over nuclear proliferation.  Projections were that the world would see thirty to fifty (probably less in fact) nuclear weapons states.

Aggressive nonproliferation efforts reduced that potential growth to a virtual stand still until the late 1990s when India and Pakistan felt compelled to move forward in pursuit of nuclear arsenals.[30]

The debate over NMD generally has taken the track that there exists no real possibility for stopping or severely hampering missile technology proliferation. Psychologically, that edge appears to have been conceded by the United States to the states of concern, formerly the rogue states. The easy solution becomes one of retreating behind a barricade, hoping that will be sufficient to keep out the demons. Pursuing an aggressive nonproliferation posture, however, requires a sense of purpose and endurance that is currently lacking. Public engagement in this issue is not irrelevant ultimately, but in the short term does not impact elite policy choices. Elites during the earlier nuclear nonproliferation scrimmages were fairly united on the necessity for success in that endeavor although their motivations for pursuing nonproliferation differed.[31] They perceived nonproliferation as maximizing U.S. power while the others pursued a more utopian vision of world peace, more or less. The consequences would be too horrifying to contemplate otherwise. By contrast, despite all the rhetoric concerning the possibility of societal devastation through missile attacks, there exists no agreement upon the necessity for stopping missile proliferation. Essentially, that part of the question has been conceded virtually without a struggle. This fatalistic acceptance was not peculiarly a Clinton administration view, but is actually shared across the spectrum. Believers do not think that success even partial success can be achieved by fostering nonproliferation while Wilsonians meanwhile are mesmerized by the NMD debate as defined by believers. Thus, one group, the believers, perceives no point to the exercise since total success cannot be guaranteed. Nuclear proliferation assumed there would be failures (i.e., states acquiring nuclear weapons) but the overall result being sought was to dramatically reduce the likelihood of nuclear war. Seeking partial solutions may be unexciting, but is absolutely critical if real progress is to be made in reducing world insecurity.

NMD deployment after all these years of debate holds the potential for rekindling the nuclear arms race not just efforts by the "bad states" but also by current American allies. The arguments for sustaining the status quo regarding NMD essentially come down to the question of whether the immediate and future benefits of deployment outweigh the overall costs when all relevant factors are aggregated together. If NMD deployment undermines international support for U.S. foreign policy initiatives or has the effect of making other states extremely anxious then the alleged benefits may not in fact out leverage the longer-term costs. The impact could be to heighten or sharpen long-term insecurities for the United States. The U.S. security dilemma becomes simply that if NMD works as advertised (an unresolved but clearly an empirical question); other states will become increasingly reluctant to support its actions. The U.S. historic role in the world was based on engaging allies in the task of international order maintenance. Back in the spring of 2000, the Russians attempted to appeal to that American tendency by offering to restrain North Korea's missile program if the Clinton administration abandoned its attempt to amend the ABM treaty.[32]    In the context of a presidential election year, that option had little likelihood of immediate success. The question whether the Russians could deliver on their promise was never resolved.

The Europeans, being geographically closer to a number of rogue states, feel excessively vulnerable to missile attack without the realistic prospect of any effective defense—whether search and destroy prior to launch or purely reactive such as NMD. The missiles already identified as under development in the Middle East all have the capability to strike Europe; the United States still lies out ·of range.    For the Europeans, their domestic political realities make expending the necessary funds for NMD (assuming the technology works as advertised) unlikely if not politically impossible. U.S. willingness to spend money upon NMD in the absence of any direct current threat reflects an economic abundance that others lack. Earlier, only Ronald Reagan suggested sharing U.S.-developed NMD technologies (then with the Soviet Union), so that there is unlikely to be a shortcut for the Europeans even if they wished to pursue it. Russian President Putin got some mileage during the summer of 2000 with his proposal for a broader defensive scheme incorporating the Europeans.[33] Official U.S. reaction was to simply dismiss this as a ploy to derail U.S.-European relations. That probably was not an inaccurate judgment, and it underestimates the attractiveness of such a proposal. Being inside the NMD tent is better than being outside; the difficulty is determining whether the tasks embodied in an NMD system can be done effectively.

From the Europeans and others' perspective, the United States becomes capable of distancing itself from at least some of the direct consequences of its actions—the often-touted shield implications of NMD are perceived as physically isolating the United States from major harm.[34] A true missile shield is not thought possible under the most optimistic scenarios. However, that assumed physical isolation is perceived as empowering the American leadership to the point of recklessness—thus, reinforcing their perceptions of a United States potentially out of control. In this scenario, the European states by default then become the aggrieved states' target of choice because of their inability to either defend or attack successfully, especially the former.[35] Republicans in Congress have proposed a NATO-oriented BMD system, but the technical aspects are fuzzy and the reality is that it would significantly expand the budget requirements.[36] The reality of European vulnerability has been true since the earliest days of NATO—a source of dissension within the alliance but irresolvable based on geography and modern military technology.[37] U.S. promises of protection to the contrary are apparently not sufficient to resolve European anxieties. This in part reflects the end of the Cold War with its overarching theme of great power rivalry where Europe was an important arena of competition. That situation no longer exists so now more particularistic views can hold sway. In this context, the United States sacrifices its capacity to lead other states due to their differing calculations as to probable outcomes.

The United States has not since the War of 1812, confronted the possibility of an invasion and occupation by another state of its home territory. Pearl Harbor represented an attack, but not an invasion, followed by the Battle of

Midway, which ended the Japanese effort to secure a forward position threatening the United States. Obviously, great patriotic fervor was aroused but the reality remained that the continental United States (the heartland of the society) remained essentially a safe sanctuary. That situation essentially persisted across the Cold War despite the peril nuclear weapons posed to the society. Subsequent to the collapse of the Soviet Union, the United States has become more, rather than less, interventionist. This aggressiveness, it could be argued, reflects the reality that the United States does not presently confront a state capable of inflicting substantial damage on its society. In fact, most have not been capable of inflicting any direct military damage outside the zone of operations defined by the United States and its partners. How aggressive the United States would be in situations of potential national peril is an interesting question. During the Cold War, the United States proved to be assertive but cautious when directly dealing with the Soviet Union and China. Actions against surrogates were more assertive but always constrained by a sense of imminent danger. NMD, from this perspective in the new international context, emboldens a national leadership already perceived by others as being somewhat outside normal international constraints. Political rhetoric from both presidential candidates in 2000 carried that implication—though phrased differently regarding specific crisis situations.[38] The United States remains a unilateral super power in a world presently devoid of others.

Even more destabilizing is the possible igniting of a new arms race across multiple states. Embedded in the present American discussions of NMD policy is a view of the correlation of forces that emphasizes even exaggerates, the status quo both politically and militarily. There are euphoric statements extrapolating American military supremacy out to mid-century.[39] Such expressions assume that other states have effectively stopped doing what most states normally do (pursue their conception of the national interest) or else are rendered permanently incapable of altering the existing power relationships with the United States placed permanently in the driver's seat.

American dominance is built upon a historically unique correlation of failed military rivals, a revolution in military affairs, and unusually favorable economic conditions. None of these conditions or American benefits from them is permanent although they can persist much longer than one might expect if there is no goad forcing change. Russia is pursuing economic reconstruction and resurrection in some form while regenerating its depleted military strength. China pursues a similar agenda. Both states will become more assertive but their hostility is not guaranteed. The Europeans and Japan are economically sounder (despite the latter's current problems) but presently reject such major military expenditure. But, those views could all change.

Currently, the list of global military rivals to the United States is short, effectively none. But, that fact represents a historical anomaly rather than a permanent condition. The great military rival collapsed just as certain technologies accelerated, creating unique conditions for U.S. dominance, at least in the short term. Many forget how quickly, historically speaking, many states have transformed themselves into significant military powers. Duplicating that performance demands three things, all of which are fungible. Those are political will, resources, and technology access.

Political will is a situational construct in that national elites are often willing to pursue armament programs in defiance of international censure and embargo. India and Pakistan provide specific and recent evidence to the latter point. Sufficiently motivated by fear, pride, avarice, or competitiveness, governments have acted to pursue the pathway thought most supportive of their national interest. Such endeavors have led to great social sacrifices and economic costs being inflicted upon their populations. Regardless, their intensity of motivation and single-mindedness lead to the accumulation of the resources necessary to aggressively pursue such activities.

Even more critically, access to relevant technologies has become easier rather than more difficult. One does not need to steal military secrets or the like, but rather through acquiring dual-use technologies many militarily critical technologies can be accessed and converted to military uses. Globalization incorporates knowledge of militarily relevant dimensions that is available worldwide. U. S. efforts to control or limit access to certain military-grade technologies through export controls have proven more difficult to implement than many imagined. For most military technologies, there exist multiple sources of high-quality material. In fact, in several areas of electronics, the United States is not necessarily the dominant player, a problem earlier publicly identified during and after the Gulf War.[40]

The larger point is that NMD in this scenario will not be a one-time commitment, but will return the world to the earlier Cold War situation in which very bright and imaginative technologists strive to develop new penetration aids or delivery modes capable of breaching the defense. Proponents continually brush off this argument by asserting that completing such tasks is much more difficult than most imagine. Granted that argument, the players, it is being suggested, are not going to be the "rogue states"—typically underfunded and technologically challenged. Rather the players now will include experienced military powers (Russia and China) or states with significant, though latent, military technological capabilities (Japan, India, and Europe, possibly in combination or several states separately). The technological challenge of sustaining NMD credibility may be much greater to achieve than is currently imagined. As potential sources of danger proliferate, the NMD deployment of necessity grows larger and more complex, meaning expensive.[41]

For example, even as NMD was being debated, the alarm was sounded with suggestions that existing BMD systems especially at the TMD level do not cover all the likely threats. Missiles with 2,500–4,000 kilometer range are not defended against adequately. So, Congress in the 2001 Defense Authorization Act directs "the BMDO [Ballistic Missile Defense Organization] to 'adapt ballistic missile defense systems and architectures to counter potential threats' posed by certain medium-range and intermediate range ballistic missiles."[42] Thus, even prior to the first new NMD deployment, serious holes are alleged to have been identified that need to be plugged. This action has occurred even though no state has explicitly embarked upon a program aimed at defeating U.S.

BMD systems. Using hypothetical scenarios as one's guide means that the variations are endless and the costs unlimited. Whether the United States is committed to sustaining a long-term effort is unclear in the absence of viable threats beyond those already existing in their present form. But, by its actions, the United States may force (from their perspective) other states to respond, despite their reluctance to do so given other national priorities.

No state necessarily sets out to become a threatening military rival to the United States, but the logic of its independent pursuit of its perceived national interests will directly conflict with the United States. No other state perceives the United States and its behaviors as totally benign. In fact, many conflicts with the United States arise over U.S. inattention or apparent indifference to seriously considering other states' needs and priorities. In that situation, those states may form alliances to check what is seen as excessive American assertiveness. That could have three effects: the United States becomes more confrontational in asserting its independent interests, retreating into a quasi-isolationist situation—striking only upon fairly direct provocation, however that action is defined—or the United States rethinks NMD and returns to earlier positions employing traditional diplomatic options combined with a deterrence-based force structure. NMD therefore can be internationally and domestically destabilizing both politically and militarily for all parties, including the United States. Adding NMD to the American arsenal is not simply adding another weapon system.

Other states are not disinterested evaluators of the American NMD debate—their reactions and perspectives are driven by where they presently sit within the international system. Clearly, Russia and China, given their respective domestic economic issues do not wish to embark immediately upon another arms race. The required expenditures could be internally destabilizing, possibly leading to anarchy and repression. China's internal stability is premised upon an implicit bargain of continued economic prosperity in lieu of political and social freedoms. Russia is struggling to restore economic prosperity to large segments of the society—a task made much more difficult if enlarged military expenditures are demanded. Either situation would be threatening to the United States since both possess nuclear weapons over which control might be lost to less stable leadership elements or those committed to a more direct and immediate military response to what they perceived as hostile U.S. actions. In a self-fulfilling prophecy scenario, if NMD deployment does occur, the United States might truly need its protection against the consequences of its opening gambit in this new international chess game.

If the United States chooses not to deploy NMD or selects a deployment option clearly limited in scope to treaty conditions (unlikely as that might be), the status quo albeit somewhat tattered, could continue. Such a choice would allow these very interested observers a holiday from having to engage or consider the possibility of engaging, in massive weapons expenditures. For domestic reasons, that option would obviously be preferred since the sacrifices are likely to be socially destabilizing. Also, in some cases, the choice might well be to drop out—a damaging choice internationally for states desiring to remain influential. This has been a recurring debate within Europe with France the most consistent advocate of enhanced military engagement while the United Kingdom has been more erratic. The European rapid reaction military force represents one response to perceived U.S. slights and indifference to their wishes. Kosovo illuminated even for the reluctant the degree to which the U.S. military operated at a different level than most of Europe. Their respective relationships with the United States influence their choices but those ties could fray even further, leaving the United States isolated from its historically strongest allies.

A choice not to deploy NMD, however, further enhances the existing military capabilities of the affected states. Their weapons systems are not rendered obsolete nor are vastly increased numbers of more sophisticated weapons demanded. For the Russian Federation, this permits a further rundown of their strategic missile forces to a level commensurate with their economic capacity to adequately support them. Mutually assured destruction (MAD) has a cruel simplicity to it if there exists no effective defenses. One's nuclear forces only have to be redundant and effective enough to do the job. Mutual arms reductions help decrease the potential level of violence inflicted but do not prevent that action from taking place if it is deemed necessary. No NMD deployment permits those intercontinental ballistic missile (ICBM) numbers to drift lower, reducing the military burden upon all societies and hopefully reducing the probability of nuclear war. NMD deployment adversely affects the strategic situation of states that already possess nuclear weapons, not those struggling to acquire them. Therefore, conflict would escalate quickly. The democratic peace hypothesis might encounter a rough and more realistic test when the stakes are high, national survival.

There are no disinterested parties in this debate. The problem is that their separate agendas lead them to advocate totally disparate solutions. Successful NMD deployment increases insecurity among states that are otherwise neutral if not positively predisposed toward the United States. Hostile states are unaffected in their hostility although the expectation is that their behavior will become more publicly circumspect. The larger fear is that the actual outcome will be more sophisticated weaponry capable of battering down any defensive system.

## THE ULTIMATE IRONY

Ballistic missile defense at both levels, national and theater, has insinuated itself into the American domestic political calculus to the point that failure to deploy either would dramatically alter the U.S. world role. Theater missile defense (TMD) appears a political given programmatically in that future deployments of U.S. forces abroad are dependent upon acquiring such protection. If the United States wishes to remain an activist international power then TMD becomes absolutely necessary unless the U.S. public truly accepts the view that significant numbers of casualties are a cost of doing business. The British empire earlier was premised upon a willingness to occasionally suffer such losses but then to later avenge them terribly, at least in the colonies. Use of mercenaries by the British also reduced the social impact of such losses. World War I undermined that psychological willingness with its unprecedented massacres of essentially citizen-soldiers at Somme.[43]

The United States has always been much more casualty sensitive, reflecting its earlier isolationist history, avoiding the series of European wars. Joint Vision 2010, with its battlefield dominance concepts, draws sustenance from that focus upon minimal casualties. TMD becomes a political-military necessity if intervention is to occur—casualties will doubtlessly occur but no administration could, politically speaking, permit the hint or suggestion of indifference to providing that total security TMD advocates claim is possible. This becomes especially true, given that most military interventions clearly have not involved countering direct security threats against the United States.

On the other hand, NMD, while dealing with more problematic national threats, becomes critical if the United States itself is to remain immune from certain forms of attack. Future adversaries will, if at all possible, strike back at the heartland of the United States, endangering the population as a leverage point to deter possible American actions. Serbian hacker efforts in 1999 to disrupt U.S. communications were attempted, although with minimal success apparently. Deterrence is a two-way street. The United States has historically speaking been sheltered from the realities of domestic military danger compared to other states. The threat of nuclear holocaust during the Cold War, while real, remained abstract in nature and faded rapidly in public attention although it constantly lurked in the shadows. Yes, the threat existed but, much like the rain, there was not much to be done about it. Normal life overrode such concerns most of the time.[44]

In a world generally thought peaceful despite hot spots and flare-ups, threatened attacks by other states could be politically paralyzing if their success appeared imminent. Even an ineffectual attack would dramatize U.S. vulnerability to such events. Therefore, the next demand to intervene may be politically impossible to pursue due to overwhelming domestic fears of attack. NMD in principle allays those fears unless the system fails to work. In that context, all bets are off regarding future American foreign policy. Psychologically if not physiologically, the United States still operates as if it is removed from any current military threat. Shattering that barrier will be a politically totally disorganizing event—the United States will discover the difficulties of operating in the face of direct foreign military threat in way not confronted for over two centuries.

## CONCLUSION

Societies operate on the basis of mythologies or perspectives that assume certain things about the world at large. For the United States, technological optimism and the associated technological imperative dominate our perceptions of military affairs regardless of the individual's worldview. The thread running through the NMD controversy is the firmly held belief that all remaining technological problems can and will be overcome given sufficient resources and time, especially the latter. Failures are rationalized away regardless of why they occurred and the difficulty of the technological fix. Success is assured for those who have sufficient faith.

Since failure becomes inconceivable in this larger sense, deployment truly becomes a when, not if, proposition. Premature deployment never happens from the believers' perspective because any deployment is better than none. Why? Because if deployment occurs, one then has the opportunity to fix possible problems. Problems become merely opportunities looking for solutions not permanent obstacles. This is why believers are so oblivious to what appears to others as very negative outcomes, that is, persistent testing difficulties. All are brushed off as only temporary glitches that can be remedied.

By their fervor and persistence, the believers structure the NMD debate because they are beyond convincing by facts or reason. Other participants in the controversy in the end bend to their intensity since certain arguments they put forth do have historical resonance among all groups: protecting American troops and population being the most critical. The negative factors are obvious: the cost and the real probability of catastrophic failure during combat. Cost is partially negated by American national wealth and the overriding moral imperative to protect the population, especially from any harm. The arguments sometimes sound like debates over health care and the question of costs when the cures become exorbitantly expensive. Should the state subsidize such treatments or focus its scarce resources upon preventive medicine? Failure by the NMD system, if it occurs, will be obvious but too late for any effective reaction. NMD pushes the nation quickly toward automated warfare, including the first volley. It is likely that the NMD system will enter into action without any explicit authorization by the national political authority. In that sense, the system returns the United States to the Cold War when it was discovered nuclear weapons were closer to being on automatic response than commonly acknowledged.[45]

NMD deployment appears a foregone conclusion because the domestic pressures for deployment are much more intense than those saying no. Other approaches, international agreements and deterrence acknowledge that occasional failures might occur (i.e. "war" possibly including nuclear war) while NMD advocates deny technological failure will ever occur and imply NMD's mere existence will so cower other states as to render them harmless. One must admit to an optimistic view of human nature or rationality despite their often-pessimistic rhetoric.

NMD advocates have clearly moved along the learning curve in that earlier objections have been systematically removed or reduced in their political effects. Nuclear warheads on interceptors are gone, with hit-to-kill (HTK) weapons now employed. The question of whether an endo-atmospheric interception might set off a nuclear warhead is generally not addressed, or at least not loudly. More critically, more recent deployments have all been away from urban areas, negating an immediate public reaction as occurred during the first deployment controversy. That physical distance from American society also helps explain public indifference to the larger NMD question despite the fact it involves fundamental questions of national survival and how best to go about pursuing that goal.

There are no succinct wrap-up thoughts concerning NMD because the reality is that the issue will not die. NMD deployment is a long-running political show, demanding resources—especially as potential adversaries upgrade their military assets. When the economy is good and budget choices are comparatively easy, NMD becomes affordable. If the economy tightens down, as it normally does, the choices will become more difficult. That will reinvigorate opposition on grounds of domestic need—a much more potent argument than abstract discussions regarding national interest. NMD is fundamentally a debate about worldviews rather than the technology itself. For this reason, the technology at times has become effectively irrelevant to the actual points being made. The ultimate question is whether or not NMD deployment will make the world truly safer for the United States. On that, there is no agreement, just firmly held positions.

## EPILOGUE

George W. Bush came to the presidency in January 2001 with only a barely discernable mandate. His election follows two Clinton presidential elections in which no candidate received a popular majority regardless of the final electoral college tally. Both the closeness of the vote and the drawn-out vote recount in the Florida phase sharpened partisan differences more than the election itself did. Specifically, the NMD question never broke the surface of the public's attention during the 2000 election. Even after President Clinton's September 1 decision delaying initial construction in Alaska and effectively pushing off deployment at least another year, if not two, the public visibility of the issue remained minimal. The advocacy groups tried to seize the issue but never gained traction.

Clinton's rationale was that his successor should be the one to render such a choice since the budget commitment would occur on his watch. That rationale went effectively unchallenged by Bush or his vice-presidential nominee, Dick Cheney. Even when Cheney made early forays into defense issues, those died from lack of interest. The level of threat perception in terms of the public still remained low, sufficiently distant so as to keep the NMD question on the margins of the election. Republican stalwarts were loudly supportive, but their attacks were mostly preaching to the choir who needed no persuasion. Disinterested voters, regardless of their presidential vote remained distant from the issue of defense except in the most general of terms. Other issues loomed much more prominently, especially morality and economic issues.

The largest difficulties that NMD confronts in the new environment are the same as before the election: system cost and effectiveness versus likely threat. Electing a Republican president does not represent a simple waving of the magic wand overriding those previous concerns. In fact, NMD deployment may be worse off in the short term (through 2002) because of the closely divided

Congress. Republicans will hold nominal control over the Senate despite its 50–50 partisan split (Vice President Cheney provides the tie-breaking vote) while the House is closely split with a nine-vote Republican majority. Both houses will be hard pressed to move extremely partisan and expensive items expeditiously through the legislative process. The tax cut question will consume political interest initially since that decision will structure the resources available for everything else.    Secretary of Defense Donald Rumsfeld will not change those dynamics unless the perceived threat level is heightened significantly. The external situation will remain central to any deployment decision, especially one regarding the size and scope of the deployment chosen. NMD advocates are willing to accept a thin national coverage option at first because they see the deployment as the down payment on a larger system.

There will likely be several symbolic votes, with both parties attempting to set the agenda for the next round of elections in 2002 and beyond. Whether those votes will penetrate public consciousness is not known at present. Having a president in favor will bolster one side but not necessarily convince either opponents or the public at large. The Democrats as a party have proven adept to this point at insulating themselves from accusations of being "soft" on defense issues. That issue rings more clearly in times of national peril or threat. Votes on NMD are not likely to entangle politically vulnerable Democrats in a situation of being tagged as soft. The party has a long tradition of being resolute on defense although not overwhelmingly enthusiastic while remaining liberal on domestic issues. That stance may be suitable for a situation at least in the short term of economic uncertainty. The arguments for NMD will demand more than scare tactics for the simple reason that the program represents a multi-year possibly never-ending, fiscal commitment. Other states hostile to the United States will not quit their efforts to advance their missile technologies. This is especially true if the United States repeatedly reaffirms its concerns about such weapons.    Technology diffusion over the years means that multiple states possess the capabilities to either build and/or improve such missile technologies. Public support therefore becomes a marathon affair, not a sprint easily finished.

Furthermore, arguments that the United States is defenseless against ballistic missile threats have a clearly different ring when one's party controls (at least on paper) both the legislative and executive branches. Asserting that past decisions were the cause for the present sad situation is an argument with a limited shelf life once the out party assumes office. This argument is particularly difficult to sell when one party has controlled both houses of Congress since 1995 (the period when the danger intensified) and now assumes the presidency. Incumbents by tradition and logic prefer to point with pride to achievements not publicize problems they have apparently failed to correct.    In fact, if the situation darkens dramatically, the argument will be made by opponents that Republican actions and rhetoric have actually inflamed the situation, creating hostilities and possibly endangering the United States. NMD remains a long-term issue, not a quick fix and then move on to something new. Dismantling the present international security arrangements in order to accommodate NMD may prove more difficult to sustain as a policy when the costs come due—both politically and fiscally.

For a new Republican president likely desirous of securing reelection, there will be more easily attainable ways to manifest his interest in improving national defense. Fixing defense procurement and readiness problems represents one obvious avenue for such action. In that broader context, NMD may fare poorly when the services total up their shopping lists. One must remember that NMD is now less closely tied to any individual military service's priorities.[46] For a president, a defense feeding frenzy will not improve matters unless a careful balance is maintained between simple replacement of worn-out equipment and acquiring new more versatile systems. The services all have extensive shopping lists of new technologies—all of which are of the highest priority, according to them. Those new weapons represent the future but are expensive and prone to glitches when first fielded. The risk comes in eliminating the old but still useful systems with unproven replacements. Regardless of the final weapon mix decided upon, upgrading or replacement are both expensive and necessary propositions and can consume all available funds. Existing funding shortages for procurement in the outlying budget years are in excess of $100 billion already, even using Clinton administration estimates.[47] Given other campaign promises especially regarding a tax cut, striking a balance becomes difficult. In this context, NMD fades as a priority given that its technological issues remain troubling and are not subject to quick fixes.

The Bush administration in early 2001 was grappling with two problems if NMD was to be quickly implemented. First, the BMD technology that was most advanced and deployable in the short term was the land based system developed during the Clinton years. That ground-based interceptor (GBI) however, still confronts significant developmental challenges. Those challenges likely can be overcome, but how long that process will take remains somewhat unclear. NMD history is littered with technology signposts that have been pushed back because of developmental problems. Any sea-based system appears to be a 2010 projection while space-based BMD assets are further out than that.

The GBI therefore represents the best short-term prospect for deployment even though it may not be optimal. At the same time, early reports are that the Bush administration is confronting the prospect that possible negotiations with the People's Republic of China may lead to such a land-based American deployment to forestall rogue state's ballistic missile attacks upon the United States. The United States, however, would still be vulnerable to a Chinese ICBM attack. Such an approach would incorporate Russia, by implication if not directly. Both nuclear powers would be guaranteed a deterrence relationship with the United States. An attack by any of the three would leave the attacker vulnerable to counterstrikes. In effect, a mini-arms race would be initiated with the goal of assuring the capacity to retaliate by all concerned.

What appears to be suggested is a partial MAD perspective among the three powers while denying that capability to lesser WMD powers. Such an approach represents a revision of the believers' position that NMD is absolutely essential. NMD is still essential necessary just more selectively targeted—ironically that has been the point of the U.S. NMD program since the original Bush administration 1991 reforms of SDI into global protection against limited strikes (GPLAS). The political effects would be to split the believers between those advocating some form of total NMD and others who accept some lesser level of protection (i.e., against rogue states).

The second item that further confuses the situation and makes NMD in its purest form more problematic are the musings by President Bush and Secretary of Defense Donald Rumsfeld that the United States should pursue deterrence at every level of threat. Such an approach clearly implies an expanding DoD budget—a political given based on earlier Bush and Republican rhetoric. To be effective, the United States will have to develop a different strategy to incorporate all the services along with new programs, including NMD.[48] Earlier discussions were of catching up shortfalls in readiness and procurement of new weapons systems. This new perspective shadows earlier Kennedy administration initiatives under the rubric of "flexible response," which meant creating the capacity to respond to communist threats at every level of potential conflict. Such an approach fits into the rhetoric about "skipping a generation of weaponry." In fact, the emphasis is to move away from nuclear weapons as much as possible.[49] Regardless of this rhetoric, the result will be significantly higher defense budgets even without NMD. Paying for all this in the absence of a demonstrated military threat will be difficult if significant tax cuts occur. Tax cuts rank as a higher priority than NMD in this administration's hierarchy of accomplishments. Thus, NMD will not disappear but its reality may take longer and it may assume a different form than many advocates expected. Seizing the presidency is not the same as implementing maximum NMD.

The large-scale NMD deployments favored by some Republicans, especially those in the House, remain even more technically challenging and expensive. Ironically, the land-based option is the most robust technically speaking but is clearly not a done deal. Sea-based systems are more flexible in theory, but the technological challenges remain significant especially once you move away from a close-in launch phase interception configuration.[50] At present, space-based NMD lies clearly twenty to thirty years out and is not assured of success if developed. Donald Rumsfeld's appointment as secretary of defense provides some impetus to the space-based option if for no other reason than his personal identification with issues, NMD and military space policy.[51] But, moving forward on both might prove both too costly and technologically challenging in the short term. Technological optimism does not trump physical reality in the end.

Clearly, the international political ramifications of NMD will continue to weigh heavily upon any choices made. Brave rhetoric about the United States going its own way will confront the reality that the country works from a position of cooperation with its allies. Disrupting those linkages will be a high price to pay and likely one the administration will shrink from incurring.[52] Rhetoric alone does not guarantee any semblance of enhanced national security. Security policy cannot stand on a single leg since the threats are multifaceted. NMD in the short term may result in the diversion of attention and energy away from the real security issues. Pushing the technological limits developmentally does not have to undermine the existing international security regime, at least for a time. Deployment represents such an event, with unknown security benefits. Deterrence remains the most reliable aspect of American national security although not an infallible defense. Its implications are scary at times, but even with its imperfections, deterrence can still work if the policies and tools are kept in place. Selecting which road to pursue most aggressively will be the most critical early decision made by the young Bush administration. However, regardless of the choice made, NMD will continue on the national political agenda.

## NOTES

1. Richard Smoke, *National Security and the Nuclear Dilemma* 3rd ed. (New York: McGraw Hill, 1993), 22–25. Smoke quotes Abraham Lincoln in 1837 speaking thusly: "All the armies of Europe, Asia, and Africa combined with all the treasure of the earth (our own excepted) in their military chest, with a Bonaparte for a commander, could not by force take a drink from the Ohio or make a track on the Blue Ridge in a trial of a thousand years." This attitude was based on geography and the hidden hand of the British navy, which made a large invasion force almost impossible to move from Europe to the United States.

2. Martin Van Creveld, *Supplying War: Logistics from Wallenstein to Patton* (London: Cambridge University Press, 1978).

3. The War of 1812 was explained away as a beating not a defeat since the British, being occupied in Europe, could not conquer the United States, a nationalistic rationalization to be sure but one congenial to building American self-esteem.

4. Benjamin S. Lambeth, *The Transformation of American Air Power* (Ithaca, NY: Cornell University Press, 2000), 260–261.

5. Karl-Heinz Kamp, "Specious NMD Arguments Stress Trans-Atlantic Relations," *Defense News* (August 21, 2000): 15, 18.

6. Donald M. Snow, *When America Fights: The Uses of U.S. Military Force* (Washington, DC: CQ Press, 2000): 99–112.

7. Thomas E. Ricks and Edward Walsh, "Bush Military Spending Move Viewed as Reform Signal," *Washington Post* February 8, 2001, A15.

8. Eugene Fox and Stanley Orman, "Make Commitment to National Missile Defense," *Space News* (December 4, 2000): 19. The argument advanced here is that any NMD deployment "will require several years of refinement. That is why it is so important to get a rudimentary system deployed as soon as possible." Also, then the force of inertia hopefully kicks in order to keep the program on track.

9. James Dao and Steven Lee Myers, "Bush Warning on Military Spending Challenges Pentagon," *New York Times* February 5, 2001.

10. *Washington* Post Survey based on random telephone interviews with 1,447 registered voters nationwide between September 7 and 17, 2000.

11. *Washington Post* poll based on random telephone interviews with 1,065 self-identified registered voters nationwide conducted between September 4 and 6, 2000.

12. Ibid.

13. "Lori's War," *Foreign Policy* 118 (Spring 2000): 28–55.

14. Clinton administration policies played to this middle group, see the speech by Under Secretary for Policy Walter B. Slocombe, "National Missile Defense Policy," *Statesmen's Forum* (Washington, DC: Center for Strategic and International Studies, November 5, 1999).

15. Mike Allen, "Bush Affirms Defense Plans," *Washington Post* January 27, 2001, A10.

16. Lawrence F. Kaplan, "Containment," *The New Republic* (February 5, 2001): 17–20.

17. Colleen Barry, "Russian Warns US on Missile Defense," *Washington Post* February 4, 2001; Richard Lister, "The Battle over Missile Defense," *BBC News* (January 27, 2001); Patrick E. Tyler, "The Missile Shield's Tough Sell," *New York Times* February 4, 2001; and Gopal Ratnam, "National Missile Defense: U.S. May Face Fallout," *Defense News* (June 4, 2000): 12.

18. David Hoffman, "Russian Criticizes U.S. Missile Plans," *Washington Post* May 5, 2000, A21.

19. James Hackett, "Double Standard on Missile Defense Leaves U.S. Vulnerable," *Defense News* (October 19, 2000): 31.

20. For an analysis dismissive of European fears, see Eugene Fox and Stanley Orman, "Divisive Missile Defense: U.S. Protection Could Put Allies in Crosshairs," *Defense News* (January 31, 2000): 15.

21. Thomas E. Ricks, "Strike Force, Missile Defense Split U.S., Allies," *Washington Post* February 5, 2001, A13.

22. Jeff Sallot, "Support Missile Project or Else, Ottawa Warned," *Globe & Mail* (Toronto) May 3, 2000; "'There Are Nuts Out There,'" *Globe & Mail* (Toronto) May 4, 2000.

23. Anthony H. Cordesman, *Defending America: Redefining the Conceptual Borders of Homeland Defense, Taking Advantage of Delay: A Success-driven Approach to NMD* (Washington, DC: Center for Strategic and International Studies, September 2000).

24. James Miles, "U.S. Missiles: China's View," *BBC News* (July 6, 2000).

25. "European Politicians Oppose US Missile Defence," *BBC News* (January 30, 2001).

26. Luke Hill, "Putin Readies Details of Russian Missile Defense," *Defense News* (June 19, 2000): 1, 28; idem, "National Missile Defense: U.S. May Face Fallout," *Defense News* (June 5, 2000): 12.

27. Thomas E. Ricks, "Rumsfeld Defends Missile Shield to Apprehensive Allies in Europe," *Washington Post* February 4, 2001, A24; Michael R. Gordon, "U.S. Tries Defusing Allies' Opposition to Missile Defense," *New York Times* February 4, 2001.

28. Michael R. Gordon, "News Analysis: Allies' Mood on 'Star Wars' Shifts," *New York Times* February 5, 2001; "US Missile Plan 'a Long Way Off,'" *BBC News* (February 7, 2001). The latter were the reported comments of United Kingdom Foreign Secretary Robin Cook, indicating that much could happen between today and actual deployment in a thick shield.

29. Dennis Gormley, "Place Equal Focus on Cruise Component of Missile Threat," *Defense News* (January 29, 2001): 15–18.

30. "The World's Nuclear Arsenal," *BBC News* (May 2, 2000).

31. Ronald E. Powaski, *Return to Armageddon: The United States and the Nuclear Arms Race, 1981–1999* (New York: Oxford University Press, 2000), 3–13.

32.  Walter Pincus, "Russia Has Offer on Missile Defense," *Washington Post* April 29, 2000, A1.

33.  Luke Hill, "Putin Readies Details of Russian Missile Defense," *Defense News* (June 19, 2000): 1, 28.  President Putin's counter NMD offense included a proposal for a pan European BMD system.

34.  Gopal Ratnam and Amy Svitak, "Foes Charge That NMD Push Jeopardizes Weapon Treaties," *Defense News* (January 29, 2001): 8.

35.  Eugene Fox and Stanley Orman, "Divisive Missile Defense," *Space News* (January 31, 2000): 15.

36.  Gopal Ratnam and Amy Svitak, "U.S. Leaders Proffer NATO Missile Defense Network," *Defense News* (February 5, 2001): 1, 19.

37.  Karl-Heinz Kamp, "Specious NMD Arguments Stress Trans-Atlantic Relations," *Defense News* (August 21, 2000): 15, 18.

38.  David E. Sanger, "World Views: Rivals Differ on U.S. Role in the World," *New York Times* October 30, 2000.

39.  Cora Bell, "American Ascendancy—and the Pretense of Concert," *The National Interest* 57 (Fall 1999): 55–63.

40.  Richard Jo Samuels, *"Rich Nation, Strong Army"*, National Security and the Technological Transformation of Japan (Ithaca, NY: Cornell University Press, 1994) 26–27.

41.  David Smith, "Stay Firm on Missile Defense," *Defense News* (January 22, 2001): 19.

42.  Gopal Ratnam, "Congress Orders BMDO to Bridge Emerging Gaps," *Defense News* (October 23, 2000): 4, 12.

43.  As one author said, World War I was "the apogee of the defense" when infantry died en masse.  Archer Jones, *The Art of War in the Western World* (Urbana: University of Illinois Press, 1987; New York: Barnes & Noble Books, 1997), 434.  John Keegan describes the slaughter of entire communities of young men (the "Chums" and "Pals" units) in the maw of the Western Front.  *The First World War* (New York: Alfred A. Knopf, 1999), 299.

44.  On a personal note, in October 1962, at the height of the Cuban Missile Crisis, I was a high school senior playing football.  Despite the fact that I lived in Tallahassee, Florida and traveled to Orlando (in the center of the state) during that time, the most dangerous days in the nuclear confrontation passed unobserved by my teammates and I. A year later, I became aware of the event only by reading newsmagazines from the time. Reading the daily newspaper in 1962 was inconclusive because I read the sports page first and skipped the A section, so much for living through history.

45.  Bruce G. Blair, John E. Pike, and Stephen I. Schwartz, "Targeting and Controlling the Bomb," in Stephen I. Schwartz, ed., *Atomic Audit: The Costs and Consequences of U.S, Nuclear Weapons Since 1940* (Washington, DC: Brookings, Institution Press 1998), 206–207.

46.  Robert Holzer and Gopal Ratnam, "Missile Defense on Budget Battlefield," *Defense News* (January 22, 2001): 1, 28.  Already in January 2001, moneys were being diverted from NMD and Navy Theater Wide to help the Navy Area Defense and Patriot PAC-3.  This action reflected a desire to speed up development of the latter two programs without adversely impacting other, more traditional military functions outside the BMD arena.  The Bush administration will likely reverse or reduce the exchange but the realities are that the services have long and expensive needs lists.

47.    Congressional Budget Office, *Budgeting for Naval Forces:    Structuring Tomorrow's Navy at Today's Funding Level* (Washington, DC:    Congressional Budget Office October 2000); idem *Budgeting for Defense:    Maintaining Today's Forces* (Washington, DC:    Congressional Budget Office, September 2000).

48.    Thomas E. Ricks, "Pentagon Study May Bring Big Shake-Up," *Washington Post* February 9, 2001, A01.

49.    Steven Lee Myers, "Bush Takes First Step to Shrink Arsenal of Nuclear Warheads," *New York Times* February 9, 2001.

50.    Gopal Ratnam and Amy Svitak, "Interest Grows in Sea-Based Missile Defense," *Defense News* (August 2, 2000): 1, 20.

51.    Commission to Assess United States National Security Space Management and Organization, *Report* (Washington, DC:    U.S. Congress, January 11, 2001). Accessed at http://www.defenselink.mil/pubs/space20010111.html January 17, 2001.

52.    Eugene Fox, Stanley Orman and Robin Ranger, "Preventing National Missile Defense from Splitting NATO," *Space News* (January 15, 2001): 15.

# Selected References

The works cited below represent a selection of important references that have influenced the writing of this book. The authors may disagree with the interpretation put upon their work but all of them had an impact upon the approach traced out in this book. Clearly, ballistic missile defense (BMD) and especially national missile defense (NMD) has been a bitterly contested issue since at least the late 1960s—that intensity is often reflected in contemporaneous and subsequent writings. The articles cited are ones of particular interest and appear in the chapter endnotes along with other materials germane to the discussion at that point. The voluminous think tank literature is cited where appropriate in the chapter endnotes as is testimony before congressional committees by various players.

## GOVERNMENT DOCUMENTS

Ballistic Missile Defense Organization. Various Dates. *Fact Sheets*. Washington, DC: Ballistic Missile Defense Organization.

———. June 1, 1999. *Summary of Report to Congress on Utility of Sea-based Assets to National Missile Defense*. Washington, DC: Department of Defense, Ballistic Missile Defense Organization.

Cohen, William S. 1997. *Quadrennial Defense Review*. Washington, DC: Government Printing Office.

Congressional Budget Office. September 2000. *Budgeting for Defense: Maintaining Today's Forces*. Washington, DC: Congressional Budget Office.

Department of Defense. 1992. *Conduct of the Persian Gulf War: Final Report to Congress*. Washington, DC: Department of Defense.

———. 1999. *Report to Congress on Theater Missile Defense Architecture Options for the Asia-Pacific Region.* Washington, DC: Department of Defense.

Government Accounting Office. May 2000. *Missile Defense: Schedule for Navy Theater Wide Program Should Be Revised to Reduce Risk.* Washington, DC: United States Government Accounting Office.

———. May 2000. *Missile Defense: Status of the National Missile Defense Program.* Washington, DC: United States Government Accounting Office.

House of Representatives. January 1999. *Final Report of the United States House of Representatives Select Committee on U.S. National Security and Military/Commercial Concerns with the People's Republic of China.* Washington, DC: U.S. House of Representatives, Government Printing Office.

Rumsfeld, Donald H. July 1998. *Report of the Commission on the Ballistic Missile Threat to the United States.* Washington, DC: U.S. Congress, Government Printing Office.

U.S. Space Command. 1998. *U.S. Space Command Long Range Plan.* Peterson Air Force Base: U.S. Space Command.


**BOOKS AND MONOGRAPHS:**

Adams, Benson D. 1971. *Ballistic Missile Defense.* New York: Elsevier.

Bailey, Kathleen C. 1991. *Doomsday Weapons in the Hands of Many: The Arms Control    Challenge of the '90s.* Chicago: University of Illinois Press.

Ball, Desmond. 1980. *Politics and Force Levels: The Strategic Missile Program of the Kennedy Administration.* Berkeley: University of California Press.

Baucom, Donald R. 1992. *The Origins of SDI, 1944–1983.* Lawrence: University Press of Kansas.

Bruce-Briggs, B. 1988. *The Shield of Faith: A Chronicle of Strategic Defense from Zepplins to Star Wars.* New York: Simon & Schuster.

Bundy, McGeorge. 1988. *Dangers and Survival: Choices About the Bomb in the First Fifty Years.* New York: Random House.

Carter, Ashton B. and David N. Schwartz. 1984. *Ballistic Missile Defense.* Washington, DC: Brookings, Institution Press.

Carus, W. Seth. 1990. *Ballistic Missiles in the Third World.* New York: Praeger.

Day, Dwayne A., John M. Logsdon, and Brian Latell, eds. 1998. *Eye in the Sky: The Story of the Corona Spy Satellites.* Washington, DC: Smithsonian Institution Press.

Fitzgerald, Frances. 2000. *Way Out There in the Blue: Reagan, Star Wars and the End of the Cold War.* New York: Simon & Schuster.

Friedman, George, and Meredith Friedman. 1996. *The Future of War.* New York: Crown Books.

George, Alexander L., and Richard Smoke. 1974. *Deterrence in American Foreign Policy.* New York: Columbia University Press.

Gordon, Michael R., and Bernard E. Trainor. 1996. *The Generals' War: The Inside Story of the Conflict in the Gulf.* Boston, MA: Little, Brown.

Gray, Colin S. 1997. *The American Revolution in Military Affairs: An Interim Assessment.* Occasional Paper No. 28. London: The Strategic and Combat Services Institute.

Hadley, Arthur T. 1986. *The Straw Giant, Triumph and Failure: America's Armed Forces.* New York: Random House.

Hall, Lauren. 1997. *Weapons under Fire.* New York: Garland Publishing.

Handberg, Roger. 2000. *New World Vistas: Militarization of Space.* Westport, CT: Praeger Books.

Holst, Johan J., and William Schneider, Jr. eds. 1969. *Why ABM? Policy Issues in the Missile Defense Controversy.* New York: Pergamon Press.

Hunter, Kerry L. 1992. *The Reign of Fantasy: The Political Roots of Reagan's Star Wars Policy.* New York: Peter Lang.

Huntington, Samuel P. 1961. *The Common Defense: Strategic Program in National Politics.* New York: Columbia University Press.

———. 1996. *The Clash of Civilizations and the Remaking of World Order.* New York: Simon & Schuster.

Jervis, Robert. 1976. *Perception and Misperception in International Politics.* Princeton, NJ: Princeton University Press.

———. 1984. *The Illogic of American Nuclear Strategy.* Ithaca, NY: Cornell University Press.

———. 1989. *The Meaning of the Nuclear Revolution.* Ithaca, NY: Cornell University Press.

Kahn, Herman. 1968. *On Escalation: Metaphors and Scenarios.* Baltimore, MD: Penguin Books.

Kanter, Arnold. 1979. *Defense Politics: A Budgetary Perspective.* Chicago: University of Chicago Press.

Kaplan, Fred. 1983. *The Wizards of Armageddon.* New York: Simon & Schuster.

Karp, Aaron. 1996. *Ballistic Missile Proliferation: The Politics and Technics.* Oxford: Oxford University Press.

Kaufman, William W. 1964. *The McNamara Strategy.* New York: Harper & Row.

Keegan, John. 1989. *The Second World War.* New York: Penguin Books.

———. 1999. *The First World War.* New York: Alfred A. Knopf.

Kennedy, Paul. 1989. *The Rise and Fall of the Great Powers: Economic Change and Military Conflict from 1500 to 2000.* New York: Vintage Books.

Kingdon, John W. 1995. *Agendas, Alternatives, and Public Policies.* 2nd ed. New York: HarperCollins.

Lambeth, Benjamin S. 2000. *The Transformation of American Air Power.* Ithaca, NY: Cornell University Press.

McDougall, Walter A. 1985. *The Heavens and the Earth: A Political History of the Space Age.* New York: Basic Books.

McMahon, K. Scott. 1997. *Pursuit of the Shield: The U.S. Quest for Limited Ballistic Missile Defense.* Lanham, MD: University Press of America.

Miller, Steven E., and Stephen Van Evera eds. 1986. *The Star Wars Controversy.* Princeton: Princeton University Press.

Newhouse, John. 1989. *Cold Dawn: The Story of SALT.* New York: Pergamon.

O'Hanlon, Michael. 2000. *Technological Changes and the Future of Warfare.* Washington, DC: Brookings Institution Press.

Pape, Robert A. 1996. *Bombing to Win: Air Power and Coercion in War.* Ithaca, NY: Cornell University Press.

Pikayev, Alexander A., Leonard S. Spector, Elina V. Kirichenko, and Ryan Gibson. 1998. *Russia, the US and the Missile Technology Control Regime.* Adephi Paper 317. New York: Oxford University Press.

Powaski, Ronald E. 2000. *Return to Armageddon: The United States and the Nuclear Arms Race, 1981–1999.* New York: Oxford University Press.

Quester, George H. 1966. *Deterrence before Hiroshima.* New York: Wiley.

Richelson, Jeffrey T. 1999. *America's Space Sentinels: DSP Satellites and National Security.* Lawrence: University Press of Kansas.

Sagan, Scott D. 1989. *Moving Targets: Nuclear Strategy and National Security.* Princeton, NJ: Princeton University Press.

Samuels, Richard J. 1994. *"Rich Nation, Strong Army": National Security and the Technological Transformation of Japan.* Ithaca, NY: Cornell University Press.

Schwartz, Stephen I., ed. 1998. *Atomic Audit: The Costs and Consequences of U.S. Nuclear Weapons Since 1940.* Washington, DC: Brookings Institution Press.

Smoke, Richard. 1993. *National Security and the Nuclear Dilemma.* 3rd ed. New York: McGraw-Hill.

Snow, Donald M. 1998. *National Security.* 4th d. New York: St. Martin's Press.

————2000. *When America Fights: The Uses of U.S. Military Force.* Washington, DC: CQ Press.

Snyder, Glen H. 1961. *Deterrence and Defense: Toward a Theory of National Security.* Princeton, NJ: Princeton University Press.

Spires, David N. 1997. *Beyond Horizons: A Half Century of Air Force Space Leadership.* Peterson Air Force Base, CO: Air Force Space Command.

Stine, G. Harry. 1991. *ICBM: The Making of the Weapon That Changed the World.* New York: Orion.

Weigerly, Russell F. 1973. *The American War of War: A History of United States Military Strategy and Policy.* New York: Macmillan.

Wilkening, Dean A. 2000. *Ballistic-Missile Defence and Strategic Stability.* Adelphi Paper 334. New York: Oxford University Press.

Yanarella, Ernest J.    1977.    *The Missile Defense Controversy:    Strategy, Technology, and Politics, 1955–1972.* Lexington:  University Press of Kentucky.

York, Herbert F.    1970.    *The Race to Oblivion:  A Participant's View of the Arms Race.* New York:  Simon & Schuster.

# Index

## About the Author

ROGER HANDBERG is Professor of Political Science at the University of Central Florida. His research has focused on space policy, defense policy, law and courts, both American and comparative, and science policy with regard to public opinion. His work has appeared in five books, 138 articles, and over 130 papers and other published materials.